Hegel's *Philosophy of Right* After 200 Years

Hegel's Philosophy of Right (1820) articulated a startling new vision of modern society as an integrated whole governed by the principle of freedom—a vision that profoundly altered political theory and, through Hegel's influence on Marx, deeply changed the world in which we live. Yet Hegel's thought is so notoriously obscure that it is difficult to pull together its many complex threads in order to understand what he accomplished and how he managed to do it.

In this volume, leading political theorists and philosophers attempt to illuminate the impact of Hegel by looking back on the *Philosophy of Right* after two centuries, shedding light on some of its most controversial elements. Among the topics discussed are Hegel's theory of bureaucracy, Marx's critique of that theory, Hegel's alternative to nationalism, his political cosmology, his critique of natural law, his organic idea of the good, and his view of totality. The contributors are Frederick Beiser, Shterna Friedman, Darren Nah, Frederick Neuhouser, Angelica Nuzzo, Alan Patten, Terry Pinkard, Paul Rosenberg, and Jacob Roundtree.

This book was originally published as a special issue of *Critical Review*.

Shterna Friedman, the Managing Editor of *Critical Review*, is a doctoral candidate in Political Science at the University of California, Berkeley, USA; an exchange scholar in the Department of Government at Harvard University, USA; and Visiting Lecturer in Political Theory at Tufts University, USA.

Hegel's *Philosophy of Right* After 200 Years

Edited by
Shterna Friedman

Routledge
Taylor & Francis Group
LONDON AND NEW YORK

First published 2023
by Routledge
4 Park Square, Milton Park, Abingdon, Oxon, OX14 4RN

and by Routledge
605 Third Avenue, New York, NY 10158

Routledge is an imprint of the Taylor & Francis Group, an informa business

British Library Cataloguing-in-Publication Data
A catalogue record for this book is available from the British Library

ISBN13: 978-1-032-35531-3 (hbk)
ISBN13: 978-1-032-35533-7 (pbk)
ISBN13: 978-1-003-32731-8 (ebk)

DOI: 10.4324/9781003327318

Typeset in Minion Pro
by codeMantra

Publisher's Note
The publisher accepts responsibility for any inconsistencies that may have arisen during the conversion of this book from journal articles to book chapters, namely the inclusion of journal terminology.

Contents

Citation Information

The chapters in this book/following chapters were originally published in the journal *Critical Review*, volume 33, issue 3–4 (January 2022). When citing this material, please use the original page numbering for each article, as follows:

Introduction

Three Pictures of Hegel's Holism: Mystical, Instrumentalist, Intrinsicist
Shterna Friedman
Critical Review, volume 33, issue 3–4 (January 2022) pp. 265–276

Chapter 1

A Mayfly for Prof. Hegel: Herbart's Forgotten Review of Hegel's Rechtsphilosophie
Frederick Beiser
Critical Review, volume 33, issue 3–4 (January 2022) pp. 277–288

Chapter 2

Hegel, Weber, and Bureaucracy
Darren Nah
Critical Review, volume 33, issue 3–4 (January 2022) pp. 289–309

Chapter 3

Hegel on "the Living Good"
Frederick Neuhouser
Critical Review, volume 33, issue 3–4 (January 2022) pp. 310–331

Chapter 4

Hegel's Philosophy of Right *and the Idea of the World: Dialectic's "Political Cosmology"*
Angelica Nuzzo
Critical Review, volume 33, issue 3–4 (January 2022) pp. 332–358

Chapter 5
Hegel's Alternative to Nationalism
Alan Patten
Critical Review, volume 33, issue 3–4 (January 2022) pp. 359–377

Chapter 6
Hegel's Own Time Grasped in Our Thoughts after Two Hundred Years
Terry Pinkard
Critical Review, volume 33, issue 3–4 (January 2022) pp. 378–391

Chapter 7
Hegel's Political Philosophy
Paul Rosenberg
Critical Review, volume 33, issue 3–4 (January 2022) pp. 392–430

Chapter 8
Marx's Democratization of Hegel's Philosophy of Right
Jacob Roundtree
Critical Review, volume 33, issue 3–4 (January 2022) pp. 431–461

Notes on Contributors

Frederick Beiser is Professor of Philosophy at Syracuse University, USA. He is the author, most recently, of *Johann Friedrich Herbart: Grandfather of Analytic Philosophy* (2022).

Shterna Friedman, the Managing Editor of *Critical Review*, is a doctoral candidate in Political Science at the University of California, Berkeley, USA; an exchange scholar in the Department of Government at Harvard University, USA; and Visiting Lecturer in Political Theory at Tufts University, USA.

Darren Nah is a doctoral candidate in the Department of Political Science at Yale University, USA. He has published on Aristotle's critique of slavery and on Hegel's fight against aristocracy.

Frederick Neuhouser is Professor of Philosophy at Barnard College and Columbia University, USA. He is the author, most recently, of *Diagnosing Social Pathology: Rousseau, Hegel, Marx, and Durkheim* (2022).

Angelica Nuzzo is the Professor of Philosophy at Brooklyn College and the CUNY Graduate Center, USA. She is the author, most recently, of *Approaching Hegel's Logic, Obliquely: Melville, Molière, Beckett* (2018).

Alan Patten is the Howard Harrison and Gabrielle Snyder Beck Professor of Politics and Chair of the Department of Politics at Princeton University, USA. He is the author, inter alia, of *Hegel's Idea of Freedom* (1999).

Terry Pinkard is Professor of Philosophy at Georgetown University, Washington, DC, USA. He is the author, most recently, of *Practice, Power, and Forms of Life: Sartre's Appropriation of Hegel and Marx* (2021).

Paul Rosenberg was an independent scholar who died in Los Angeles in August 2021. This paper is adapted from his 2001 University of

Cambridge dissertation, "The Pattern of Large-Scale History: Hegel's System and Its Political Transformations in Marx and Postmodernism." It is published with the permission of his estate.

Jacob Roundtree is a doctoral candidate in Political Theory in the Department of Government at Harvard University, USA.

Shterna Friedman

INTRODUCTION: THREE PICTURES OF HEGEL'S HOLISM: MYSTICAL, INSTRUMENTALIST, INTRINSICIST

ABSTRACT: *The two-hundredth anniversary of the publication of Hegel's* Philosophy of Right *allows us to provide an array of exciting interpretations of his work. In one interpretation, exemplified by the reactions of Johann Friedrich Herbart (discussed here by Frederick Beiser) and of Karl Marx (discussed here by Jacob Roundtree), Hegel's holism is a product of a romantic or mystical metaphysics that prioritizes the invisible reality of the Idea over visible realities. In another interpretation (advanced here by Roundtree himself and by Darren Nah, Alan Patten, and Paul Rosenberg), Hegel's holism is instrumental to preserving individual freedoms or interests by embedding them in a larger cultural or institutional context. A third interpretation, not necessarily incompatible with the second (and exemplified here by contributions from Frederick Neuhouser, Angelica Nuzzo, and Terry Pinkard), treats the Hegelian whole as rational intrinsically, not merely because it is instrumental to other ends.*

This volume commemorates Hegel's *Philosophy of Right* 200 years after the (inaccurate) printer's date of publication (1821, despite its actual appearance in 1820). It is a pleasure to be able to include reflections on *The Philosophy of Right* by Frederick Beiser, Darren Nah, Frederick Neuhouser, Angelica Nuzzo, Alan Patten, Terry Pinkard, Paul Rosenberg, and Jacob Roundtree. Together, these reflections provide a dynamic portrait of Hegel's political philosophy, seen from a variety of angles—so many that it is difficult to come up with a comprehensive theme on which to hang a group portrait of the contributions to the symposium.

Difficult, but not impossible: one issue that is raised, directly or indirectly, by each contributor is the role of the whole in Hegel's *Philosophy of Right*. This is hardly surprising, as Hegel's holism so permeates his thought that it would be challenging to offer an interpretation of Hegel that completely got away from the subject of the whole.

There might not be a better time than the present to grapple with Hegel's holism, now that politics has suddenly taken a "systemic" turn—grasping our present as a whole in order to wrestle with systemic racism, systemic oppression, and systemic injustice. It is true that in contemporary systemic accounts, the whole is described as irrational, unfree, and unjust, in marked contrast to Hegel's account of a rational, free social organism. Like Hegel, however, contemporary systemic theorists treat social wholes not just as metaphors describing the *effects* of individuals' interactions, but as *causes* or *sources* of social ills, and thus as capable of bearing responsibility for injustice and domination (just as, for Hegel, the whole is responsible for justice and freedom). Further, systems of oppression are now seen as autonomously maintaining and reproducing themselves, just as Hegel saw modern society as doing—a feature of such systems that, in the absence of a Hegelian moment of reconciliation, accounts for the persistence and intensification of injustice and oppression. Might aspects of this systemic understanding of society, then, stem from Hegel's concept of society as a system, despite the radically different (positive) valence of this system for Hegel? Regardless of the answer to this historical question, reflecting on Hegel's holism might better help us understand the promises and challenges of our own turn to the systemic, as there was no theorist who devoted more thought to the concept of a system than Hegel.

Yet as our symposium indicates, there are many ways to assess and react to Hegel's systemic holism, and there is much disagreement about the role it plays in his political philosophy and his philosophical system as a whole.

At the risk of overschematization, I will group the symposium papers into three types. First, there is the picture of an irrationalist metaphysical Hegelian system that emerges in Beiser's depiction of Johann Friedrich Herbart's critique of Hegel, and in Roundtree's account of Marx's much better-known critique. This is the Hegel who propagates the full-throated holism of an organic, self-differentiating totality, the Hegel whose conception of the whole falls into a "logical, pantheistic mysticism," as Marx ([1843] 1970, 7) put it. Second, there is the more familiar sociological, institutional, and liberal or quasi-liberal thinker who emerges from the portraits painted by Nah, Patten, and Rosenberg, and from Roundtree's own account of Hegel. Sometimes this Hegel's holism disappears into the background, as when Nah attributes Hegel's political theory to his attempt to counter the power of the Junkers in the "agricultural estate," who had resisted Prussian efforts at reform. Yet it is difficult to extirpate Hegel's holism entirely. Even in Nah's historical contextualization of Hegel as a latter-day Prussian reformer, society as a whole was the object of reform efforts, which were undertaken from the center in the interest of a rationalized modern whole as envisioned by the Hegelian bureaucrat. In Patten's, Rosenberg's, and Roundtree's more textually oriented interpretations of Hegel, he articulated the outlines of a social whole that takes center stage and serves the interests and freedom of individuals. A third type of holism emerges from Neuhouser's, Nuzzo's, and Pinkard's interpretations of Hegel's treatment of the whole as rational not merely because it promotes individual freedom and interests, but because it is rational in itself. This Hegel deliberately patterned his concept of the social whole on the model of a biological organism (Neuhouser). Or he saw the concept of a certain kind of whole in the making of the "world" as central to his account of politics and philosophy (Nuzzo). Or his holism might better be elucidated by means of the concept of a form of life rather than that of an organism (Pinkard).

Hegel 1: A Mystical, Unrealistic Holist

The first Hegel is an irrationalist whose holism stemmed less from a sophisticated assessment of reality than from a reckless Romantic or mystical disregard of it. This picture arises from Beiser's and Roundtree's reconstructions of the critiques of *The Philosophy of Right* offered by Herbart and Marx.

In 1822, Herbart wrote a long review of *The Philosophy of Right* that took Hegel to task for a number of reasons, such as Hegel's conflation, as Herbart saw it, of the science of the state with the science of natural law, and his assignment of far too much power to the state. I take

Beiser's article to imply that these complaints stemmed from Herbart's individualism and empiricism. Thus, he found Hegel's conception of a social totality—a whole that evolves from primal unity to greater unity through a process of increasing self-differentiation and self-enrichment—to be an unproved and unprovable assertion: a fantasy. Herbart attributed this fantastic element in *The Philosophy of Right* to what he saw as Schelling's Romantic influence on Hegel. In relying on the notion of intellectual intuition—the notion that we can attain knowledge not merely through the discursive mediation of concepts, but immediately and intuitively—Schelling opened the door to unverifiable assertion, to "dogmatism and irrationalism." Herbart did not seem to realize that Hegel himself had criticized Romanticism on similar grounds, namely that Romantics attributed unwarranted confidence to their immediate thoughts and feelings. If one does not note the strongly rationalist side of Hegel, it is easy to ridicule his metaphysics of a self-evolving totality.

Incredulity towards Hegel's holism was by no means anomalous, as we are reminded by Roundtree's analysis of Marx's critique of Hegel. Marx scoffed at Hegel's "mysticism" as well as a different aspect of Hegelian social holism—its application to the present. What Marx found absurd was the claim that the Idea is a subject that differentiates itself into the moments of an organic whole, moments that we happen to find instantiated in the institutions (such as the monarchy and bureaucracy) of Prussia and European societies in general. For Marx, to treat the Idea as a subject is to invert the relationship between actuality and appearance by depicting non-ideal individuals, families, economies, monarchies, and bureaucracies as ideal, treating fantasy (the Idea) as real. Unlike Herbart, however, Marx embraced Hegel's organicism in principle. He thought only that Hegel had illegitimately used the pattern of his own *Logic*'s categories to create the illusion that the real Prussia of 1820 was a functional organic whole.

Hegel 2: A Liberal Instrumentalist

Over the past several decades we have become familiar with a Hegel who has been stripped of the metaphysical baggage to which Herbart so harshly responded. This new, more familiarly liberal Hegel aims to protect individual freedom and a degree of social equality, yet has not lost all interest in organic unity. But the organic social whole is instrumental to protecting the freedom of individuals.

Nah's article subordinates Hegel's institutionalism to the achievement of social reform in the face of Junker resistance. Thus, Hegel not only confined "agricultural"—including Junker—influence to one of the two chambers of the legislature, but he insulated the bureaucracy from legislative control. This depiction of Hegel leaves only a non-metaphysical concern with the social whole, in the limited sense of a social body to be directed from its center (or its head) by the unelected officials of the "universal class." The key question, for Nah's Hegel, regards these officials' motivation. Uncontroversially, Nah's controversial article is predicated on Hegel's defense of a group of bureaucrats who have the common good—the universal—as their motivation.

Although Patten's contribution does not deal directly with the bureaucracy, it situates Hegel's motivational concerns in the context of those of his predecessors, Kant and Fichte—who took selfishness to be one of the primary reasons for the divergence of social reality from moral ideals. Kant therefore wanted institutions to check selfish inclinations by pitting these inclinations against one another. Fichte, on the other hand, advocated a program of national education that would inculcate children with a love of the nation rather than the self. Patten's Hegel turned toward ethical habituation, not nationalist education, to encourage other-regarding dispositions. For Hegel, according to Patten, "the central problem of political philosophy" was to "articulate a social order that was at once hospitable to freedom *and* stable and self-reproducing." The freedom in question was subjective or, in Hegel's terms, "abstract" individual freedom, the freedom embodied in the rights of "personality." Hegel thought that the protection of freedom requires that individuals be embedded in a cultural framework that cushions the destructive effects of unregulated self-seeking: *Sittlichkeit*, which encourages the development of ethical habits and other-regarding dispositions.

Rosenberg likewise depicts Hegel's holism as instrumental to protecting individual freedom by limiting it and embedding it in a larger whole. In Rosenberg's telling, the *Philosophy of Right* is structured around a critique of the natural-law ideology that Hegel saw as threatening the stability of modern society. Natural-law theory deprives people of the ability to distinguish between finite needs and infinite wants. Their pursuit of the latter can destroy the institutional structures that make individual freedom possible. Hegel attempted to isolate unlimited self-seeking by confining it to the mercantile estate, where it could be softened by *Sittlichkeit* and countered by the universal estate and the traditionalist agricultural estate—which, in direct contrast to Nah's interpretation, Rosenberg's Hegel considered an ally to be protected. Like Nah, however, Rosenberg sees Hegel as placing the greatest hopes, and the most political power, in the bureaucratic hands of the universal estate, which, unlike the mercantile estate, is motivated not by its own good but the good of the whole.

Unlike Nah, Rosenberg does not interpret Hegel's interest in staffing the bureaucracy with members of universal class as stemming from a desire to shield it from the Junkers; rather, the universal class was to serve as a counterweight to the self-interested ideology that infused the consciousness and activities of the mercantile estate. Thus, the knowledge required of the highly educated universal estate is primarily ethical—knowledge of the distinction between needs and wants—and the main qualification for being a member of the universal state is ethical rather than technical training. This training, Rosenberg speculates, would be provided by educating the universal class in Hegelianism itself, providing it with both the motivation to work toward the universal and knowledge of the difference between the universal and the particular, and thus with the ability to distinguish between universal needs and particular wants. The bureaucrats' regulation of civil society would draw on this distinction, and on a knowledge of the organic structure of the state. This knowledge is, in Rosenberg's telling, instrumental to the preservation of a social whole that, in turn, enables a sustainable brand of individual freedom that does not run amok.

Roundtree's account suggests that Marx had a similar interpretation of Hegel's intentions, even though he thought that the *Philosophy of Right* betrayed them. Marx's critique of Hegel's universal estate asserted that it is untrue that the bureaucracies of Prussia and other European countries *did* promote universal interests rather than their own interests, because Marx denied that bureaucrats knew the interests of the whole organism rather than their own interests as members of a hierarchical organization of (false) knowledge. Thus, Hegel's insulation of the bureaucracy from popular control ensured only that the interests of the whole, i.e., of the people as a whole, would *not* be served by the state. While Roundtree's Marx agreed with Hegel that the state must embody the universal will (*allgemeiner Wille*)—Rousseau's *volonté générale*—Marx was more like

Rousseau than Hegel in arguing that this meant that state sovereignty must necessarily be popular sovereignty. Marx disagreed with Hegel about whether the people's interests can be represented by an executive bureaucracy or whether the people must manage their own affairs if their interests are to be served, presumably because he assumed that only those who cared about their own interests would try to further them. By contrast, Hegel did not find evidence that the untutored people knew its *rational* interests—those served by the organic whole.

Despite the gulf this established between the young Marx and Hegel, it would appear that if we accept Roundtree's interpretation, both figures treated the central challenge of politics to be the alignment of motivations with interests, as in Nah's interpretation of Hegel. However, unlike Nah, Roundtree, like Rosenberg, brings out the role in Hegel's thought of bureaucrats' knowledge, which is instrumental to ensuring that the alignment of bureaucrats' motivations with the genuine interests of the whole leads to the actual satisfaction of those interests. For Roundtree, this knowledge is knowledge of the whole.

Hegel 3: The Intrinsicist Holist

Yet a third picture of Hegel emerges in Neuhouser's, Nuzzo's, and Pinkard's contributions, which treat the social whole as having intrinsic value even apart from the value it may have for individuals.

Neuhouser and Pinkard build on recent work on Hegel's account of life [*Leben*] to emphasize Hegel's description of society as organic. Yet they have rather different interpretations of the value of this organicism. Neuhouser takes up Hegel's relatively overlooked description in PR §142 of *Sittlichkeit* as the "living good" [*das lebendige Gute*], and unpacks the significance of this term for Hegel. To draw on Hegel's *Philosophy of Nature* in order to discuss his social and political philosophy is, almost necessarily, to bring back the metaphysical Hegel. But this approach allows Neuhouser to unpack Hegel's view of the complex relationship between life, understood as a natural phenomenon, and spirit, understood as a type of social and political life that transcends mere natural life. As Neuhouser puts it, in society, life "is both transcended and preserved within the spiritual." Life is transcended in society (which is included in the sphere of "objective spirit," for Hegel) because mere life lacks self-consciousness of its purposes and is thus unfree to a degree, while in society we have the ability to become aware of our purposes and ends, and we are thus free to a degree. Yet life is also preserved within society, most obviously by the family but also by civil society, which enables us to try to meet our material needs.

However, Neuhouser's account goes beyond the relatively uncontroversial claim that for Hegel, social interactions both preserve life and transcend its unconsciousness. Hegel's references to society as organic were not merely metaphorical, Neuhouser contends, but ontological. Thus, he did not merely model society on the metaphor of an organism, but actually believed that it *is* an organism, with its own internal organization and differentiation, its own functionality, its own purposiveness, and the ability to regulate and reproduce itself. Life provides Hegel with a model of autonomous self-organization and self-regulation and, thus, a blueprint for diagnosing social pathology; for just as life can flourish, so can it become diseased. This occurs, for Hegel, when any organ or social sphere overreaches itself and is no longer content with being a subordinate, functional element of the whole, but rather seeks to make its own subordinate end the purpose of the whole. In contrast, a social organism is healthy when its elements are functionally integrated in such a way that, together, they serve the purposes of the whole. From this perspective, Hegel's is an intrinsicist rather than instrumentalist holism that treats the social whole as rational not only because of its effects—its ability to serve individual interests and freedom—but because it is organized in such a way that it can serve its own end.

This intrinsicist holism may raise worries of the sort that Pinkard takes up in his contribution. For example, Hegel "relied on his philosophy of nature to import and underwrite his view that the difference of the sexes did not itself have a merely natural but also a deeper metaphysical and ethical significance (that of the polarity in the universe at large) that, in turn, underwrote the domination of women in his conception of civil society supposedly committed to the freedom and equality of all." Pinkard therefore suggests that, precisely to the extent to which we would like to appropriate Hegel's political philosophy, we should treat his organicism as a metaphor, not an ontology (presumably because the ontology of organicism legitimizes the "functional" subordination of some in the interest of the health of the social whole). Pinkard's alternative account of holism instead emphasizes Hegel's concept of a form of life, as manifested in conceptually inflected shared practices, habits, and dispositions. As I understand Pinkard, while organic life relies on functionalist imperatives that specify necessary relationships among various elements, thus demanding a strict integration between components, a form of life permits a looser type of relationship between various elements that need not constitute a strictly integrated, organically functional whole. I take Pinkard to suggest, moreover, that the notion of a form of life more appropriately captures Hegel's attempt, in his political philosophy, to observe the modern social "baselines," a term that literally translates the first word in *Grundlinien der Philosophie des Rechts*. Pinkard describes the principle of equal freedom as Hegel's modern baseline, for it provides both the standard for determining the legitimacy of modern society and also a bird's-eye view from which we can understand ground-level contradictions within it. Thus, finding a more comprehensive standpoint by which to resolve contradictions does not require treating society as an ontological organism, but accepting only that collective patterns—forms of life—are formed on a baseline principle.

Nuzzo's account of Hegel's view of the "world" [*Welt*], however, suggests that Hegel was referring to a non-metaphorical whole that is larger than any organic social totality. Hence what Nuzzo calls Hegel's "political cosmology." Comparing Hegel to Kant, she argues that the latter held that if we are to make progress in realizing our human vocation, we must assume the presence of a unitary moral world that is, however, epistemologically closed to us; we must therefore "act *as if* the world were amenable to moral and free action, *as if* the world made human sense." In contrast, Hegel spoke of an *actual* world in which nature and moral freedom are joined. However, this world is not, as Nuzzo tells it, a given whole or "fully constituted object." The world is constantly being made and remade and so is never fully complete; the world is more appropriately seen as a processual whole than an object. As I understand Nuzzo's argument, the fluidity of the world-whole, its ungiven, *poietic* status, grounds the dialectical method, for the processual nature of the world stems from its constant unspooling of immanent contradictions. But at the same time the dialectical method grounds the world, for the world is simply the process of turning the content of philosophy into actuality. In this way, the world both "checks" philosophy—for only content that can be actualized as world can truly be philosophical—and also justifies philosophy (for philosophy sees itself in the actual world). With this working account of Hegel's concept of the world in hand, Nuzzo suggests that we can make sense of Hegel's critique of utopian political theories such as Plato's and positivist historicist theories such as Gustav Hugo's. The first type of theory fails to recognize that the world must check philosophy, while the second fails to recognize that philosophy must check the world.

Nuzzo's account of the world has similarities to Pinkard's account of forms of life and Neuhouser's account of society as an ontological organism. The concept of the world maintains the openness and sense of possibility captured by the concept of forms of life, but also presumes an immanent normative standard that is akin to, even if different from, the immanent normative standard provided by the notion of purposive life (health, as opposed to disease).

Hegel's Holisms

Hegel was not shy about relying on holist language and concepts. He spoke of organic wholes; criticized mechanical wholes; talked about the world as a spiritual whole; loosely referred to epochs, eras, and ages as wholes; wrote extensively about objective, relative, and absolute totalities and "systems" (of philosophy, sensibility, irritability, etc.); treated love as a type of whole; unpacked spirit as a type of whole; spoke of the Absolute; and treated various types of wholes as having triadic, syllogistic structures. He had a rich conception of unity as more than simple oneness, and as constituting more than the aggregation of a group of components. Given the multifariousness of Hegel's holism, it is not easy to specify the purpose it served in the "whole" of his philosophical system or, in particular, in his political philosophy.

One response is simply to write off Hegel's holism as fantastic or unrealistic; a second is to replace it with an aggregative or mechanical view of the whole. More sympathetically, instrumentalist holism views Hegel's *political* whole as primarily instrumental to preserving individual freedom. This became the most palatable reading of Hegel in response to Cold War criticisms of Hegel's holism as having inspired Soviet and Nazi totalitarianism.

Instrumentally holist interpretations do help undo the picture of a dangerous, fantastically metaphysical Hegel. Yet Neuhouser and Nuzzo suggest that Hegel's system was more robustly, intrinsically holist, treating the social whole as having its own purposes and autonomy over and above the purposes of individuals—which does not require, however, treating individuals as merely instrumental to the whole. The array of intrinsicist holisms provided by our symposiasts, however, raises the question of how to interpret this holism. For example, while an organicist ontology might easily accommodate the concept of world, treating it as perhaps a super-organism, Hegel tends to align the concept of the world with God. While God, for Hegel, is indeed a living, self-developing process, the concept of world and the concept of organism may be infused with different connotations—theological in one case, biological in the other—which may therefore rely on different presuppositions that might be in tension with one another. Likewise, as Nuzzo foregrounds the neglected topic of Hegel's concept of world, as Neuhouser foregrounds the concept of life, and as Pinkard foregrounds the concept of forms of life, it might be time to focus on yet another neglected whole in Hegel's holist arsenal: *Totalität*, one of the overarching concepts in Hegel's philosophy (with the striking exception of the *Phenomenology*), but perhaps the one that has been most shunned since the Cold War.

While a hard look at Hegel's holisms and their purposes might gain us a better understanding of Hegel, it might also be a first step to evaluating to what extent Hegel's influence might be found in the contemporary interest in the systemic, such as in the politics of systemic injustice and systemic oppression. Further research might reveal whether affinities between Hegel's account of a social whole and contemporary understandings of systemic oppression are merely conceptual or also genetic. Moreover, conceptual differences between Hegelian and systemic theorizing might be signs not of lack of influence, but of mediated influence, as Hegel's systemic theorizing was appropriated, modified, and critically preserved by a raft of systemic social thinkers after him, most immediately Marx. A return to Hegel's systemic theorizing, then, may illuminate newer problems or provoke us to rethink them, a process that we can already see taking place in this symposium.

REFERENCES

Beiser, Frederick. 2021. "A Mayfly for Prof. Hegel: Herbart's Forgotten Review of Hegel's *Rechtsphilosophie*." *Critical Review* 33(3-4).

Marx [1843] 1970. *Critique of Hegel's Philosophy of Right*, ed. Joseph O'Malley. Cambridge: Cambridge University Press.

Nah, Darren. 2021. "Hegel, Weber, and Bureaucracy." *Critical Review* 33(3-4).

Neuhouser, Frederick. 2021. "Hegel on 'The Living Good.'" *Critical Review* 33(3-4).

Nuzzo, Angelica. 2021. "Hegel's *Philosophy of Right* and the Idea of the World: Dialectic's 'Political Cosmology.'" *Critical Review* 33(3-4).

Patten, Alan. 2021. "Hegel's Alternative to Nationalism." *Critical Review* 33(3-4).

Pinkard, Terry. 2021. "Hegel's Own Time Grasped in Our Thoughts After Two Hundred Years." *Critical Review* 33(3-4).

Rosenberg, Paul. 2021. "Hegel's Political Philosophy." *Critical Review* 33(3-4).
Roundtree, Jacob. 2021. "Marx's Democraticization of Hegel's *Philosophy of Right.*" *Critical Review* 33(3-4).

Frederick Beiser

A MAYFLY FOR PROF. HEGEL: HERBART'S FORGOTTEN REVIEW OF HEGEL'S *RECHTSPHILOSOPHIE*

ABSTRACT: *Herbart and Hegel were contemporaries and both became famous, in their time and thereafter. It would be interesting therefore to know what they thought of one another. We could easily answer this question if they reviewed one another. Hegel never reviewed Herbart; but Herbart did review Hegel. Though in his later years Herbart protested that he did not want to engage with Hegel, he had already written, in 1822, one of his longest and most important reviews, which was of Hegel's* Philosophie des Rechts. *Herbart maintained that there is a Spinozistic element to Hegel's political philosophy which equates right with might. Hegel tried to avoid the implications of this equation by bringing Kantian transcendental freedom into his system, which for him boiled down to the idea of dialectical development. But Herbart rejected the fundamental idea behind dialectical development: that the ego posits the opposite of itself. Herbart then criticized Hegel's attempt to revive natural law and his theory of the state. Herbart contended that reason cannot prove the fundamental principles of natural law, that reason by itself is an abstract and formal power and as such cannot demonstrate any principle having substantive content. And Herbart criticized Hegel's doctrine that the individual finds his identity only in the state. Much more liberal than Hegel, Herbart stressed the importance of individuality outside the state.*

It would surprise many contemporary philosophers to learn that Johann Friedrich Herbart was once more famous than George Wilhelm Friedrich Hegel. But he was.

Fate was very fickle in its treatment of Hegel and Herbart. The reputation of one rose as the other fell. With the collapse of the 1848 Revolution, Hegel's fortunes plummeted in Germany. All the Hegelian schools—left, right and center—disappeared into the mists of history, and the strife between them ceased to matter. But as Hegel declined, Herbart ascended. From the 1850s until the end of the century, there was a Herbartian school in Germany and Austria,[1] and a Herbartian journal, *Zeitschrift für exakte Philosophie*,[2] which lasted until the beginning of the next century. By the 1930s, however, both the movement and the journal had expired, and memory of the man behind their inspiration faded away. No one talked about Herbart anymore. It was now the turn of Hegel to rise from the dead. The scholarship of Kojève and Hyppolite in France, and the widespread European interest in the origins of Marxism, called Hegel from the grave and made him a focus of attention again. In turn, the Anglo-American Hegel renaissance of the 1970s made him an established figure in the history of philosophy. Now, as Hegel rose, Herbart fell. Nowadays, hardly anyone talks about Herbart. But perhaps the fortunes of these philosophers will reverse yet again. It might only be a matter of time before analytic philosophers, in search of their roots, will discover "the grandfather of analytic philosophy"—Herbart, leaving Hegel once again to take his place in the shade.

Despite their contrasting fates, there are some remarkable parallels in the lives of Hegel and Herbart. They shared so much one might think that they were brothers. Hegel lived from 1770 to 1831, Herbart from 1776 to 1841. They went to the same university, Jena, and both met the intellectual celebrities of that time and place. Both were house tutors in the same Swiss household, that of Baron von Steiger. Their first major publications were in the first decade of the 1800s: Hegel published his *Phänomenologie des Geistes* in 1807, a year after Herbart's *Hauptpunkte der Metaphysik*. Yet the two never met. They knew of one another well enough, though, and eyed one another with all the suspicion that comes with professional jealousy.

The parallels between Hegel and Herbart end when it comes to their doctrines, which could hardly be more opposed. Hegel was an absolute Idealist who believed in the identity of reason and reality. Herbart rejected the central premise of absolute idealism: teleology. In his

Psychologie als Wissenschaft (1820), he struggled to reassert two doctrines that Hegel had deposed: mechanism and atomism. And in his *Allgemeine Metaphysik* (1828-29), Herbart attempted to rid metaphysics of the heritage of absolute Idealism, whose monism he regarded as a terrible mistake.

For all their differences, there was still one point on which Hegel and Herbart agreed: Romanticism. In the early 1800s both were drunk with it, but both of them quickly sobered up and grew out of it; in their mature writings they had cast off its legacy. What united Hegel and Herbart in their opposition to Romanticism was their shared rationalism, which led to a similar critique of intellectual intuition. What was grasped in intuition, they both believed, had to be articulated in concepts and demonstrated by reasoning. From their shared opposition to Romanticism came their common suspicion of Schelling and his school.

But even here, where Herbart and Hegel were closest, their affinity remained concealed to at least one of them. Herbart was convinced that Schelling was behind some of the more objectionable features of Hegel's metaphysics: its monism and its teleology. He saw Hegel's metaphysics as only a more elaborate and obscure form of Schelling's philosophy of identity. He could not see within Hegel's metaphysics an attempt to refute Schelling and to reaffirm rationalism. This was a crucial mistake on Herbart's part.

Origins and Context of Herbart's Review

In June 1836 Herbart published his last major work, *Analytische Beleuchtung des Naturrechts und der Moral.*[3] The work was a compendium to accompany his lectures on practical philosophy, and it was meant as an introduction to the field. Herbart told his friend Martin Wilhelm Drobisch that his aim in writing the book was to prepare the reader for his *Allgemeine praktische Philosophie,*[4] which he still regarded as his final word on the subject, even though it had first been published in 1808.

The *Analytische Beleuchtung* is in large part a critical commentary on previous works in its field. Herbart examines some of the leading works on natural right, among them those of Grotius, Kant, Hufeland, and Fichte; he also investigates seminal works in morals, especially those of Plato, Aristotle, Spinoza and Schleiermacher. But there is one figure missing in Herbart's otherwise broad survey: Hegel. He had become one of the most important thinkers in natural right and morals in the 1830s; but Herbart never mentioned him. Gustav Hartenstein, Herbart's student and later editor, wrote him that this was a shortcoming of his work, because modern readers would expect him to take account of Hegel.[5] Furthermore, Hartenstein added, Hegel had questioned the independence of ethics from natural law, which it was Herbart's intention to defend. All the more reason, then, to write about Hegel.

The very day he received Hartenstein's letter, July 3, 1836, Herbart took up the issue of Hegel with Drobisch: "Please do not refer me to the *Berliner Jahrbücher* nor to the Hegelei;[6] for I ignore these without boasting of it. My age excuses me; and for my person, I am outside the realm of this nonsense."[7] From Herbart's letter to Drobisch, one would infer that Herbart had never paid serious attention to Hegel, let alone attempted to rebut him; after all, Hegel was "nonsense" and there could not be any reward for the effort of writing about him.

But this inference would be incorrect. In 1821, shortly after it first appeared, Herbart wrote a long review of Hegel's *Grundlinien der Philosophie des Rechts.*[8] It was a serious examination of Hegel's work, and it reveals an intense effort to grapple with its contents. It was one of the most important reviews Herbart ever wrote, and one of the longest. It fully betrays Herbart's recognition, despite his passing attempt at belittlement, that he was dealing with an important philosopher. The review, though it is dense and difficult, deserves the effort to examine it.

Before we examine the content of Herbart's review, we do well to consider its context. In 1822, when the review was published, Herbart's alienation from the German intellectual establishment was at its height. He felt isolated in the Prussian hinterland as a professor in Königsberg; he held Kant's chair there, a prestigious appointment, but it did not help him escape his isolation. The heart of things, the center of philosophy in Germany, was Berlin. But it was Hegel who was the professor in Berlin, which made him, for Herbart, the epitome of the German establishment. When Hegel died, Herbart wanted that chair; but he knew he would never get it because of the power and influence of the Hegelian school in Berlin. Given these circumstances, one should expect a measure of envy and resentment in Herbart's review, as there was.

One other contextual factor shaped Herbart's review: namely, the perceived influence of Schelling on Hegel. Herbart knew that Schelling was Hegel's ally in Jena; and he greatly exaggerated his influence on Hegel. So much the worse, then, for Herbart's review of Hegel. Herbart regarded

Schelling as the source of all the evil in contemporary philosophy. Schelling's mode of philosophizing, which stressed the role of intellectual intuition, was behind the dogmatism and irrationalism in contemporary philosophy, Herbart believed. Despite Hegel's own later attempts to distance himself from Schelling, Herbart still believed that Schelling was a major influence on Hegel. It was all the more reason for him to be critical of Hegel.

The First Part of the Review

For Herbart, the problems with Hegel's *Rechtsphilosophie* began with the subtitle: *Naturrecht und Staatswissenschaft im Grundrisse*. This was very misleading, Herbart thought, because it made it seem as if *Staatswissenschaft* is exhausted by *Naturecht* or *Rechtslehre*, as if the science of the state were fully encapsulated by the study of its laws. This is incorrect because the science of the state is more than the science of its laws. The science of the state also has to examine the *natural necessity* by which the state came into being; it has to show historically how the association of families came together to form a state, a process which took place before its formulation into laws and their articulation into a system. The affairs of the state have often taken place, for historical or natural reasons, independently of any process instituted by human beings to construct a legal system. Much of the science of the state should be regarded as analogous to physiology, Herbart says (1822, 141). Just as the body exists before the formulation of a science of medicine to treat it, so the state exists prior to the formulation of a science of laws to organize and legalize it.

Herbart recognizes, however, that Hegel had systematic reasons for integrating the science of the state with the science of law. There was a deep element of Spinozism in Hegel's philosophy, and for Spinoza there is no distinction between fact and norm, between might and right. God's power is the same as God's right; every finite being has as much right as it has power within itself (141). The science of the state, which is about power, therefore should be incorporated into the science of law or right.

Herbart also saw, though, that Hegel's Spinozism is not as crude as it first appears. Hegel does not simply equate right with might: the will of the stronger or most powerful. There was also a Schellingian moment to his Spinozism, an injection of Kantian transcendental freedom and Platonic ideas into Spinoza (142). It was this Kantian and Platonic dimension of his Spinozism that allowed Hegel to polemicize against positivist jurors who accepted unjust Roman laws about the treatment of children and slaves. Because of the Kantian and Platonic element, Hegel did not simply equate rationality with actuality; there was an ideal element in rationality that could not be reduced to a matter of fact.

Herbart was still not satisfied with Hegel's theory, however. The fundamental question, then, was whether it is possible to integrate Kant's theory of freedom with Spinoza? Herbart was skeptical that this could work. It is characteristic of Spinozism to emphasize the unity and wholeness of the universe; but how can a plurality of free beings, each of which is contingent for the others, ever fit into such a universe (142)? Free beings should each be self-determining; and should they establish an institution of laws among themselves, this should be their goal, which would be impossible without their independent wills. According to Spinoza, however, these beings are originally and primally one, and only through the divergence in their unity do they become many. According to Kant, by contrast, these beings are originally and primally many, and only through free association can they become one. For Spinoza, unity is the truth and the many is the appearance; but for Kant, the many is the truth and the unity is only in representation (143). In Spinoza's substance, the many free beings will not really be free; they will be like unfortunate Siamese twins, or they will have the freedom of oysters or polyps (143).

However, to think that Hegel's system is guilty of such an obvious and naked fallacy, Herbart admits, would be "unfair and incorrect." There is still possible a third mediating term between Kant and Spinoza, Herbart tells us. It is only after examining this term that we will be in a position to evaluate Hegel's theory. To understand the term, Herbart says that we first have to go back in history and examine Spinoza's original problem, and consider how Schelling attempted to solve it through Fichtean means.

The problem Spinoza faced was how to explain, from his absolute substance, the plurality of finite things (143). Spinoza's solution to this problem was to see the limits between finite things as only negations, nothing real, which is virtually to confess that the sum of finite things does not really exist (144). The new Spinozist school, including Schelling, had a better solution to the problem: they claimed that in the absolute substance, there is an original power of dividing and reuniting itself, so that the multitude of finite things was reincorporated and reunited in their primal unity. There was, in other words, a process in the absolute that moved from unity, to difference, and then to difference in unity. Difference, then, is not something unreal that stands outside the absolute, but is the process by which the absolute realizes itself.

Herbart admitted that there was something fantastic about this solution. How could the absolute substance, which is pure unity, negate itself and reproduce its unity from its self-negations? But for those who could not understand how anyone could believe or utter such nonsense, Herbart duly cited, word for word, §7 of the *Philosophie des Rechts* (144).[9]

It was through attributing this process of development to the Spinozian substance that Hegel managed to integrate Fichtean freedom into Spinozism. For the freedom of the Fichtean ego consists in an analogous process of development. It moves from self-positing, to the self-oppositing of a non-ego, and then to the reunification of ego and non-ego in an absolute ego. And so Herbart explains: "One now sees how through the thought, '*I am only limited because I so posit myself*' the finitude of Spinozism is inoculated with freedom" (144).

There can be no doubt that Herbart interpreted Hegel "fairly and correctly" in giving such importance to the idea of dialectical development, i.e., the idea that spirit develops in a pattern from unity, to difference, to unity-in-difference. This was indeed Hegel's mediating term between Spinoza and Fichte. Yet Herbart thought that Hegel's effort to unite such opposing thinkers in this way was imprudent and only led to more nonsense. "From absolute substance, absolute freedom, finitude, infinitude, etc. one can produce many forms just like in the familiar Chinese game. . . . Spectators will stand transfixed by the myriad forms but then turn away and each go its own way, as if nothing happened—for the simple reason *that nothing has really happened*" (145).

Though Herbart did not explain himself in detail in his review, in some of his earliest philosophical essays he had critically examined Fichte's idea of the ego and came to some similarly damning conclusions.[10] He rejected the very idea of the dialectical development of the ego. How could the ego, which is only what it posits itself to be, negate or limit itself by positing a non-ego? How can the ego be *both* self-positing and self-oppositing? The whole theory was absurd. Herbart alluded to this argument in his review of Hegel, though he did not spell it out explicitly, as he did earlier. It was not least because of this critique that Herbart had ceased to be a Fichtean and abandoned the idea of the ego as a central concept of philosophy.

The Second Part of the Review

So far we have analyzed only the first part of Herbart's review; it remains to examine the second half.[11] The second half considers the topics of natural law and the state. Natural law was a subject about which Herbart had always felt suspicious. One of the theses he defended for his Inaugural Disputation in Göttingen, in 1802, was that "there is no perfect and absolute science of natural law."[12] Herbart maintained this skepticism toward natural law for the rest of his career. It surfaces clearly and powerfully in his review of Hegel.

The thrust of Herbart's critique of natural law is that it attempts to prove by reason what cannot be determined by reason at all. It pretends to be a purely rational science about a subject matter that, not being rational, exceeds its competence. This criticism appears in the very first paragraph of the second half of the review. Herbart states that "the most familiar and most stressed principle of natural law is that there should be no conflict in the external use of freedom" (145). Why there should be no conflict, however, is left totally unclear. Only one thing *is* clear: that this principle is affirmed if one thinks that its denial leads to a contradiction; but there is no more contradiction in the conflict of wills than in that conflict of natural powers we see every day (145). Though he does not cite it, Herbart here seems to rely on Kant's distinction between logical contradiction and real or physical conflict, in a text he knew very well.[13] The conflict between people is a real logical possibility, whereas a contradiction is a logical impossibility.

It should at least be clear, Herbart contends, that the above principle is insufficient to prove all the relations of right (*Rechtsverhältnisse*) that one wants to build upon it (145). One attempts to derive from this principle all external relations of property. It seems that a right to property should protect the right of everyone to something; but the question is never answered *how much* does everyone deserve (145)? One cannot determine a priori the quantity of deserved goods or the degree of their convenient distribution. Who is to say through pure reason what is too much or what is too little (146)? For a Napoleon, a whole island would be too little "for the external use of his freedom." And what is too much or too little for a whole nation of Napoleons? Behind attempts to determine the limit of rights there lies a false principle, Herbart says, namely "that the external use of freedom has a dignity, and one upon which right as such can rest" (146). Though Herbart does not mention Hegel here, it is clear that he had him in mind as one of the propagators of this false principle.[14]

There is no a priori, logical, or purely rational basis for the distribution of property rights, Herbart contends. The only way to prevent strife between people, he is convinced, is through the consensus of all. The right to property has to be determined through agreement between people; and there is no a priori limit on what their agreement should or can be (146). If there is no consensus, no agreement, then there is no property. One cannot justify property, therefore, by appeals to first occupancy. The old rules of right—*res nullius cedit primo occupanti* or *qui prior tempore, potior iure*—are for Herbart nothing more than remnants of barbarism.

Although Herbart disputes the existence of a natural law as an ethical norm justified by reason itself, there is another sense in which he acknowledges the existence of a natural law, though it would give no comfort to Hegel or anyone else in the natural-law tradition. In this other sense, natural law is how people would behave by nature, i.e., according to their instincts and feelings, independent of any education or social norms. We all know well enough, Herbart says, how people would behave in a "state of nature" where there is no law, morality, or education: "what would happen then we see every day when a bunch of rascals get together: they grab one another and fight" (147). Natural right is nothing less than "the right of the strongest" (148). When the ideas of natural right and natural law are consistently developed, Herbart says, they lead inevitably to Spinozism. Just as Jacobi once claimed that all philosophy leads to Spinozism, so Herbart now says the same of natural law and right. Like Jacobi, Herbart thought that this was a *reductio ad absurdum*.

Herbart has as many criticisms of Hegel's theory of the state as he has of his theory of natural law. He does not accept Hegel's signature doctrine that the individual has "objectivity and truth" only insofar as he is a member of the state. He can hardly believe that Hegel is actually saying this.

> Really the state? Which connects some citizens only as it separates others? Which concerns itself only with external actions and does not bother with inner dispositions? For whom good and evil are equal so long as one and the other show the same conformity to law? Is it really the state that should

> express those thoughts about the return of the individual into the absolute substance? (151)

The skepticism that Herbart expresses here comes from his own more liberal and more individualistic ethics, which made the development of individuality the foremost task of ethics. Against Plato and Fichte, Herbart believed that it is dangerous to give the state the leading role in the education of the individual. Private education is the best protection of the individual against the forces of conformity and state hegemony.

If Herbart is incredulous about the role Hegel assigns to the state in the education of the individual, he is no less amazed by Hegel's statements about the role of philosophy *vis-á-vis* the state. Hegel famously claimed that it is not the business of philosophy to teach how the state ought to be, but that its only task is to grasp it as it is (152). In reply, Herbart could only ask: "Is that really serious?" He could not really believe that it was more important for Hegel to fit into the world as it is rather than as it ought to be. All excellent thinkers have always strived, he insists, to stand above the world and to judge it as it ought to be (ibid.). It was part and parcel of Hegel's stand against prescribing how the world ought to be that he said, "Every nation has the constitution adequate to it and that belongs to it" (Hegel, PR §274R). This was a useless statement, Herbart felt. For what is the constitution that best serves France? The constitutions in France have changed erratically since 1789, so how can we conclude that the right one is the present one? Hegel seems to have in mind a kind of relativism by saying this; but this does not allow anyone to judge, in the case of a conflict of opinion, which is the best constitution for a country.

In concluding his review, Herbart makes one passing compliment to Hegel: "The author of the book shows himself as a masculine thinker to whom one can ascribe more acumen than invention, and who has in his own manner tried to bring order and distinctness into his views, [an effort] which shows insight in many places" (153). But, Herbart tells us, he would have seen the whole with more insight if he had avoided "the Schellingian lapse of sinking into Spinozism" (ibid.). In ascribing such importance to Schelling, Herbart did Hegel an injustice. Schelling's Spinozism—"the night when all cows are black"—was not Hegel's Spinozism; and behind Schelling's Spinozism stood the romantic love of intuition and feeling that Hegel rejected no less than Herbart.

The conflation of Hegel's and Schelling's Spinozism was fatal for Herbart's opinion of Hegel, for it meant that all the vices he attributed to the Schellingian school he also saw as afflicting Hegel. What Herbart said against Schelling he also said against Hegel. And so he concludes his review: "Herr Hegel speaks in his preface of the contemptible vices into which philosophy has sunk in our age; but he should be silent; because this decay has happened at a time when no one has spoken louder and sharper than the school to which he belongs. Nothing else is guilty of this decline than the boldness and insolence of this school, which asserts rather than proves, which fantasizes rather thinks rigorously and acutely" (153). This was the final nail in the coffin which Herbart had built for Hegel; but the deceased did not fit into it well.

Such were, if only in a brief summary, the contents of Herbart's review of Hegel. Why Herbart never mentioned it when Hartenstein urged him to write about Hegel in 1836 is something of a mystery. It was an incisive and thorough review, not a piece that someone would need to disown or want to forget. But Herbart's contempt for all reviews, including his own, might have led him not to mention it. "Reviews are mayflies. Who will catch them when they die?" That was his opinion of all reviews, as he told his friend Griepenkerl.[15] The review of Hegel, despite its weight and density, was a mayfly.

NOTES

1. On the Herbartian school, see Siebert 1898, 136-83.
2. The complete title of the journal was *Zeitschrift für exakte Philosophie im Sinne des neueren philosophischen Realismus;* it was edited by Friedrich Allihn and Tuiskon Zille.
3. In *Sämtliche Werke* (abbreviated SW) X, 315-460.
4. An Drobisch, 26 February 1836, SW XVIII, 192.
5. Hartenstein an Herbart, 3 July 1836, SW XVIII, 215.
6. The *Berliner Jahrbücher* was the journal of the Hegelian school. "Hegelei" is a derogatory reference to Hegelian discourse.
7. Herbart an Drobisch, undated, SW XVIII, 216. Though undated, this letter was written the same day Herbart received Hartenstein's letter, 3 July 1836. The postmark is from 9 July 1836.
8. The review was originally published in the *Leipziger Literatur-Zeitung,* 1822.
9. See *Werke* VII, 54-55.
10. See "Spinoza und Schelling: Eine Skizze," SW I, 9-11; and "Versuch einer Beurteilung von Schellings Schrift 'Über die Möglichkeit einer Form der Philosophie überhaupt," SW I, 12-16.
11. The first half is from SW XII, 140-45; the second half from SW XII, 145-54. These parts are not marked in the text itself.

12. The thesis states in the original Latin: "X. *Jus naturae, tanquam scientia in se perfect atque absoluta, ab ethica et politica separanda, nullum est.*"
13. See Kant 1763.
14. See Hegel 1820 §§41-42, Werke VII: 102-4.
15. Herbart to Griepenkerl, 24 September 1827, SW XVII, 157.

REFERENCES

Hegel, G.W.F. 1820. *Grundlinien der Philosophie des Rechts*, in *Werke* VII.

Hegel, G.W.F. 1970. *Werke in zwanzig Bänden*, ed. Karl Michel and Eva Moldenhauer. Frankfurt: Suhrkamp Verlag.

Herbart, Johnan Friedrich. 1822. "Hegel, Dr. Georg Wilhelm Friedrich, ordentl, Prof. der Philosophie zu Berlin, *Naturrecht und Staatswissenschaft im Grundrisse, zum Gebrauch für seine Vorlesungen*. Berlin, 1821." *Leipziger Literatur-Zeitung*, Nr. 45-47, reprinted in SW XII, 140-154.

Herbart, Johann Friedrich. 1836. *Analytische Beleuchtung des Naturrechts und der Moral*. Göttingen: Dieterich. In SW X, 315-460.

Herbart, Johann Friedrich. 1887-1912. *Sämtliche Werke* (SW), 19 vols., ed. Karl Kehrbach and Otto Flügel. Langensalza: Hermann Beyer & Söhne.

Kant, Immanuel. 1763. *Versuch den Begriff der negativen Größen in die Weltweisheit einzuführen*. Königsberg: Kanter. In the Akademieausgabe, vol. II, 165-204.

Siebert, Otto. 1898. *Geschichte der neueren deutschen Philosophie seit Hegel*. Göttingen: Vandenhoeck & Ruprecht.

Darren Nah

HEGEL, WEBER, AND BUREAUCRACY

ABSTRACT: *Hegel gave the bureaucracy a distinctively corporatist and collegiate structure and insulated it from legislative control. The close match between these features of the* Philosophy or Right *and the structure of the Prussian bureaucracy, which had been used by reformers to insulate progressive decisions from Junker resistance, suggests that Hegel, too, wanted the bureaucracy to spearhead reform within a hostile environment.*

In the *Philosophy of Right*, civil servants drawn from what Hegel calls the "universal estate" (*allgemeiner Stand*) are at the executive helm of the government and are given very wide latitude to set its priorities.[1] This is why the Hegelian state, as Bernard Yack argues, can be aptly described as "the rule of public officials" (1980, 715; cf. Avineri 1972; Bowman 2013; Jackson 1986; Shaw 1992; and Tunick 1991).

Hegel's vision of bureaucracy markedly differed from that of, say, Max Weber, who saw bureaucracy as a passive and dispassionate instrument whose job is to realize the will of a parliamentary majority, which the bureaucrats ought to have no part shaping (Sager and Rosser 2009; Tijsterman and Overeem 2008; Spicer 2004, and Gale and Hummel 2003).

Since Hegel argued that responsible government can be achieved only when the bureaucracy is insulated from external political pressures, many are inclined to reject Hegel's vision of the state as anti-democratic, in contrast to the conventional Weberian vision of the bureaucracy.[2]

This reading of Hegel is true as far as it goes, but it ignores the historical context. Hegel, I will suggest, defended a relatively insulated bureaucracy as a way of combatting the traditionalist landowning aristocracy, which dominated the Prussian legislature.[3] Unlike Weber, for whom the main issue was to bring the German state under democratic control, Hegel worked to insulate the state apparatus from the power of traditionalist elites by undermining the Junker-dominated parliament, and by giving the bureaucracy itself a distinctively non-Weberian corporatist and collegiate structure.[4] By "corporatist" I mean that the bureaucratic establishment is publicly recognized as one of the three estates, while by "collegiate" I refer to the fact that top-level Hegelian bureaucrats "work together in groups" (PR §289). Corporatist and collegiate features, Hegel seemed to think, would allow the bureaucracy to spearhead reform against the aristocracy.

Hegel's proposed regime appears to be a continuation and idealization of the agenda of the early nineteenth-century reformers, such as Stein and Hardenberg, who ultimately failed to realize their efforts due to changing geo-political and domestic tides. The context of the battle over reform is too often ignored in attempts to make sense of Hegel's political philosophy. Before fleshing out this context, section I begins by laying out Hegel's theory of bureaucracy and, by contrast, Weber's. Section II then explains their differences and the insufficiency of contemporary explanations of these differences that appeal to their philosophies of freedom. Section III concludes with the historical context of Hegel's defense of a relatively insulated bureaucracy.

I. HEGEL AND WEBER ON BUREAUCRACY

The profound conceptual difference between Hegel's and Weber's visions of bureaucracy centers on Hegel's rejection of the strict separation of politics from administration, which would be central to Weber's schema. Because Hegel did not strictly separate the two, arguing that an unelected bureaucracy should have wide political initiative in the shaping of government policy, many today are inclined to see in his vision of an unaccountable executive a threat to democratic accountability (e.g., Hardimon 1994, 220-27). After all, if unelected bureaucrats set the government's agenda on their own, how can the people hold the government to account? Weber's strict separation of politics and administration appears more conducive to democracy, since it puts representative institutions in charge of the bureaucracy. Blake Emerson (2019, 53) applies this view to the post-Hegelian course of German political history:

> The most significant failure of the Hegelian tradition of German state theory . . . was that it did not appreciate the need to democratize the state as a whole and the administrative process in particular. Hegelian legal scholars did not adequately recognize that individual freedom would require active popular involvement in the exercise of public power if the principle of self-determination were to have real purchase. When the state had finally been democratized under Weimar, this occurred only at the level of the parliament and the president. With the decline in parliamentary control, the "democratic" nature of administration was thus identified with the plebiscitary mandate of the president rather than with deliberation in the public sphere, in parliament, or within administrative bodies themselves.

I want to question assessments such as Emerson's, so let us first see where Hegel and Weber meet and where they diverge. Doing so allows us to map the two visions of how the executive relates to the legislature under varying constitutional arrangements.

It is well known that both Hegel and Weber saw in bureaucracy an organization that institutionalizes impersonal and rational forms of authority, which are embodied in the notion of the civil servant (PR §294).[5] Rejecting the patrimonial and feudal personalization of premodern governmental authority, both Hegel and Weber shared the view that bureaucracy is a novel form of public administration that centers on the rule of professionals who (1) do not own their offices but are salaried by the state according to a systematic pay scale indexed to seniority; (2) are chosen based on criteria determined by the functional needs of the organization, as opposed to nepotism or such purely extraneous considerations as noble birth; (3) are bounded in public action by clear and explicitly written rules and procedures of operation; (4) are interpersonally structured according to a well-defined chain of command and career promotion; (5) work within relatively differentiated and specialized spheres of competence and expertise; and (6) are full-time careerists, not amateurs (PR §§274, 277, 288-289, 290, 291, 294). Yet as much as their theories of bureaucracy are alike in these respects, Hegel and Weber differ on *whom* the bureaucrat is ultimately accountable to.

In rejecting the authoritarian thrust of Imperial German politics and in defending the Weimar parliamentary regime, Weber found it imperative that the bureaucracy be subordinated to the "political" organs of government, by which he meant those institutions that decide upon the agenda of state policy through a competitive electoral process (Beetham 1985, 95-118). The subordination of the bureaucracy to parliamentary decision-making upholds the strict and indispensable separation of public administration from politics by placing bureaucrats who implement the day-to-day running of the state under the direction and supervision of party politicians in a parliament sensitive to public opinion (Overeem 2005; Fry and Nigro 1996). This distinctive Weberian separation of politics from bureaucratic administration, which renders the latter politically "neutral," is intuitively appealing to democratic sensibilities. In order to subordinate bureaucratic elites to the people, it is strictly the job of unelected public agents dutifully and impersonally—*sine ira et studio*—to carry out the wishes of the democratic majority (Weber 2004, 53-54). For bureaucrats to countermand, alter, or question their orders or shirk their duties would be to insert an element of democratic unaccountability into the state and call into question the extent to which the people govern themselves.

By contrast, Hegel dispenses with the strict separation of politics and administration.[6] Indeed, one might question whether there is even a distinction between the two in Hegel's theory of the state, since Hegel accords bureaucrats extremely wide latitude to set government priorities. It is true that in certain passages, Hegel argues that the bureaucrats are subordinate to the "sovereign" monarch, who is technically the head of the entire public administrative apparatus. But the formal nature of the monarch's powers and his dependence on the skill and expertise of his bureaucratic ministers effectively puts political power in the hands of his "subordinates" and makes the civil servants the drivers of political initiative in the Hegelian state. Thus, neither the personality nor the initiative of the monarch matters much in the actual development of government priorities. Hegel writes:

> A frequent objection to monarchy is that it makes the affairs of the state subject to contingency—since the monarch may be ill-educated or unworthy of holding the highest office—and that it is absurd for such a

> situation to be regarded as rational. But this objection is based on the invalid assumption that the monarch's particular character is of vital importance. In a fully organized state, it is only a question of the highest instance of formal decision, and all that is required in a monarch is someone to say 'yes' and to dot the 'I'; for the supreme office should be such that the particular character of the monarch is of no significance. (PR §280, Addition)

This suggests that most of the work done in the executive branch is done not by the monarch himself but his agents, the bureaucrats. As Hegel soon specifies,

> the task of *upholding*, within these particular rights, *legality* and the *universal interest of the state*, and that of bringing these rights back to the universal [i.e., common good], need to be performed by delegates of the executive power, i.e., the executive civil servants and the higher consultative bodies. The latter work together in groups and they converge in their supreme heads who are in touch with the monarch himself. (PR §289)

These descriptions of the bureaucratic state mirror earlier reformers' creation of centralized Prussian power, which Gianfranco Poggi describes this way:

> An essential component [of bureaucratic absolutism in Prussia] was a new body of law—'public law'—specifically concerned with the construction and operation of the administrative system. The system's members operated not immediately on a commission from the ruler, nor as the direct executors of his personal commands, but rather, under the guidance and control of a body of enacted norms that articulated the state's power (unitarily conceived) into a number of functions each of which was entrusted to an organ, i.e., a set of coordinated offices empowered to form and enforce authoritative decisions. Each organ possessed precisely delimited competencies, standards by which to evaluate their exercise, and formal and material faculties for operations. The individuals manning such operations were functionaries (*Beamte*) duly appointed to the component offices of each organ and supposedly trained and tested in the business of those office. . . . Except at the highest level, where peculiarly "political" decisions were taken on matters concerning the internal and external security of the state or the broader direction of its policy, all individual decisions were to be reached through juristic reasoning—applying general legal provisions to carefully ascertained and documented circumstances. . . . Thus *the state was intended to operate as the instrument of its own enacted laws, thereby making its activities systematized, coordinated, predictable, machinelike and impersonal.* (Poggi 1978, 74–75)[7]

In reproducing these features in his theory of the bureaucracy, Hegel, unlike Weber, insulates the bureaucratic establishment from external political pressures by emphasizing the corporatist and collegiate structure it is to have. So let us attend to these two key features of Hegel's vision of bureaucracy

First, Hegel says that the bureaucrats of his state are to belong to one of the three recognized corporate bodies. The universal estate of bureaucrats, the estate of industry and trade, and the estate of agriculture comprise civil society (PR §250). The reason for a tripartite division of society into corporations of civil servants, businessmen, and agrarians has been the subject of much speculation, with some portraying it as reflecting Hegel's triadic logic and/or his dialectical form of reasoning applied to society, while others claim that it was an attempt to rationalize Prussian feudalism (Lee 2008; Nederman 1987). For my purposes, however, what is important to note is that the integration of the universal estate with the other corporate bodies in the Hegelian state, and its simultaneous control of the executive branch of government, are in direct contrast to the Weberian paradigm. Hegel's bureaucracy resembles more, for lack of a better term, a powerful clique in control of government than the rational and impersonal instrument of a parliamentary majority advocated by Weber.

Second, this cliquish aspect of the Hegelian bureaucracy is enhanced by the collegial structure of the higher levels of public administration (PR §289). Unlike the Weberian civil servant, who is accountable to the ultimate authority of parliament in the conduct of public affairs, the high-level Hegelian bureaucrat, by dint of his corporate standing and membership in a college of bureaucratic peers, is free of legislative control. "Control," Michael W. Jackson (1986, 149) therefore concludes, "must come from within the bureaucracy and ultimately from within each bureaucrat."[8]

The decisive issue is that, at the highest echelons of government in the Hegelian state, the deciding, adjudicating, and implementing functions of public administration are jointly exercised by one group of men, the bureaucrats (cf. PR §297).

II. WHY DID HEGEL INSULATE THE BUREAUCRACY FROM LEGISLATIVE ACCOUNTABILITY?

Contemporary scholars have come up with several explanations for Hegel's theory of bureaucracy that, when they go beyond merely noting the unfortunate naïveté of Hegel's trust in the universal class, typically fall into two broad categories: finding philosophical justifications for Hegel's view or apologizing for its antidemocratic consequences. Let us take each in turn and see why these attempts fall short.

Taking the philosophical route, Sebastiaan P. Tijsterman and Patrick Overeem (2008) argue that Hegel gave such wide political latitude to bureaucrats to determine the public agenda because his notions of freedom and rationality fundamentally differed from those of Weber. For Weber, modern human rationality cannot, in a disenchanted world, decide upon the ultimate ends of life, and so can only instrumentally decide upon the means to achieve a given set of priorities whose ultimate ordering is inscrutable to reason, being the product of an existential decision. In politics, this means that the ultimate priorities (ends) of a government are decided in an agonistic political arena between parties struggling to win a majority. The task of the bureaucracy under such a regime is to carry out the majority party's decision, not to question it. Weber's separation of public administration, which decides on the means, and high politics, which decides on the ends, is thought therefore to flow directly from his view that values are irreconcilable and that ends are set by arbitrary decision, not ratiocination—a view of human choice that, in obvious respects, Hegel's systematic way of thinking rejects (Overeem 2005).

Hegel's is a processual and social understanding of human reason that underscores how the ends and means of human agency mutually condition each other in a community (Pinkard 1994). That is, Hegelian rationality is a collective and reflective process in which individuals try to grasp their own consciousness in relation to that of others. By being involved in the crafting of policy, by actively adjudicating disputes, and by being a party to the collective decisions affecting all—*ira et studium*—the Hegelian civil servant is integrated into every stage of the process of government. For Hegel, there can be no question of reducing reason to simply developing the instrumental means of pursuing an externally given end. Accordingly, the bureaucracy does not fulfill this function. Instead, the highest bureaucrats act as a collegial mini-deliberative body whose job it is to take an expansive, "universal" view of affairs, shape policy in light of their own "educated" insights, and hold each other to account for their public duties, embodying social rationality, in contrast to Weber's instrumentalism. Emerson (2019, 46) nicely articulates this point:

> The disparity between this Weberian vision of bureaucracy and the Hegelian account is remarkable. Hegel and Weber described the same general kind of institutional phenomena—a merit-based public officialdom carrying out the laws, organized in a hierarchical, functionally differentiated system. But for Hegel this administrative staff was permeated with substantive normative commitments. Its purpose was to advance social freedom through public welfare provision, a contextually sensitive implementation of law, and a careful adjudication of social antagonisms and conflicts. Public law for Hegel was the means by which individuals were able to recognize one another as members of a common political project and community. The officials who implemented this law were therefore engaged in the interpretation and maintenance of the public rights held by this community. For Weber, by contrast, administration had become a purely instrumental form of rule. The law it implemented was distinguished by its formal generality, which was open to any substantive content. The ethic of the bureaucratic staff and the structure of bureaucratic organization both aimed to facilitate the efficient application of these statutory commands, whatever they happened to be. The bureaucrat did not think so much as calculate and obey.

However, this appeal to the philosophical differences between Hegel and Weber should not be allowed to obscure the effects of the different historical and political environments within which they operated. For instance, it is unclear that, in Hegel's time, a proto-Weberian strengthening of parliamentary control over the bureaucracy would have had desirable effects.[9] If we reflect upon a related circumstance, the development of the American bureaucracy in the late nineteenth and early twentieth centuries, it might seem that that the subordination of the state apparatus to radically changing electoral majorities would result in a hodgepodge of inconsistent policies that actually undercut the public good. Stephen Skowronek (1982) shows, in effect, that Presidents Roosevelt, Taft, and Wilson (as well as other Progressives like them) acted more like Hegel and less like Weber to insulate bureaucracy from congressional majorities, because they thought congressional influence deeply inimical to any prospect of responsible government.

A second line of interpretation succumbs to the apologetic temptation to mitigate all of the unpalatable aspects of Hegelian thought. For example, Brady Bowman (2013) tries to frame the corporatist and collegiate structure of Hegelian bureaucracy as somehow reflecting Hegel's commitment to "republican ideals," by which he means mean citizen participation in and control of government. On Bowman's account, Hegelian bureaucracy institutionalizes the ancient Greek ideal of participatory citizenship. The bureaucrat is a citizen whose position within the state as member of a corporate body permits his involvement in ruling and making decisions in a college of his peers. Bowman's hope is that, by identifying aspects of republicanism in how Hegel stresses the need for the transparency and publicity of bureaucratic processes, we can reinterpret his bureaucratism in less alien terms and bring him closer to our shared commitment to citizen self-government.

Yet it was precisely the collegiate nature of the Prussian bureaucracy that facilitated its degeneration into an insular, self-serving organization under Bismarck (Gillis 1971; Liebich 1982). This was not an accident. To associate the corporatist and collegiate nature of Hegelian bureaucracy with civic republican thought contradicts their very purpose: *restricting* the bureaucratic class to the educated elements of society. Although the bureaucratic code of professionalism "guarantees every citizen the possibility of joining the universal estate," according to Hegel, this guarantee is qualified by the possession of relevant "knowledge [*Erkenntnis*] and proof of ability" (PR §291). The need for an education that qualified one for bureaucratic office filtered out whoever could not afford to get a university degree.[10]

III. THE POLITICAL CONTEXT OF THE HEGELIAN BUREAUCRAT

Turning away from normative evaluations of Hegel's theory, pro and con, we still face the question of why Hegel suggested a corporate, collegial, and fundamentally inegalitarian bureaucracy.

One answer that has not been previously mooted is that this organizational form would advance progressive reforms and policies against the landowning nobility in Prussia, the Junkers. Had Hegel subordinated the bureaucratic establishment to an unreformed parliament, it would have had the perverse effect of strengthening the grip of the landowning aristocracy, which controlled the national legislature.

There was ample historical reason for this concern. In 1811-1812, following the Prussian defeat by Napoleon at Jena, a reform movement took hold that allowed Prince Hardenberg to oversee the establishment of a national legislature composed of 18 Junkers, 12 burghers, and 9 peasant representatives. The goal of the assembly was to obtain parliamentary agreement to levy taxes to fund the central government's priorities, especially war against France. But the nobility, under the leadership of Frederich August von der Marwitz, interpreted these reforms as an attack on their feudal privileges. The nobles' resistance went so far that the central government resorted to abolishing this early assembly and imprisoning its leaders at Spandau. Thereafter, Prussian reformers became increasingly wary of representative institutions—whose establishment in 1848, as Reinhart Koselleck (1967) argues, prevented all later reforms. (Prussia remained without a parliament from 1812 to 1848.)

Against this historical background, a Hegelian bureaucracy of collegiate and corporatist administration can be read as a rejection of the Weberian model of parliamentary control of the executive so as to undo the power of the landowning nobility to resist reform. Unlike Weber's obedient bureaucracy, the Hegelian universal estate acts as a unit insulated from legislative control, a disciplined phalanx of progressive reformers resembling a vanguard movement aimed at (1) spearheading public decisions for the sake of the whole of society, (2) controlling those tasked with implementing these reforms (lower-level civil servants), and (3) preventing competitive political forces from challenging their agenda or influencing the composition of their corporate body without their assent.

This possibility has been obscured by contemporary analyses of Hegel's historical context. Emerson (2019, 28), for example, claims that Hegelian administrative power "was organized under the monarchical executive and was constrained by the legislature, which represented the interests of bourgeois civil society." Yet it was not until 1914 (some say 1944) that the power of the Junker aristocracy in the Prussian Diet was effectively overcome. Before that, it was not the bourgeoisie but the landed aristocracy that controlled the legislature.[11]

The hold of aristocratic interests over German government was the legacy of Germany's late industrialization, which had only begun when Hegel was writing. Hegel was dealing with the problems of a largely feudal society, which was beginning to be transformed by contact with industrial England but had not yet experienced the radical structural transformations brought on by full-fledged industrialization.[12] A telltale sign of this situation is that Hegel still gave agriculture a prominent place in his state (PR §§305-307), which would have been anachronistic if agriculture had been reduced to an inconsequential element in a modern economy centered around the manufacturing, distribution, and sale of mass-marketed goods and services. Likewise, a cursory glance at Hegel's thoughts on political economy shows his inability to envision the concentrated state-led industrial growth that would eventually prove to be so important in overcoming Germany's late start in the game of industrialization. Simply put, Hegel never touched on (or even understood) how a truly industrial economy, especially one with bank-led and state-financed growth in capital-intensive industries such as iron production, would radically transform the very composition of a modernizing society, rendering an agricultural estate otiose and "bourgeois" politics rather different in Germany than it was in England.

In Hegel's day, Prussian society was dominated by three groups: the Junker nobility; the serfs; and the Hohenzollern monarchy, with its bureaucratic and military administrative arms—around which the civil servants, army officers, and professors gathered (Rosenberg 1958). For the rest of the nineteenth century the Junker nobility, the military establishment, and the bureaucracy would vie with each other for power. Unlike Great Britain, where commercial relations had, since the seventeenth-century Civil War, adapted the British peerage and gentry to a type of bourgeois "modernity" (whatever their aspirations for the bucolic and pastoral), the Junker ruling class of Hegel's time vigorously opposed every effort of the modernizing bureaucracy in Berlin to alter their traditional privileges. Prussia was still in an early transitional phase between feudal monarchism, with a strong aristocracy and a weak monarch, and what Hegel called a "fully organized state" (or "objective constitution"), where the central bureaucracy would be dominant. As he said in the *Philosophy of Right,*

> The fact that Montesquieu recognizes *honor* as the principle of *monarchy* is enough to indicate that the monarchy he has in mind is neither the patriarchal or ancient variety nor that which has developed an objective constitution, but *feudal monarchy* as that in which the relationships covered by its constitutional law [*inneren Staatsrecht*] have become firmly established as rights of private property and privileges of individuals and corporations. Since the life of the state is based, under this constitution, on *privileged personalities* to whose discretion a large part of what has to be done for the preservation of the state is entrusted, the objective aspect of their services consists not in *duties* but in *representations* [*Vorstellung*] and *opinions*; consequently, the state is held together not by duty but merely by *honour.* (PR §273)

This strike against "honor" in feudal monarchy shows that Hegel had aristocracy—government by "privileged personalities"—in his sights, for under feudal monarchy the relationship of these powerful individuals to the central government was based not on legal obligation, but on promises and oaths. Hegel was not, of course, complaining that the aristocracy broke its promises. His emphasis on "honor" in feudal monarchy implies instead the structural inability of the central government to compel obedience, especially the obedience of powerful aristocrats. Consequently, feudal monarchs had to rely on all sorts of soft powers—and, occasionally, destructive violence—to make sure that their lords and dukes obeyed. By contrast, in fully developed modern states, the concept of honor becomes less important precisely because the government, now in control of a monopoly of force, has the ability to coerce non-compliant individuals regardless of their private opinions. The goal of reforming bureaucrats, such as Stein and Hardenberg, was to build a state strong enough to overcome these discretionary relationships by centralizing and enforcing state priorities against the aristocracy. Seen in this light, it is not surprising how they were met with vigorous Junker opposition, which necessitated the insulation of the policy-making process from their control (Simon 1955).

Prussia's defeat by Napoleon temporarily discredited the strong grip of the Junker nobility and allowed the bureaucrats to seize the moment (Skocpol 1979, 108). Bureaucratic reformers moved to exclude the traditional nobility from power and rapidly proceeded to create the corporatist and collegiate bureaucratic structure that Poggi detailed for us above. This was done with the explicit purpose of centralizing the bureaucracy and insulating it from aristocratic interference, while ensuring that its members were drawn from a relatively homogeneous social group of non-noble professionals dedicated to public service (Westphal 2006). The reformers' goal was to introduce specific reforms in the agricultural economy, the military service, and education to modernize Prussia and strengthen the state, such as abolishing feudal restrictions on allodial land-holding and commercial activities, widening the tax base to include nobles, and introducing universal military conscription. The fate of these reforms depended on the Junker resistance the reformers encountered.[13]

In the realm of administrative reform, the parallels to Hegel's state structure are apparent. Under Stein's leadership, a ministry of state was introduced in 1808 that placed five functionally differentiated ministries —interior, foreign affairs, finance, justice, and war—directly under the king. This closely parallels Hegel argument that bureaucrats in the executive branch "converge in their supreme heads who are in touch with the monarch himself" (PR §289). Prior to this reform, ministerial responsibilities were divvied up geographically. By organizing offices functionally, which Hegel calls the "*division* [*Teilung*] *of* [ministerial] *labour*" (PR §290), the reformers were able to quickly centralize government efficiently to spearhead reform in ways impossible under the fragmented system before.[14]

At first, these measures prove politically successful. As John R. Gillis (1971, 14) notes,

> During the Reform Era every attempt to extend the principle of monocratic government to the bureaucratic hierarchy failed because of the resistance of the officials themselves.[15] The principle of collegiate responsibility in decision-making was retained at both the ministerial and district levels, where all matters of importance continued to require the deliberation of the entire membership of the particular unit concerned. All members of the agency involved took part in the discussion of every major question to come before their college, and all shared legal responsibility for the collective decision. The collegiate principle was the symbol of the corporate tradition of the bureaucracy. Though it was less efficient than monocratic organization, early nineteenth-century officials were strongly attached to it for reasons that were social as well as technical. Collegiate responsibility protected their profession against corruption and the threat of arbitrary intrusions from higher authorities, and officials regarded it as a reinforcement to the corporate morale and professional solidarity they believed to be necessary to the preservation of the honor and prestige of the bureaucratic estate.

Seen in this context, Hegel's defense of bureaucratic insulation idealized a regime in which reformers, buoyed by a sense of superiority and purpose, thought of themselves as "the rightful guardian[s] of the public interest," in contrast to the landed nobility. Universal equality was not their goal (ibid., 33).

However, by the time Hegel wrote the *Philosophy of Right*, the Prussian reform movement had largely been neutralized. Intense Junker opposition to reform, and geopolitical and domestic political tides of reaction, eventually ended their program. In Metternichian Europe, calls for reform became closely associated with the French Revolution, particularly Jacobinism. And the ascension to the Prussian throne of King Frederick William III, a romantic conservative, made reform efforts extremely difficult to pass. Under such pressures it is no surprise that the practically minded reformers, adjusting to the new realities that confronted them, gave up on the more radical aspects of their agenda.[16] Compromise with the landed nobility became strategically necessary even though, as many reformers realized, this reopened the door to aristocratic dominance. The *Philosophy of Right*, especially in the structural details of an insulated bureaucracy, can thus be read as an idealization of what the reformers' agenda, had they been successful, would have achieved.

The other striking fact about Hegel's historical moment is that the drive towards centralized and modern government had not emanated from the entrepreneurial and industrial "bourgeoisie," in contrast to Britain (Kemp 2013, 109-110). German modernization initiatives had to come from the bureaucratic establishment, since they not only threatened the established privileges of the traditionalist agrarian landholding elite, but because the commercial classes were unwilling to challenge that elite.[17] Prior to the arrival of a mass market (courtesy of bureaucratically imposed measures such as the *Zollverein*), there was no "consumer" or "general public" to be catered to by entrepreneurs selling their goods and investing their capital. This meant that commerce found its most (sometimes, *sole*) lucrative outlet by providing the nobility with "trinkets and baubles," as Adam Smith ([1776] 1981, 421) put it. Under such conditions, so far were the German bourgeoisie willing to question the primacy of the Junker class that they sought to ape them in manners and dress (see Berdahl 1988).[18] For these reasons, Otto Hintze (1975, 84-85) concludes that "at the beginning of the nineteenth century Prussia lacked a compact, responsible, politically active middle class that could stand on an equal footing with the landowning aristocracy." Almost by necessity, then, the driving force of reform came not from businessmen but civil servants and professionals.

Thus, in the *Philosophy of Right,* the term *die Mittlestande* excludes the commercial classes (PR §297).[19] Hegel offers all sorts of reasons for why the civil service cannot be staffed by businessmen, such as the narrowness of their views and the all-engrossing nature of industry, which prevents them from devoting themselves to the public interest (PR §§ 230, 234-238, 250-256, 306-308). Conversely, Hegel constructs a bureaucracy that draws its manpower exclusively from the educated, professional *Bildungsbürgertum,* excluding those involved in commerce or agriculture.[20] Intense training in law and *Bildung,* which stressed the cultivation of inner "spiritual" qualities, created an ethos of and justification for bureaucratic rule (Bruford 1935 and 1975). Hegel, like Humboldt, Schiller, and Goethe, was engaged in the pedagogical project of redefining what it meant to be an *élite* in the modern world. As much as this meant a rejection of commercial pursuits, it also meant a rejection of inherited privileges, martial pugnacity, and the rights of noble blood (PR §§295, 296, 297). The right to rule on the basis of "inner" merit rather than inheritance clearly excludes the aristocracy.

Hegelese about the "universal" aspect of the bureaucrats may plausibly be seen as reflecting the bureaucratic drive toward German unification at a time when conservative forces defended the parcellation of political power. Traditional elites benefited enormously from Germany's fragmentation into innumerable sovereign states, which Hegel detested. What the landed aristocracy feared above all was the rise of a unified and centralized state—precisely the form of organization that Hegel and the reformers envisioned—in which common laws, common standards, common procedures, in short, "universal" considerations, would predominate. The "universal" demanded the subordination of particularity to common measures, while aristocracy meant the triumph of particularity over the norm.

However, Hegel recognized the enduring power of the landed aristocracy, which, given the reaction against earlier reforms, could not simply be excluded from the government. This might explain why he incorporated the agricultural estate into the legislature. However, he did not give the agricultural estate explicit constitutional powers to veto government policy. Indeed, as Philippe Deranty (2001) points out, earlier notes for the *Philosophy of Right* gave this power to the legislature, but this idea did not survive in the published version. My conjecture is that Hegel thought that completely excluding the landed aristocracy would have turned them into inveterate enemies of his proposed government, while giving them some degree of representation would have made them amenable to the program of the reformers. It must be remembered that prior to the reformers, there had not been a *national* Prussian Diet, so representation in a national legislature would have given greater prominence to the landed aristocracy than they had had in their *local* Estates alone.

If so, however, Hegel severely underestimated the long-term political power of the Junkers. Hegel expectantly wrote:

> In our times, the [agricultural economy], too, is run in a reflective manner, like a factory, and it accordingly takes on a character like that of the second

> estate and opposed to its own character of naturalness. Nevertheless, this first estate will always retain the patriarchal way of life and the substantial disposition associated with it. The human being reacts here with immediate feeling [*Empfingdung*] as he accepts what he receives; he thanks God for it and lives in faith and confidence that this goodness will continue. . . . This is a simple disposition which is not concerned with the acquisition of wealth; it may also be described as that of the *old nobility*, which consumed whatever it had. (PR §203, Addition)

Yet Hegel clearly realized that feudalism was changing, taking on characteristics of capitalism, even though in this passage he suggested that the "old nobility" would rest content with what it "received" and would not be "concerned with the acquisition of wealth." In fact, the landed aristocracy would exploit the rise of unorganized popular social movements for their own gain, persuading the central government to ally with them against "democracy" and turning their feudal privileges to commercial and industrial advantage. The infamous German marriage of rye and iron resulted.

Nonetheless, Hegel's mistake here is clear only in hindsight. Criticizing Hegel's bureaucratism as "undemocratic" because he could not have done what his time simply did not permit is engaging exactly in the kind of empty moralism that Hegel, in his preface to the *Philosophy of Right*, calls "superficial philosophy." It is superficial because such philosophizing fails to understand the problem to which its answers are proffered. My hope is that by looking at Hegel's historical context, we can gain a more sympathetic appreciation for how a great thinker attempted to grapple, in a meaningful and practical way, with the problems of his time.

NOTES

1. On the use of the term *universal* and how this relates to Hegel's political philosophy in terms of "the growth of universalistic general, common, public, universal rules, roles, meanings and laws," and its legacy in subsequent thinkers, see Knapp 1986.
2. This is because Hegel's assignment of ultimate accountability to the bureaucracy itself seems to guarantee no accountability at all, especially in light of how the Prussian bureaucracy developed into a closed caste of privileged officials hostile to rising democratic and liberal calls for reform in the mid- to late nineteenth century. For this history see Gillis 1971. On how Hegel's theory of bureaucracy developed during this time, see Eisfeld and von Beyme 2012.
3. For the relationship of the Prussian bureaucracy to the king and aristocracy from Frederick William I to Hegel's own time, see Berdahl 1988, 1976, and 1973; Rosenberg 1958; and Dorn 1932.

4. It is ironic that Weber's notion of bureaucracy was not popularly received in the actual practice of German public administration; see Seibel 2010.
5. Brady Bowman (2013, 55-62) sets out a list of Weber's ten criteria of "bureaucratic" organization: (1) authority is impersonal, (2) offices are clearly and hierarchically defined, (3) each office is legally defined to manage a limited sphere of competence, (4) staffing is contractual and freely entered into, (5) candidates are selected by measurable criteria of technical qualifications, (6) salaries are fixed and clearly defined by rank, (7) office holders usually treat their responsibilities as their sole occupation, (8) there are clear career paths and "promotion" ladders using definite measures of seniority or achievement, (9) offices are not the property of the incumbent, and (10) incumbents are accountable to supervision according to procedures and are protected against arbitrary dismissal. Bowman then finds that Hegel's bureaucratism fails to secure condition (3) because the bureaucrat is given wide discretion, (4) because the bureaucracy is an estate, and (10) given that the collegiate nature of the bureaucratic estate allows for discretionary in-group disciplinary measures. In the text, I rearticulate this list so as to stress the buraucracy's wide discretion, its corporatist standing in the legislature, and the collegiate structure of bureaucratic self-regulation.
6. Carl K. Y. Shaw (1992, 383-86) writes that, in contrast to what Hegel calls "subsumption," the use of professional judgment in the application of universal norms to concrete cases is what Weber calls "discretion."
7. It should be noted that Hegel and Weber agree that having the state apparatus independent of society is key to advancing the conditions of modern politics. "Only with the bureaucratization of the state and of law in general," writes Weber (1954, 239), "can one see a definite possibility of separating sharply and conceptually an 'objective' legal order from the 'subjective rights' of the individual which it guarantees; of separating 'public' law from 'private' law. Public law regulates the interrelationships of public authorities and their relations with the subjects; private law regulates the relationships of the governed individuals among themselves. This conceptual separation presupposes the conceptual separation of the 'state,' as an abstract bearer of sovereign prerogatives and the creator of 'legal norms,' from all personal 'authorizations' of individuals. These conceptual forms are necessarily remote from the nature of pre-bureaucratic, and especially from patrimonial and feudal, structures of authority" (Weber 1964, 239).
8. Philippe Deranty (2001) shows how Hegel removes the ability of the legislature to veto government policy. This eliminates formal and explicit checks on government policy by the legislature, although it does not eliminate informal checks and pressures.
9. On Weber's pessimism about electoral politics under modern conditions, see Mommsen 1984.
10. It is true that Hegel writes that the civil service should be open to talent and merit (PR §308). But we must not forget that a career open to talent is not necessarily one that guarantees equal access of all to the perquisites of an education that prepares one for it, especially in a highly unequal society as early nineteenth-century Prussia.
11. The monarchy was finally abolished in 1918.
12. Germany really only began industrializing after the inauguration of the internal customs union in 1834. Not only was the dominance of the agrarian elite a great inhibitor of wide-scale *independent* bourgeois development, but so was

the parcellation of Germany after the Peace of Westphalia (1648) into innumerable petty kingdoms and aristocratic sovereignties with a confusing array of tariff structures and economic regulations, which Hegel often lamented. It was only after bureaucratic reformers were able to push through schemes for Germany-wide customs unions, beginning in 1834, that German businessmen could finally tap into a larger market and dare to be independent of the aristocracy. For the political economy of Germany during this time, see Kemp [1969] 2013.

13. As detailed in Simon 1955.
14. Moreover, in the *Nassauer Denkschrift*, this functional reorganization of the bureaucracy was linked by Stein to the inculcation of the spirit of self-government in citizens. It was believed that rationally reorganizing the government would allow citizens to thoughtfully support government policies. Hegel appears to share the same expectation in PR §§289-290.
15. By "monocratic" Gillis means a military-style hierarchy of top-down organization.
16. For this development, see Simon 1955.
17. "One must view the bureaucracy," Klaus Epstein (1966, 53) writes, "as the single most important progressive force in Germany at the end of the eighteenth century. . . . Their motivation was as frequently an idealistic desire to serve mankind as a personal desire to make a career for themselves. . . . Their self-respect required that they view themselves as servants of the law and the general welfare rather than instruments of the king's arbitrary whim."
18. Technically, the English "bourgeoisie" was a more ambiguous category than its Continental counterparts. In England the "bourgeois" were largely gentry, whereas in the waning feudal societies of the Continent, the distinction between "bourgeois" and "aristocrat" was more stark. By the time of Hegel, England had, in effect, "commercialized" its aristocracy.
19. PR §297. It is true that today, the German word refers both to such educated professionals as bureaucrats, teachers, and lawyers *and* independent businessmen and tradesmen, while Hegel relegates the latter to the "estate of trade and industry," which he considers incapable of "universal" (i.e., public) concerns. Translating *Stand* as "class" obscures the radical difference between an estate and a socio-economic group, strictly speaking. For more on this, see Weber 2010 and Berdahl 1973.
20. In agrarian and feudal Europe, the legacy of the drive of monarchical absolutism against the entrenched landed aristocracy created the insulated and rigid bureaucratic career path which normally starts from entrance into some state-run administrative school and then works up to the highest echelons of a specialized branch of the civil service (except, of course, for the politically appointed top positions). Hegel's notion of an insulated "Executive Power" simply tracks this historical development, detailing how the "Universal Estate" replaced the "knight errant" by consolidating its own power against the landed aristocracy. See especially PR §297. For the relevant institutional history, see further Schlesinger 1968.

REFERENCES

Avineri, Shlomo. 1974. *Hegel's Theory of the Modern* State. Cambridge: Cambridge University Press.

Beetham, David. 1985. *Max Weber and the Theory of Modern Politics*. Cambridge: Polity Press.
Berdahl, Robert M. 1988. *The Politics of the Prussian Nobility: The Development of a Conservative Ideology*. Princeton: Princeton University Press.
Berdahl, Robert M. 1976. "Prussian Aristocracy and Conservative Ideology: A Methodological Examination." *Social Science Information* 15: 583-99.
Berdahl, Robert M. 1973. "The Stande and the Origins of Conservatism in Prussia." *Eighteenth-Century Studies* 6(3): 298-321
Bowman, Brady. 2013. "Labor, Publicity and Bureaucracy." *Hegel-Studien* 47: 41-74.
Brooks, Thom. 2007. "No Rubber Stamp: Hegel's Constitutional Monarch." *History of Political Thought* 28(1): 91-119.
Bruford, Walter H. 1975. *The German Tradition of Self-Cultivation: "Bildung" from Humbolt to Thomas Mann*. Cambridge: Cambridge University Press.
Bruford, Walter H. 1935. *Germany in the Eighteenth Century: The Social Background of the Literary Revival*. Cambridge: Cambridge University Press.
Deranty, Jean-Philippe. 2001. "Hegel's Parliamentarianism: A New Perspective on Hegel's Theory of Political Institutions." *The Owl of Minerva* 32(2): 107-133.
Dorn, Walter L. 1931. "The Prussian Bureaucracy in the Eighteenth Century." *Political Science Quarterly* 46(3): 403-23.
Eisfeld, Rainer, and Klaus Von Beyme. 2012. "From Hegelianism to Neo-Pluralism." In Rainer Eisfeld, *Radical Approaches to Political Science: Roads Less Traveled*. New York: Columbia University Press.
Emerson, Blake. 2019. *The Public's Law: Origins and Architecture of Progressive Democracy*. Oxford: Oxford University Press.
Epstein, Klaus. 1966. *The Genesis of German Conservatism*. Princeton: Princeton University Press.
Fry, Brian R., and Lloyd G. Nigro. 1996. "Max Weber and U.S. Public Administration: The Administrators as Neutral Servants." *Journal of Management History* 2(1): 37-46.
Gale, Scott A., and Ralph P. Hummel. 2003. "A Debt Unpaid: Reinterpreting Max Weber on Bureaucracy." *Administrative Theory and Praxis* 25(3): 409-18.
Gillis, John R. 1971. *The Prussian Bureaucracy in Crisis, 1840-1960: Origins of an Administrative Ethos*. Stanford: Stanford University Press.
Hardimon, Michael O. 1994. *Hegel's Social Philosophy: The Project of Reconciliation*. Cambridge: Cambridge University Press.
Jackson, Michael W. 1986. "Bureaucracy in Hegel's Political Theory." *Administration and Society* 18(2): 139-157.
Kemp, Tom. [1969] 2013. *Industrialization in Nineteenth-Century Europe*, 2nd ed. London: Routledge.
Knapp, Peter. 1986, "Hegel's Universal in Marx, Durkheim, and Weber: The Role of Hegelian Ideas in the Origin of Sociology." *Sociological Forum* 1(4): 586-609.
Koselleck, Reinhart. 1967. *Preussen zwischen Reform und Revolution. Allgemeines Landrect, Verwaltung und Soziale Bewegung von 1719 bis 1848*. Stuttgart: Ernst Klett Verlag.

Lee, Daniel. 2008. "The Legacy of Medieval Constitutionalism in the *Philosophy of Right*: Hegel and the Prussian Reform Movement." *History of Political Thought* 29(4): 601-34.

Liebich, André. 1982. "On the Origins of a Marxist Theory of Bureaucracy in the Critique of Hegel's *Philosophy of Right*." *Political Theory* 10(1): 77-93.

Mommsen, Wolfgang. 1984. *Max Weber and German Politics, 1890-1920*, trans. Michael S. Steinberg. Chicago: Univeristy of Chicago Press.

Moore, Barrington. 1966. *Social Origins of Dictatorship and Democracy: Lord and Peasant in the Making of the Modern World*. London: Penguin.

Nederman, Gary J. 1987. "Sovereignty, War and the Corporation: Hegel on the Medieval Foundations of the Modern State." *Journal of Politics* 49(2): 500-520.

Overeem, Patrick. 2005. "The Value of the Dichotomy: Politics, Administration and the Political Neutrality of Administrators." *Administrative Theory and Praxis* 27 (2): 311-29.

Hegel, G.W.F. 1991. *Elements of the Philosophy of* Right, ed. Allen W. Wood, trans. H. B. Nisbet. Cambridge: Cambridge University Press.

Hintze, Otto. 1975. *The Historical Essays of Otto Hintze*. New York: Oxford University Press.

Pippin, Robert. 1991. *Modernism as a Philosophical Problem: On the Dissatisfactions of European High Culture*. Oxford: Blackwell.

Poggi, Gianfranco. 1978. *The Development of the Modern State: A Sociological Introduction*. Stanford: Stanford University Press.

Rosenberg, Hans. 1958. *Bureaucracy, Aristocracy and Autocracy: The Prussian Experience, 1660-1815*. Cambridge, Mass.: Harvard University Press.

Sager, Fritz, and Christian N. Rosser. 2009. "Weber, Wilson, and Hegel: Theories of Modern Bureaucracy." *Public Administration* Review 69(9): 1136-47.

Schlesinger, W. 1968. "Lord and Follower in Germanic Institutional History." In *Lordship and Community in Medieval Europe*, ed. Fredric L. Cheyette. New York: Holt, Rinehart and Winston.

Seibel, Wolfgang. 2010. "Beyond Bureaucracy: Public Administration as Political Integrator and Non-Weberian Thought in Germany." *Public Administration Review* 70(5): 719-30.

Shaw, Carl K. Y. 1992. "Hegel's Theory of Modern Bureaucracy." *American Political Science Review* 86(2): 381-89.

Skocpol, Theda. 1979. *States and Social Revolutions: A Comparative Analysis of France, Russia, and China*. Berkeley: University of California Press.

Skowronek, Stephen. 1982. *Building A New American State: The Expansion of National Administrative Capacities 1877-1920*. Cambridge: Cambridge University Press.

Simon, Walter M. 1955. *The Failure of the Prussian Reform Movement, 1807-1819*. Ithaca: Cornell University Press.

Smith, Adam. [1776] 1863. *An Inquiry into the Nature and Causes of the Wealth of Nations*. Edinburgh: Adam & Charles Black.

Spicer, Michael W. 2004. "Note on Origins: Hegel, Weber, and Frederician Prussia." *Administrative Theory and Praxis* 26(1): 97-102.

Tijsterman, Sebastiaan P., and Patrick Overeem. "Escaping the Iron Cage: Weber and Hegel on Bureaucracy and Freedom." *Administrative Theory & Praxis* 30(1): 71-91.

Tunick, Mark. 1991. "Hegel's Justification of Hereditary Monarchy." *History of Political Thought* 12(3): 481-96.

Weber, Max. 1964. *From Max Weber: Essays in Sociology*, trans. and ed. H. H. Gerth and C. Wright Mills. New York: Oxford University Press.

Weber, Max. 2004. *Max Weber: The Vocation Lectures*, ed. David Owen and Tracy B. Strong. Indianapolis: Hackett.

Weber. Max. 2010. "The Distribution of Power within the Community: Classes, Stände, Parties by Max Weber." *Journal of Classical Sociology* 10(2): 137-52.

Westphal, Kenneth. 2006. "The Basic Context and Structure of Hegel's *Philosophy of Right*." In *The Cambridge Companion to Hegel*, ed. Frederick C. Beiser. Cambridge: Cambridge University Press.

Yack, Bernard. 1980. "The Rationality of Hegel's Concept of Monarchy." *American Political Science Review* 74(3): 709-720.

Frederick Neuhouser

HEGEL ON "THE LIVING GOOD"

ABSTRACT: *Hegel calls social life "the living good," but what this means is unclear. The idea expresses an ontological claim about the kind of being that human societies possess, but it is also normatively significant, clarifying why the category of social pathology is an appropriate tool of social critique. Social life consists in processes of life infused with ethical content. Societies are normatively and functionally constituted living beings that realize the good similarly to how organisms achieve their vital ends: via specialized, coordinated functions. In distinction to living organisms, the living good realizes itself through the consciousness and will of individual social members.*

In his account of rational social life (*Sittlichkeit*), Hegel employs two suggestive phrases, each of which requires explanation. On the one hand, he locates social life in the domain of "objective spirit," and on the other, he characterizes it as "the living good" (Hegel Ph.R. §142).

Whereas much has been written about Hegel's conception of objective spirit, his idea of the living good has received considerably less attention, even though, once unpacked, it is arguably the more informative of the two concepts. Identifying rational social life as the living good expresses an ontological claim about *the kind of being* possessed by human societies, but it is also relevant to social critique, insofar as it clarifies why employing the category of *social pathology* is an appropriate way of conceiving of certain problems in the social domain. In this paper I explain the content and normative implications of Hegel's idea of the living good. This idea should not be understood as replacing the concept of objective spirit; rather, the two, when correctly elaborated, illuminate complementary aspects of Hegel's social ontology.

The standard English translation of *Sittlichkeit*, "ethical life," reflects the main thought underlying the idea of the living good: social life consists in processes of life infused with ethical content. Although human society is an ethical phenomenon for Hegel, his account of the rational society has ambitions beyond those of moral philosophy as normally understood. Calling rational social life "the living good" expresses the ontological thesis that human societies are normatively and functionally constituted *living* beings. They are normatively constituted not only because their functioning requires social members to act in accordance with norms they take to be authoritative (because productive of the good), but also because when social life functions as it should, its institutions *realize* the good. Moreover, human societies realize the good in a manner similar to the way living organisms achieve their vital ends, namely, through organized subsystems that carry out specialized and coordinated functions, enabling the organism to be self-maintaining and self-reproducing (Hegel Ph.N. §§350-3). In distinction to living organisms, however, the living good realizes itself in human societies through the awareness, will, and actions of its individual members (Hegel Ph.R. §142). In other words, the living good that animates rational social life and is realized within it is a *spiritual* living good. One could express this by saying that spirit, in the domain of the social, is *aufgehobenes Leben:* life that is both transcended and preserved within the spiritual.

In the first two sections of this paper I explore this idea by discussing, first, how biological life is preserved within human society and, second, how the spiritual life of human societies goes beyond mere biological life. In the third and fourth sections I examine the conception of the good at issue in Hegel's idea of the living good, and in the final section I consider how understanding the social domain in terms of the living good enables us to diagnose certain disturbances in social life as social pathologies.

Biological Life

Hegel's concept of life is complex, and it plays various roles in his philosophy (Khurana 2013, 155-93; Särkelä 2018, 220-35; Ng 2020; Hahn 2007; Testa 2020). Here I restrict myself to the aspects of his account most relevant to social philosophy, examining several respects in which human societies preserve, or retain features of, the phenomena of life. It does so in two senses: it both *incorporates* and *mirrors* (possesses the same structure as) the activities of biological life. The first of these points consists in the familiar claim that material reproduction—producing the human bodies and necessities of life required if society is to survive over generations—is an indispensable task of social life: nature imposes biological needs on living creatures, and for humans, just as for ants and bees, satisfying those needs requires cooperating with other members of the species. This does not imply that material reproduction exhausts the meaning and importance social life has for us. The fact that biology requires us to cooperate with others, and to spend large parts of our waking life doing so, does not entail that survival and reproduction of the species are social life's principal ends. Moreover, nature's placing constraints how we live does not mean that it *determines* that life, dictating specific acts or forms of organization. Hegel is well aware that there are uncountable ways in which humans can satisfy their needs for nutrition, shelter, sleep, and sex. Within material reproduction there is ample room for self-determination, even if it is always subject to very general constraints that are not themselves self-imposed.

The second sense in which Hegel takes human societies to preserve elements of animal life consists in the more obscure claim that social and animal life share a basic structure that non-living beings lack. (To be clear: all spiritual beings are living beings, but the converse is not the case.) Hegel's claim, more specifically, is that human society is purposively organized, carrying out specialized and coordinated functions that enable it to maintain and reproduce itself: the rational society "exists as living spirit only as an organized whole, differentiated into the particular functions that ... continually produce it as their result" (Hegel Ph.M. §539). Hence, the main feature of life Hegel exploits in conceiving of human societies is its functional character. A living organism, he says, "acts in accordance with ends," although it "does not know its end as an end"; in the case of non-human animals, behavior is "unconscious acting in terms of ends" (Hegel Ph.N. §360). For Hegel, both societies and living things are defined by their functions in the sense that one cannot understand what they are or why they are constituted as they are without referring to the ends their activities serve. This implies—this is what it is to say that life is purposively organized—that the various specialized functions of living beings work together to achieve those beings' vital ends.

Hegel's description of human society as an organized (and self-organizing) whole that reproduces itself by means of differentiated functions is illustrated by his doctrine that a rational feature of modern European society is its division into three semi-autonomous, coordinated spheres: the nuclear family, civil society, and the constitutional state. Regarding these spheres as relatively autonomous subsystems with distinct functions implies that it is meaningful to make the family, the economy, and the state into objects of study in their own right and to ask about each, "How does this sphere carry out its distinctive functions?" If we restrict ourselves to only the living (non-spiritual) aspects of social life, Hegel's point is easily grasped. Each sphere carries out a distinct function necessary for society's material reproduction: the family furnishes the next generation of human individuals; civil society supplies the goods needed for the sustainment of life; and the state, while less directly tied to material reproduction, shores up the two other spheres and ensures that neither functions at the other's expense. Of course, once we bring the spiritual aspects of human social life into the picture, each sphere can also be seen to carry out specialized spiritual tasks, such as realizing different forms of freedom and producing the forms of subjectivity, or self-conceptions, appropriate to each. Moreover, society's material and spiritual tasks are not carried out separately. The activities that make up life in civil society, for example, possess both material and spiritual significance—or, more accurately, their spiritual character consists precisely in their integrating two general types of ends within a single activity, making processes of life at the same time ways of realizing freedom.

Hegel's conception of an organized whole implies not only functional differentiation but also organization in accordance with an overarching telos. (If it seems implausible that the various functions of society could be explained by referring to just one end, it should be noted that the telos Hegel ascribes to rational social life is a very expansive conception of the *good* that unites various social goods—well-being and freedom of various types—that non-Hegelians might regard as distinct ends of social life.) Thus, apprehending something as an organized whole includes both ascribing an essential end, or telos, to it and grasping how the constitution of its parts—which are in truth *members* (*Glieder*) rather than parts[1]—is determined by what it requires in order to achieve its defining end. In biological organisms, this telos is the reproduction of the species to which it belongs (including the maintenance of its own individual life), and its organization takes the form of a network of functional subsystems subordinated to the end of the whole and dependent on its proper functioning (Hegel Ph.R. §270A). This means that the relation between an organism and its specialized members is one of mutual dependence. Not only does the functioning of the whole depend on each component carrying out its specific task; its members, too, depend on being united with the others if they are to realize their distinctive ends. This mutual dependence between members and whole implies that both biological organisms and rational societies achieve their defining ends not by squelching diversity but by fostering it and by bringing its diverse elements into a purposeful arrangement, thereby preserving the qualitative richness that difference implies.

A further respect in which Hegel takes society to exhibit the structure of animal life is expressed in his remark that "a being capable of holding the contradiction of itself within itself and of *enduring* that contradiction is a *subject*" (Hegel Ph.N. §359A). The *Phenomenology of Spirit* further characterizes a subject as "pure, *simple negativity*," as "the bifurcation [*Entzweiung*] of the simple" (Ng 2020 72-74, 98-99, 103-4, 106-7, 212-12, 268-69), and as a doubling that posits difference (or opposition) internal to itself and then "negates" this difference by restoring identity between the opposites it has posited (Hegel Ph.S. ¶18). Thus, the nature of a subject, according to these passages, is to engage in a distinctive activity that consists in dividing itself into two and then negating this division by unifying what it is has torn apart, albeit in a way that both negates and preserves—thus enabling the subject to "endure"—that internal division. This defining activity of subjectivity is what makes spirit a "living substance" rather than an inert, lifeless one (Hegel Ph.S. ¶18).

Various features of living beings inspire Hegel to make this odd-sounding claim (Khurana 2017 §§65-68), but I restrict myself here to those most relevant to understanding human society. The main idea is that a living being does not merely exist, inertly, like a stone; it is not a mere *Seiendes*, something that merely *is* (Hegel Ph.N. §352). Life's mode of being, rather, is like that of a subject[2] in that it exists only as a *sich Reproduzierendes*, only insofar as it constantly reproduces itself, including its characteristic form (Hegel Ph.N. §353): "the living being … exists only by making itself into what it is" (Hegel Ph.N. §352); a living being exists only insofar as it constantly (re-)makes itself.

Hegel's thesis that life exhibits the structure of subjectivity includes a claim about how a living being (or its species) reproduces itself, namely, by constantly relating to what it treats as *not* itself[3]—air, water, other organic material—or, more precisely, by assimilating what is foreign to it, not by simply ingesting its "other" but by transforming it so that it can then be subordinated to the organism's vital ends. A living being is "infinite" in the manner of a subject because it maintains its own living form only by relating to what it is not and in making its "other" into itself. A living being "*is* and *maintains itself*" (Hegel Ph.N. §352) as what it is—a purposively organized being "set up" to maintain itself and reproduce the species—only by interacting with what it is not, and it does so fluidly, without losing its identity (without flipping back and forth between states of being itself and being its opposite).

Hegel ascribes this subjective structure not only to individual living beings but also to their species: a biological species maintains itself by breaking itself up into individual living beings, each distinct from its species, even if at the same time identical to its species in the sense that its form of life is that of the species. It is these individual living beings that, in striving to live and to reproduce, and ultimately in dying, carry out the vital functions on which the continuation of the species depends. Only by positing differences internal to itself (in the form of individual members of the species) (Hegel Ph.N. §371) and then abolishing those differences does the species as a whole reproduce itself as what it is.

A further aspect of Hegel's thesis that life posits differences internal to itself and then unifies those contradictions is his claim that life's characteristic activities are *processes* (Hegel Ph.N. §§ 215, 337, 367, 369): temporally extended, self-generated series of changes (changes are "negations" of what was) in which different ("contradictory") states succeed one another. Successive states acquire a coherence and unity—become *stages* of a process—by virtue of the end the series as a whole serves, the reproduction of the species. The reproductive cycle of a fruit tree, for example, involves the sprouting of leaves, the blossoming of flowers, the transformation of the latter into fruit, the production of seeds that will begin the next generation, and so on. Hegel will claim that social practices, too, are processual in this sense, even if in this case (where life is spiritualized), in order for the changes in question to constitute a process, they must be interpreted as such by the agents of those changes, self-conscious human individuals.

Spiritual Life

This thought leads naturally into the topic of how social life, as a form of spirit, not only preserves but also goes beyond mere life, infusing processes of human life with spiritual significance. The most important respect in which spirit is more than mere life is that although a biological species maintains itself by positing differences internal to itself and then abolishing them, as well as by assimilating its external "other" to itself and making the latter serve its purposes, mere life, unlike spirit, is unconscious of itself and its characteristic activity (Hegel Ph.M. §§381A, 386A). Expressed in Hegelian language, life can exist as what it in truth is (a unified process) only for another—its nature can be apprehended only by a conscious being—whereas spirit exists "for itself," which means that members of human societies are conscious of the ends their social activities serve and that unify their various actions over time into a practice. Since the activities that constitute social processes are mediated by an understanding of their governing ends, spirit is *self-conscious life* (Hegel Ph.M. §385A), and spiritual beings are self-conscious animals.

This point raises the question: what becomes of life and its essential functions when imbued with self-consciousness?[4] It is important to avoid thinking that spirit exists *alongside* life or as the additive result of "mixing" life and self-consciousness. Rather, social activity is *spiritual life*: processes of life carried out in the mode of self-consciousness. One difference between mere life and spirit is that life's telos is transformed when living processes are imbued with self-consciousness. This is due to the connection between self-consciousness and free agency. In spiritual beings, life's supreme end, biological reproduction, expands into the end of freedom (Hegel Ph.M. §382). This does not mean that the end of biological reproduction is replaced by freedom in spiritual beings; rather, their supreme end becomes the reproduction of life in accordance with the (demanding) requirements of freedom. Spiritual life is life "infused with" freedom; it consists in life processes within which its participants achieve the panoply of freedoms made possible by self-consciousness.

The second implication of the self-conscious character of human social life is expressed in Hegel's statement that "ethical life is the *idea of freedom*, which, as the living good, becomes actual in self-consciousness—in its knowing, willing, and acting" (Hegel Ph.R. §142). Taken by itself, this is merely another way of saying that human society achieves its defining end, the free reproduction of life, in the mode of self-consciousness. If we add to this, however, that society possesses no organ of consciousness of its own, independent of those of its members, then it follows that social life accomplishes its ends only in and through the self-conscious knowing, willing, and acting of its members, who participate in it as individuated bearers of consciousness. The fact that individual members of society are themselves spiritual beings (Hegel Ph.R. 264) has implications for the normative standards appropriate to social life: if individuals are spiritual beings, then the tasks of social life must be carried out in a way that does justice to their spiritual nature. In other words, what is at stake in rational social life is the good of individuals (Hegel Ph.R. §264) and not merely (if this idea can be made sense of) the good of some collective whole.

A further respect in which self-conscious life differs from mere life follows from this one: processes of spiritual life are carried out with awareness on the part of those who do so not merely that such processes are taking place but also what their function, or point, is. Social members' activities not only have a point; they also have a point *for* those members (even if there is also room for them to have partial or mistaken understandings of what they do and why). In other words, processes of spiritual life have a *meaning* and not merely a function. This means that (potentially) self-conscious meaning is intrinsic to social reality in a way it is not in non-spiritual life. In contrast to the behavior of fish, one cannot capture what humans do in social life without referring to the meanings it has for them. Moreover, the meanings that distinguish the doings of spiritual beings from those of mere animals are *social* meanings, not only because the activities they interpret are ones we carry out together but also, more fundamentally, because they are *shared* meanings made possible only in collective practices.

What we have seen thus far about the living good enables us to say more about the meaning social members' activities have for them. As we know, the characteristic activities of human social members serve vital functions (of both society and the individuals composing it). Raising children (in the family) and producing commodities (in civil society) are two such activities, both of which satisfy needs humans have by virtue of being alive. Such activities serve vital functions, but because they are activities of spiritual beings, they are also carried out with an awareness of them as having an end, or serving a function. Moreover—and, again, because they are activities of spiritual beings—their point is not reducible to the reproduction of life; as spiritual activities, they aim also at freedom. This means that for members of human societies, more is at issue in raising children and producing goods than merely reproducing life; rather, they are ways of reproducing life that are at the same time taken to promote or express freedom, broadly conceived. One might say, then, that the characteristic activities of spiritual beings strive to unite the ends of life with the loftier end of freedom. Those activities are processes of life that at the same time aim at realizing the freedom of those who carry them out—and this is why it is appropriate to conceive of them as the living good.

Finally, self-consciousness brings with it the possibility of a type of *Entzweiung*, or internal division, as well as a way of enduring such internal opposition, that is absent in merely living beings. Whereas mere life cannot know that it both is and is not identical with what is distinct from itself, spirit is aware of itself as both identical and not identical with what it posits as its other. The most significant implication of this is that the principal other that a self-conscious subject both distinguishes itself from and identifies with is life itself. Hence, the fundamental contradiction spiritual beings must negotiate is the opposition they posit—the distinction they themselves draw—between self-consciousness, with its essential characteristic, freedom, and mere life, which is taken to be submerged in nature and hence unfree. This means—and represents another sense in which spirit is *aufgehobenes Leben*—that it is characteristic of spiritual beings to be conscious of themselves as participating in life and at the same time as something more (and "higher") than life. Implicit in this claim is that spiritual beings have a conception of their own ("essential") nature, a conception of life, and a conception of their own ambiguous relation to life. Spirituality involves a form of divided consciousness in which what from one perspective appears as alien to spiritual being (our embeddedness in life) is, from another, grasped as essential to one's nature as self-conscious and free. Spiritual, and therefore social, life is characterized by activities that "mediate," or negotiate, the opposition between free self-consciousness and mere life.

The Good

The thought that ethical life unites the ends of life with those of free self-consciousness lies at the core of Hegel's characterization of ethical life as the living good, for the basic components in terms of which Hegel defines the good are freedom and human well-being. Before examining this spiritual, or ethical, conception of the good, it is worth noting that animal life, too, exemplifies the living good insofar as organisms are naturally set up so as to realize both their good and that of their species. Even if only spiritual beings can bring about what is ethically good, living organisms realize the good in a more limited sense: their instincts lead them to seek what is good for them *qua* living beings, namely, survival, reproduction, and freedom from unnecessary suffering. Being constituted so as to achieve one's good "naturally" (or "spontaneously") is a feature shared by both animal and spiritual life, and it represents another sense in which the two are similarly structured.

Hegel articulates his concept of the ethical good in "Morality," the section of the *Philosophy of Right* immediately preceding his account of ethical life. Here he characterizes the good as a unity of freedom and human well-being (*Wohl*) (Hegel Ph.R. §§129-30), where unity consists not in mere compatibility or co-existence but in a mutual dependence that is both existential and conceptual (Heisenberg 2019, 62-78). With regard to existential dependence, freedom is realized in the world only insofar as self-conscious human beings aim in their practices at realizing the good—hence only insofar as their aims include realizing their own and others' well-being; and, conversely, well-being is achieved only insofar as individuals are motivated by the ideal of freedom. The good, then, requires that freedom not be achieved at the expense of well-being (and vice versa) as well as, more robustly, that each be realized through the other.

Beyond this, freedom and well-being, when united so as to constitute the good, are conceptually interdependent in the sense that the requirements of freedom place constraints on what genuinely good well-being consists in, just as the requirements of well-being place constraints on what qualifies as genuine freedom. Well-being in general counts as good only to the extent that it is compatible with the realized freedom of all, and the "true" conception of freedom (as a component of the good) is subject to realizability constraints deriving from the nature of human well-being. The latter claim means that a fully determinate conception of freedom must take into account whether it can be realized in a self-sustaining manner by socially related individuals who by their nature cannot help but care about their own well-being.

The details of why Hegel thinks modern European social institutions realize his demanding concept of the good are too complex to be set out here.[5] But his main idea is that those institutions are rational because, working in concert, they carry out the specialized tasks required for realizing both freedom (in a variety of senses) and human well-being. To mention just one example: the nuclear family produces the next generation of human individuals on which social reproduction depends. It produces those individuals not only biologically but also spiritually, which is to say that it forms them subjectively such that, as adults, they are motivated to create their own families. In addition, children are brought up to be adults who are able and motivated to realize their moral agency (as subjects who know, endorse, and act in accordance with the good) as well as their personal freedom (as bearers of rights and owners of property). Moreover, the family promotes the well-being of its members, both children and parents, since it is the source of love and emotional attachment—a form of recognition—as well as, for parents, sexual satisfaction. At the same time, family life, despite its obligations and sacrifices, is itself an instance of living freely—an instance of determining the contours of one's life in accordance with one's own understanding of the good—insofar as family members endorse the ends of family life and regard them as good.

Rational social life, as the living good, is a good that perpetually realizes itself in the world in and through the self-conscious practices of real human beings. Thus, the good is not only self-realizing;[6] it also acquires an extra-mental (objective) existence in social life that, similarly in this respect to the being of ordinary things, persists independently of its presence in the consciousness of any single individual. (Of course, the living good cannot exist, as stones do, independently of *all* human consciousness.) This means that the good enters Hegel's social theory not as a subjective conception of the good consisting in my own, perhaps idiosyncratic, ideas regarding the kind of life most suitable to me. If a "conception of the good" plays a role for Hegel, it is not one that exists in social members' minds in the form of self-fashioned life plans.

Rather, the good exists in, and hence can be read off of, the objectively knowable features of the society in which it is widely realized. In this respect, too, social reality is similar to life. For living beings are constituted such that the ends ascribed to them by the biologist are inscribed within their empirically accessible features and behavior. This implies that social theory must not only interpret the subjective understandings of social members but also acquire empirical knowledge of a society's structure and actual functioning, as embodied in laws and institutions.

The self-conscious nature of the living good implies that the agency of social members is best described in terms of their interpreting what their institutions require of them in light of their understanding of the human good to be achieved in social life. This makes social life expressive of their shared values. That what is at issue is the *human* good does not mean that Hegel presupposes a determinate picture of what that good consists in at all times and places. No one is more aware than he that conceptions of the good are historically and culturally variant. One reason it nevertheless makes sense to talk of the human good is that the good at issue in the fundamental institutions of social life is the *living* good, incorporating needs that spring from our biological nature. Another reason is that the human good includes two goods distinctive of spiritual beings, freedom and recognition. Because biological needs can be satisfied in numerous ways, and because conceptions of freedom vary historically, the requirement that the human good both satisfy our biological needs and accommodate our freedom is compatible with the fact that determinate conceptions of it vary with time and place.

Following Aristotle, Hegel places habit at the center of his account of social life conceived of as the living good: the ethical takes the form of mores (*Sitten*), or ethical habits that have become the "second nature" of participants in social life, which, as "the penetrating soul, meaning, and actuality of their existence," makes spirit "living and present" in the world (Hegel Ph.R. §151).[7] Habits of the relevant sort have a meaning because they are end-directed and because the purposive behavior they make possible is something the human animal must learn to be able to do. The feature of habit most important to Hegel is that it is a species of meaning that penetrates the bodies of the habituated and through their habit-mediated actions becomes living and present in the world. Habit is mind that has taken on a bodily existence and body that has acquired the significance of mind.[8]

Another reason habits are important for Hegel is that those acquired through socialization form our desires, dispositions, and values so as to enable us to participate in social life in a way that is largely "spontaneous," or that "comes naturally," analogously to how the vital behavior of living beings comes naturally to them. When habituation takes place in the right way—through socialization in rational social institutions—it forms our inclinations so as to accord with our duties, such that we do not normally experience our social participation as dictated by external "oughts" but rather as "what we do" and as what we must do in order to be who we take ourselves to be. Even if habituation makes the demands of social life appear to us immediately, under the guise of "what we do," they are not experienced as arbitrary—as nothing more than "what we, in this specific community, happen to do." Rather, the habits on which social life depends are value-infused in that they make a claim, usually implicit, to realize the good, where this claim purports to have more than merely parochial validity. It is mistake, then, to assume that social life's habitual character excludes the possibility of having reasons for what one habitually does or of stepping momentarily outside those habits to ask whether the life they animate is good. That human habits need not be "blind" is apparent even in low-level habits, such as brushing one's teeth at bedtime. It is even more obvious in the endlessly repeated daily routines in which we feed our children or iron our spouse's clothes; demonstrate both concern and professional distance to our students; or take the symptoms of our patients as more than just whining of the spoiled. Habits of the right sort are essential to there being a *living* good, but they do not rule out the possibility of *knowing* the practices they make possible as good.

Recognition and the Living Good

One aspect of the good Hegel takes to be realized in social life is that of recognition (*Anerkennung*). It is a central claim of his that in performing their social roles, social members secure the esteem of others and the foundations of their self-esteem as well. They achieve, in other words, the recognition of their fellow social members and thereby satisfy an aspiration that Hegel, following Rousseau, regards as fundamental to being a self-conscious subject, namely, the aspiration to "be someone," to count as a being of value for oneself and for others. In Hegel's words, individuals find in social life their "feeling of self" (*Selbstgefühl*) and "dignity" (Hegel Ph.R. §147, 152), their "recognition and honor" (Hegel Ph.M. §527). Recognition is closely connected to the idea of "who we take ourselves to be" referred to above. In characterizing love and friendship, two essentially recognitive relations, Hegel says that "one constrains oneself gladly in relation to another but in this constraint is aware of oneself as oneself... and wins one's feeling of self" (Hegel Ph.R. §7A). Thus, giving expression to "who one takes oneself to be" as a social member involves not only being committed to fulfilling the obligations of one's various roles but also knowing one's social commitments as a source of one's sense of self—finding one's identity in them as a self that matters, such that to be deprived of them is to experience oneself as "defective and incomplete" (Hegel Ph.R. §158A). Recognition, one could say, is a "spiritual need" (Hegel [1817-19] 1983, 80) that provides "*subjective* satisfaction" to its recipients (Hegel Ph.R. §124).

Even if recognition is a spiritual need, its significance extends beyond being part of the well-being individuals must achieve if social life is to realize the good. For recognition is central also to the normative character of social life; as Hegel's talk of "constraining oneself in relation to another" suggests, recognition is essentially practical and normative. When one person recognizes another, she does so in the name of some conception of the value or standing of the other, and she takes this value or standing to place constraints on her own will. When, in Hegel's master-slave dialectic,[9] the bondsman recognizes the lord as the only free subject of the two, he regards the lord's free status as a normative constraint on his actions. Recognizing the master as free, or sovereign, means accepting the validity of a norm—roughly, "the wishes of a free will count as my commands"—that determines how a being of that sort is to be treated, and this defines the terms of their interaction. Love counts as recognition for similar reasons: when I love another, I regard him as worthy of my love—and, hence, as in some sense valuable—and I make his desires and interests into constraints (although not absolute constraints) on my actions. For both the bondsman and the lover, the desires and interests of a recognized other count as an "ought"; they have the status of something I am to respect or promote through my actions.

For Hegel, reciprocal recognition is what makes voluntary self-constraint for the sake of others possible without self-sacrifice or the loss of freedom, for in working for others I win my own identity. It is this that enables us to understand a large part of the glue that holds societies together. That is, recognition explains how individuals who cannot help but care about their own particular good can be motivated to follow the egoism-constraining norms that make their interactions collectively beneficial and coordinate them so as to accomplish the business of social life. Recognition provides the recognized with a publicly acknowledged confirmation of a specific identity that is secured by the norms of the institutions within which social life is carried out. Individuals who live within such institutions have publicly recognized identities that give meaning to their lives and shape their practical engagement in an intersubjectively constituted social world. This is one reason recognition is crucial for Hegel: it enables socially united individuals to enjoy certain goods they could not achieve outside social life.

When recognition is reciprocal, the actions and identities of individuals are guided and defined by norms or values they jointly endorse. In Hegel's conception of the modern family, for example, husband and wife occupy distinct roles, the rights and obligations of which are defined by institutional norms accepted by both. In each case, the two spouses win particular identities—as husband and wife, respectively—that are recognized by the other spouse as well as, through the institution of marriage, by society at large. The tight connection between my being recognized by others and my recognizing them is due to the fact that the norms around which social institutions are oriented are such that to abide by them is to recognize the normative status of those who occupy the other roles of the same institutions. To fulfill the role of father is to act in ways that demonstrate to other family members a valuing of them in their respective familial roles.

If relations of recognition are to coordinate the different (specialized) actions of social members so that together they achieve the good of individuals and society, then the specific content of the norms expressed in recognition is important. Not just any set of recognitive statuses, with whatever rights and obligations, will both provide social members with satisfying identities and coordinate their interactions in socially beneficial ways. (Think of the destructive social consequences of the rights and obligations accorded to the role of mafia boss or feudal lord.) One requirement of the institutions of ethical life is that the identities they make possible provide social members with complementary desires and characteristics. Such individuals possess distinct but complementary qualities that enable them to fulfill the specific functions—as children and parents, or farmers and tailors—essential to achieving the ends of social life. The desires and characters of such individuals are not similar but complementary: a mother can realize her desires and ends (as a mother) only if her spouse and children have different desires and ends complementary to hers (and vice versa), and the same is true of farmers and tailors. When family members interact as such—when they reciprocally constrain themselves by the desires and needs of fellow family members—they find in the world, not mirror images of themselves, but qualitatively distinct counterparts whose particular qualities and actions are necessary for their being the particular selves they take themselves to be. To experience such complementarity in one's dealings with others is, for Hegel, to be "at home" in one's social world, or "with oneself in another" (Hegel [1830] 1991, §24A2; Hegel Ph.R. §7), which counts for him as an especially important sort of freedom.

The Living Good and Social Pathology

Although Hegel never offers an explicit account of social pathology, his social philosophy is fertile ground for theorists who concern themselves with this concept. Not surprisingly, this is due to the central role that life—the native domain of the concept of illness—plays in his understanding of human society. Because processes of life are essentially end-directed, or functional, disturbances in them are aptly described as *dysfunctions*, and it is this idea that lies at the core of the concept of illness, whether animal or spiritual. Hegel's account of ethical life provides many resources for diagnosing dysfunctions in social life; in the following paragraphs I indicate some of the social pathologies his account enables us to diagnose.

One conception of social dysfunction available to Hegel—indebted no doubt to Plato's account of the unhealthy polis—involves what is properly a subordinate moment of society arrogating to itself the function of ruling the whole (Hegel [1802-3] 1975, 124). This dysfunction—a kind of unhealthy imbalance or disharmony—would be present in a society in which a "lower" social sphere, such as civil society, dominated the others and became the organizing power of society as a whole. Thus, one way a society can be ill is if the "principle" appropriate to civil society—that of contract—comes to govern all spheres, including the family and state. Civil society's domination of the whole would occur if the freedom distinctive of contracts were taken to be the ideal appropriate to all spheres of social life, and if the social relations characteristic of contracts—where individuals decide what they want in abstraction from their relations to others, and act together only when their independently constituted wills "overlap"—became the model for social relations *tout court*. A society in which relations among family members or citizens were modeled on contracts would be one in which the spiritual benefits available to social members outside the economic domain would go unrealized and those spheres themselves would be unable to function as they should. Treating my spouse as just another contracting party and determining my will in accordance only with what I want for myself, independently of my relations to my spouse and children, would mean both that I would miss out on the distinctive goods afforded by family membership and that my family could not function as it should.

A further class of social pathologies involves dysfunctions internal to a specific institution or sphere. Civil society's non-accidental tendency to produce poverty (Hegel Ph.R. §§241-45) is such a pathology. Poverty is internal to civil society because its causes—overproduction and bad luck in the market—derive from the very nature of an unregulated market economy (Hegel Ph.R. §§241, 243, 245-46). Poverty produces material want, of course, but it is also a spiritual pathology because its primary danger is not the malnutrition or death of social members but their exclusion from the spiritual benefits—freedom, recognition, and a subjective attachment to social life—that membership in civil society affords.

Another possible form of social pathology depends on a specific danger Hegel associates with civil society: the possibility that the appetites of participants in a market economy will be "infinitely aroused" by the nearly unlimited possibilities it offers for satisfying ever more specific and complex desires, leading individuals to acquire limitless "needs" that render enduring satisfaction impossible (Hegel Ph.R. §§185, 190, 195, 253A). The potential for acquiring unlimited desires in civil society is heightened by the fact that its members' activities and relations to others are mediated by money, which measures value only quantitatively (Hegel Ph.R. §204). Hegel's worry, taken over from Rousseau, is that individuals in civil society, especially members of the commercial estate, will be tempted to seek *recognition* from others by accumulating wealth rather than by pursuing less abstract, "finite" ideals. In contrast to qualitatively defined aims—being a good plumber, doctor, or school-teacher—measuring one's worth by quantitative standards admits of no natural stopping point in the quest for recognition. The satisfaction to be had from this way of pursuing recognition is both thin and unstable since there is no reason not to seek ever larger "quantities" of recognition and hence no reason to place limits on one's quest to acquire more. The problem is not so much that satisfaction in *consumption* becomes elusive—Hegel was unfamiliar with the orgies of consumption we revel in today—as that the stable recognized identities to be had as *producers* in civil society give way to a frenzied, never-resting quest for recognition.

Yet another conception of social pathology draws on the idea that spiritual beings act with an understanding of what they do and why and that this self-consciousness makes rationality of a certain kind possible: a commitment to aligning one's ideas with the reality they purport to be of. This function of rationality, as Hegel thinks of it,[10] aims to bring inner experience in line with an objective world subject to generally binding norms, and it goes awry when what social members take themselves to be accomplishing in the world fails to track what they actually do. If a mismatch of this sort has its source in a basic feature of institutions—as in Marx's account of commodity fetishism (Marx [1867] 1978, 319-29)—then it makes sense to think of that mismatch as a spiritual defect of society itself. In other words, some forms of *ideology* are social pathologies, and even though Hegel never uses this term, the phenomenon it names lies at the heart of the *Philosophy of Right*'s account of the alienation faced by modern subjects (Hegel Ph.R. 13-17, 22).

Finally, what I take to be Hegel's most important conception of social pathology is best illuminated in reference to his account in the *Phenomenology of Spirit* of forms of (premodern) social life organized around the categories of bondsman and lord.[11] The relation between bondsman and lord is depicted there as a rudimentary and ultimately unsatisfying attempt to unite the aims of life and freedom within social life. Perhaps the easiest point to see about this social relation is that the activities of bondsman and lord serve the material ends of both: the lord commands, the bondsman labors, and together these complementary activities produce the goods needed to reproduce life (Hegel Ph.M. §434). Of course, these activities are marked by a radical asymmetry in that the two moments of material reproduction—production and consumption—are torn apart, with each ascribed principally to only one of the relation's poles: the bondsman labors, while the lord "enjoys" the fruits of that labor.

At the same time, these material activities have a significance in relation to freedom. The lord's commanding and the bondsman's obedience are grounded in a shared conception of what it is to be free (being completely independent from "foreign" determination) and in the fact that in the struggle preceding those relations, the future bondsman affirms the independent value of his life, while the future lord persists in valuing only freedom in the guise of absolute independence from life's demands. This is what explains the asymmetric recognitive relation between them: only the lord has *demonstrated* that he is free in the struggle unto death, and for this reason both participants acknowledge that his will alone carries normative authority for both. In other words, the bondsman-lord relation is a form of ethical life because it consists in cooperative practices among biologically needy subjects regulated in accordance with shared norms grounded in the supreme value of freedom. If we recall Hegel's characterization of spirit as a being capable of enduring the contradiction between freedom and life, it becomes clear that both the bondsman's servile labor and the lord's enjoyment are *spiritual* activities because they are ways, however rudimentary, of negotiating the opposition between freedom and life.

Where, though, does social pathology enter this picture? One might locate the pathological character of the bondsman-lord relation in any number of its features: neither party finds satisfying recognition from its counterpart; their relation manifests itself in domination rather than freedom; and the bondsman is alienated from his true essence (since he is potentially a free subject but regards only his lord as belonging to that category). None of these responses is incorrect, but a more comprehensive description of what has gone wrong comes into view if we focus on the fact that in a society of bondsmen and lords, those who labor satisfy no end of their own other than survival, while those who "enjoy" have a spiritual end in view—realizing freedom—but are moved by an impoverished vision of what freedom is (complete independence from the demands of life). In other words, a society of bondsmen and lords fails in its spiritual mission to negotiate the opposition between freedom and life in a satisfying way. This failure shows up in the inability of social members to integrate, in what they do and how they think of themselves, their dependence on the conditions of life with their understanding of freedom. This means that the ways in which social members participate in life are not, at the same time, expressions of their freedom and that, conversely, the activities they regard as expressions of freedom are not, at the same time, ways of participating in life. Expressed differently, failure here consists in the inability of social members to sustain conceptions of themselves as *free animals*, where the tension between being free and participating in life is (somehow) both present to consciousness and overcome. Spiritual satisfaction, in contrast, requires that life be elevated to freedom and that self-consciousness be filled with the aims of life. On this view, social pathology exists whenever the basic conditions of a society prevent its members from bringing together their membership in both the realm of freedom and the realm of necessity. Success in doing so would mean that there is no essential life activity that is not also a site of freedom and no expression of freedom that is not at the same time a material practice.

NOTES

1. "The so-called parts of an animal organism are not parts but members or organic moments whose isolation and separate existence constitute disease" (Hegel Ph.R. §278). "In an organic relationship, the units in question are not parts but members, and each maintains the others while fulfilling its own function" (Hegel Ph.R. §278). Parts, for Hegel, exist only in a mechanical relationship, while members exist in an organic relationship. I am indebted to Shterna Friedman for impressing this point on me.
2. Recall Fichte's claim that a subject has no being beyond its own self-positing activity (Neuhouser 1990, 102-16).
3. One basic feature of organisms is the capacity to distinguish inner from outer (Hegel Ph.N. §§357, 359; Pinkard 2012, 24).
4. For more on the relation between self-consciousness and life, see Ng 2020, 101-12 and *passim*; and Ng 2015, 393-404. Alznauer 2016, 196-211 examines the normativity appropriate to spiritual phenomena and compares it to that of living beings.
5. I attempt this in Neuhouser 2003, chs. 3, 4, 5, and 7.
6. This makes the living good self-sufficient, a good that continually produces and maintains itself.
7. That habituation is compatible with—indeed, necessary for—free social life is argued for in Novakovic 2017, 20-68. The literature on habit and second nature in Hegel is vast; see Khurana 2017, §§82-89, 99-101; Testa 2008, 286-307 and 2020; Haase 2017; and Menke 2018, 119-48.
8. For the relation between habit and *living* spirit, see Heisenberg 2019, 37, 43-44, 144-53, and 161-62.
9. Although this is the name it is usually given, Hegel's terms are "lord" (*Herr*) and "bondsman" (*Knecht*) (Hegel Ph.S. ¶¶189-96).
10. "Illness occurs in *psychic life* (*Seelenleben*) when the organism's merely psychic elements (*das bloß Seelenhafte*) become independent of the power of *spiritual* consciousness and presume to arrogate its function, with the result that spirit loses its rule over the psychic elements that belong to it and, with that, power over itself" (Hegel Ph.M. §406A).

11. A different attempt to glean resources for an account of social pathology from the bondsman-lord relation is found in Särkelä 2018, 328–59.

REFERENCES

Alznauer, Mark. 2016. "Hegel's Theory of Normativity." *Journal of the American Philosophical Association* 2: 196–211.

Haase, Matthias. 2017. "Geist und Gewohnheit." In *Selbstbewusstes Leben: Texten zu einer transformativen Theorie der menschlichen Subjektivität*, ed. Andrea Kern and Christian Kietzmann. Berlin: Suhrkamp.

Haase, Matthias. 2013. "Life and Mind." In *The Freedom of Life: Hegelian Perspectives*, ed. Thomas Khurana. Berlin: August Verlag.

Hahn, Songsuk Susan. 2007. *Contradiction in Motion: Hegel's Organic Concept of Life and Value*. Ithaca: Cornell University Press.

Hegel, G.W.F. [1820] 1991. *Elements of the Philosophy of Right* [PR]. Cambridge: Cambridge University Press.

Hegel, G.W.F. [1830] 1991. *The Encyclopedia Logic*. Hackett.

Hegel, G.W.F. [1802–3] 1975. *Natural Law: The Scientific Ways of Treating Natural Law, Its Place in Moral Philosophy, and Its Relation to the Positive Sciences of Law*. Philadelphia: University of Pennsylvania Press.

Hegel, G.W.F. [1807] 2018. *The Phenomenology of Spirit* [Ph.S.]. Cambridge: Cambridge University Press.

Hegel, G.W.F. [1817–19] 1983. *Die Philosophie des Rechts: Die Mitschriften Wannenmann (Heidelberg 1817/18) und Homeyer (Berlin 1818/19)*. Stuttgart: Klett-Cotta.

Hegel, G.W.F. [1830] 1971. *Philosophy of Mind: Part Three of the Encyclopedia of the Philosophical Sciences* [Ph.M.]. Oxford: Oxford University Press.

Hegel, G.W.F. [1830] 2004. *Philosophy of Nature: Part Two of the Encyclopedia of the Philosophical Sciences* [Ph.N.]. Oxford: Oxford University Press.

Heisenberg, Lars Thimo Immanuel. 2019. "Hegel on Social Critique: Life, Action, and the Good in Hegel's 'Philosophy of Right.'" Ph.D. diss., Department of Philosophy, Columbia University.

Khurana, Thomas. 2013. "Life and Autonomy." In *The Freedom of Life: Hegelian Perspectives*, ed. Thomas Khurana. Berlin: August Verlag.

Khurana, Thomas. 2017. *Das Leben der Freiheit: Form und Wirklichkeit der Autonomie*. Berlin: Suhrkamp.

Marx, Karl. [1867] 1978. *Capital* (excerpts). In *The Marx-Engels Reader*, ed. Robert C. Tucker. New York: W. W. Norton.

Menke, Christoph. 2018. *Autonomie und Befreiung*. Berlin: Suhrkamp.

Neuhouser, Frederick. 1990. *Fichte's Theory of Subjectivity*. Cambridge: Cambridge University Press.

Neuhouser, Frederick. 2003. *Actualizing Freedom: Foundations of Hegel's Social Theory*. Cambridge, Mass.: Harvard University Press.

Ng, Karen. 2015. "Ideology Critique from Hegel and Marx to Critical Theory." *Constellations* 22: 393–404.

Ng, Karen. 2020. *Hegel's Concept of Life: Self-Consciousness, Freedom, Logic*. Oxford: Oxford University Press.

Novakovic, Andreja. 2017. *Hegel on Second Nature in Ethical Life*. Cambridge: Cambridge University Press.

Pinkard, Terry P. 2012. *Hegel's Naturalism: Mind, Nature, and the Final Ends of Life*. Oxford: Oxford University Press.

Särkelä, Arvi. 2018. *Immanente Kritik und soziales Leben: Selbsttransformative Praxis nach Hegel und Dewey*. Frankfurt am Main: Klostermann.

Testa, Italo. 2008. "Selbstbewusstsein und zweite Natur." In *Hegels Phänomenologie des Geistes*, ed. Klaus Vieweg and Wolfgang Welsch. Berlin: Suhrkamp.

Testa, Italo. 2020. "Embodied Cognition, Habit, and Natural Agency." In *The Palgrave Hegel Handbook*, ed. Martina F. Bykova and Kenneth R. Westphal. London: Palgrave.

Angelica Nuzzo

HEGEL'S *PHILOSOPHY OF RIGHT* AND THE IDEA OF THE WORLD: DIALECTIC'S "POLITICAL COSMOLOGY"

ABSTRACT: *Foregrounding Hegel's political cosmology allows us to set his dialectic-speculative theory of the political world in contrast both to ideal theories and to historicist-positivist theories. Against these positions, Hegel upholds his "realism of the idea": the claim that a rational world is neither a pre-given whole nor an unattainable ideal, but the dynamic, immanent orientation of reason that continually constructs and animates the world. Hegel's view of the world thus provides him with a way of reconceiving the relationship between philosophy and actuality. In this view, philosophy is not immune from, or external to, the world it theorizes, but is produced and checked by that world, which it, in turn, produces.*

It seems to be the "peculiar fate"[1] of Hegel's major works to bring their interpreters, admirers and detractors, followers and critics alike, back to a discussion of the fundamental issue that in any other comparable work of the tradition is instead taken for granted: the issue of what these works are really about; of what their topic really and properly is.

That is certainly the peculiar fate of the Logic and the *Philosophy of Right*. Indeed, in the case of the first division of the system, the longstanding discussion has centered on what kind of "logic" Hegel is presenting in the works that carry this title (the *Science of Logic* and the *Encyclopedia Logic*)—the candidates being an ontology, a metaphysics broadly construed (pre- or, alternatively, post-Kantian), an epistemology, a unique doctrine of the categories, a formalizable (or, alternatively, not-so-easily formalizable) system of thought determinations, or a spurious (indeed even ideological) collection of abstractions from historical reality. All these possibilities have repeatedly led to the interpretive task of assessing what kind of logic is Hegel's "science of logic." The *Philosophy of Right* has not fared any better in this regard. The clear-cut separation between a theory of ethics and a theory of politics has been, from early on, a contentious, interpretive issue, one reason being the difficulty of mapping such a distinction onto Hegel's dialectical relation of *Moralität* and *Sittlichkeit*. The apparent lack of a clear-cut separation between these two spheres, and certainly the difficulty of conceptualizing their relationship, has led interpreters to the occasional claim that Hegel lacks a genuine ethical or moral doctrine, that his ethics is utterly reduced to political philosophy. Additionally, the relationship between the descriptive and the normative value of Hegel's pronouncements in this work has also been repeatedly addressed, often investing the issue of justification, alternatively read as the justification of the historical present or of an ideal (again, perhaps, ideological) theoretical construct. Moreover, while the designation of "natural right" appears in the subtitle of the work (next to "science of the state"), Hegel's book is uniquely positioned, among its contemporaries, outside of the natural right and social contract tradition, harkening back more to Aristotle than to the early modern tradition. Hence the basic but still widely unsettled question arises: what kind of theory is the theory developed by Hegel's "philosophy of right," which is framed as a doctrine of "objective spirit"?

Ultimately, in both the case of the Logic and that of the *Philosophy of Right*, the array of possible thematic alternatives discussed by the interpreters is often instrumental to casting doubt: doubt about whether Hegel's Logic is "truly" a logic (at least in the traditional formal and Kantian sense of "logic"); doubt about whether his *Philosophy of Right* is "truly" an ethics or a political philosophy (at least in the early modern and contemporary sense, which is, in fact, a matter of controversy in its own right).

There is no question that in these two cases, the root of these thematic uncertainties lies in the interpreter's difficulty in grappling with Hegel's peculiar way of presenting his subject matter—the *Sache selbst* that, Hegel contends, properly *presents itself* in its immanent, specific development, and is never there in its full-fledged, already given and constituted form. To put this point in a different way, what often puzzles the interpreter is Hegel's dialectic-speculative method. This, however, is what I find most fascinating in Hegel's philosophical enterprise.

The radical import of the method can be measured, in the most general way, precisely by its capacity to challenge and destabilize disciplinary divides and unquestioned distinctions, hence, specifically, by its capacity to re-frame traditional understandings of logic, ethics, and political philosophy in an utterly fresh and unprecedented way. As the mode (*Art und Weise*) in which the *Sache selbst* presents itself in the immanent, dynamic movement that makes it what it truly is,[2] and not as a way of disclosing an already fixed and determined essence or thing (or topic), Hegel's method challenges, from the outset, the very understanding of the issue at hand—be it the chief issue of logical thinking or that of practical philosophy writ large. Moreover, the method is also responsible for the particular type of theory that Hegel's *Rechtsphilosophie* offers within his philosophical system as a whole—for the peculiar cognitive objectives and practical aims he assigns to it. And finally, the issue concerning the proper topic or "object" of a "philosophy of right" goes hand in hand with the question of the function that such a philosophy has (or ought to have) with regard to—and, as we shall see, within—the ethical-political world.

This essay is the first part of a larger study in which my concern is, first, the very general question of the type of ethical-social-political theory that Hegel develops in the *Philosophy of Right* on the basis of his dialectic and speculative method. At stake is the specific model or type of philosophical reflection on politics, political institutions, and ethical and social life articulated by the dialectic-speculative method. This is the question that directly interests me here. The indirect upshot of this question, or the second concern that constitutes the background of this essay, is the issue of its fruitfulness in understanding our historical present—a present characterized by the ongoing, multifaceted global crisis unfolding under everybody's eyes. For, ultimately, this is "*das Bekannte*" (the familiar or the known) from which any current reading of Hegel's *Philosophy of Right* unavoidably starts and in which it is unavoidably always implicated.[3] Since both issues are much too broad to be fully addressed here, let me begin by narrowing them down.

The Philosophy of Right *and Hegel's Dialectic-Speculative Method*

Hegel's dialectic-speculative method comes to the fore with regard to the question of the type of theory of politics developed in his philosophy of objective spirit.

To consider this issue, let me start with Hegel's contrast of the project of a "philosophy of right" as a theory of "objective spirit" against, on the one hand, the ideal, even utopian theory of the political world—*à la* Plato or Kant—and against, on the other hand, the "positive" science of right and jurisprudence of the historicist school: Gustav Hugo is, in this regard, Hegel's famous polemical target. This contrast needs more explanation than one might think necessary.

For one thing, Hegel's *Staatswissenschaft* is a "speculative" science of right in dealing with the "concept" and properly the "idea" of the state viewed as the full realization of the "idea of right" and as the "actuality of the ethical idea" (PR §1; §257). But what is Hegel's type of "ideality," especially in contrast to that, most obviously, of Plato or of Kant, and in contrast to doctrines that are based on the theoretical fiction of a social contract? Conversely, in what sense can it be claimed that Hegel's theory is "realistic" or that actuality is central to it, despite its being based on the "idea" of freedom—in fact, perhaps precisely because such a theory is based on the idea of freedom?

For another thing, Hegel's doctrine of objective spirit is a developmental account of (the idea of) freedom's progressive actualization in the world of social and political institutions that is deeply sensitive to the historical, changing nature of that actualization process and, consequently, of those institutions. Indeed, the thematization of world-history in the moment of *Weltgeschichte* constitutes the conclusion of the *Philosophy of Right*, the final step that brings the process of objective spirit to the threshold of absolute spirit.[4] This raises the question of the relation between the idea (of freedom, right, the state) and history, or the question of the historical nature of freedom, right, the state considered in their idea; and requires, in addition, a clarification of the harsh opposition that Hegel sets up between his own theory and that of the historicist school. What role does history play in a dialectic-speculative theory of right? What is the relation between, on the one hand, the historicity of "positive" right and jurisprudence, and, on the other hand, the historicity of the speculative concept of right—or, to put it with Hegel, what is the relation between the way ethical and political structures "arise" historically and their "arising out of the concept" (PR §3A, W7, 37)? Ultimately, Hegel contrasts the historical justification of political structures with their philosophical—the conceptual or logical—justification.

This is the problematic that will orient my discussion. Within this methodological framework, I am interested in the issue of social and political change—the change that takes place in collective life forms. This is an issue that one can easily assume must be ingrained in a theory such as Hegel's—a theory that is programmatically both developmental and mindful of the historical dimension of freedom's actuality in all its forms. At stake is, first, the descriptive question of how and under which conditions social and political life forms change; and, second, the practical, pragmatic, and normative question of how and under which conditions institutional and social forms can or must be changed.

It should be noted that change is not always and not necessarily for the better; it is not always and not necessarily progressive. Change may imply falling back into less advanced manifestations of freedom (and unfreedom); and change may be resisted and delayed or hampered; change may be illusory or take place only at the surface, as it were (or, following Hegel, only at the level of *Existenz* and not at the deeper structural level of *Wirklichkeit*), leaving the substance of life forms and institutions untouched. Dialectically, change implies—and is always confronted with—the possibility of not-changing, i.e., ultimately, with the "positivity" always ingrained in spirit's objective forms. For the speculative moment of rationality—*das Vernünftige*—is always animated (and indeed propelled forward) by its tension with the negative, intellectual moment—*das Verständige*—that aims at the absolutization of the status quo, at rejecting and resisting the transition or the change proper to speculative rationality.[5]

To further refine this approach to Hegel's political philosophy, I am interested in how the dialectic-speculative method mobilized in the *Philosophy of Right* and inherited from the Logic (PR §2, Remark) can help us in understanding social and political change *from within*, as it were, or from what I call the "position of immanence." Since the method is the development of the *Sache selbst*, not an instrument imposed from without on a given and already concluded topic or object,[6] the method is placed *within* the matter at hand; it is immanent within it and indicates a position, a dynamic taking place within it. As Hegel repeatedly states, the method is the living "soul" of the *Sache selbst*. It is at this juncture that the separation between theory and practice is overcome. The method that allows for the *comprehension* of the *Sache selbst* in its true conceptual and rational form is that which the matter at hand itself *does* when allowed to perform according to its own logic (and not following an external viewpoint). Thus, to understand change is to perform change. Ultimately, it is to accept change in ourselves.

What happens, then, when the position of immanence (in which change is required but also, contradictorily, resisted) is the position within a global historical crisis? This is the predicament that Antonio Gramsci famously called *interregnum*.[7] What can the *Philosophy of Right* and its method offer to this question when at stake is the immanent development of the idea of freedom in social, political, juridical institutions?

This is, to be sure, an ongoing open question—a question that in recent years I have found myself answering time and again, yet necessarily never conclusively since our present crisis has certainly evolved but not ended. In this essay, then, at the intersection between the methodological structure of the *Philosophy of Right* and the issue of the immanent change of social and political life forms in moments of historical crisis, I shall place the concept of the "world." My claim is that the position of immanence articulated by Hegel's 1820 work is a dynamic *within the world of spirit* that is responsible for *producing and instituting the world of spirit*. While my starting point is, yet again, the famous passage of the preface claiming philosophy's rootedness in the "contemporary world" (TW 7, 26), I shall now emphasize the idea of the world over that of the historical present. This will lead me to the central claim of this essay: Hegel's doctrine of objective spirit or his "science of right" (PR §2) is a philosophical account of spirit's "world." This latter is the dialectic-speculative successor of both the metaphysical concept of the world and Kant's criticism thereof. Accordingly, within the framework of his system, Hegel's philosophy of right offers the model of what I propose to call a practical or "political cosmology." In Hegel's dialectic-speculative philosophy, cosmology becomes a practical, worldly science: it becomes the account of the ways in which spirit constructs, produces, and comes to know its own world. The totality of the world—or its idea—is not a (given and fixed) object but a process. *The world is a historical process.* In this way, the *Philosophy of Right* should be seen as offering Hegel's *Weltbegriff* of philosophy—that cosmo-political concept that Kant formulates, uniquely, in the Doctrine of Method of the *Critique of Pure Reason.* Finally, the concept of the world turns out to be the discriminating concept that separates the *Philosophy of Right* from both idealistic ("otherworldly," as it were) and historicist accounts of the political realm.

I will begin with an account of Hegel's concept of the world as the dialectical successor of both the metaphysical and the critical cosmological concept. Herein I examine some famous passages of the *Philosophy of Right* in light of Hegel's *Weltbegriff* as a cosmopolitical concept. Then I turn to the method's immanence within spirit's world, but I only begin to tackle this problem.[8] Because of its immanence in spirit's world, and as the practice whereby spirit's world is progressively constituted, the dialectic-speculative method offers important hints as to how social change is carried out in relation to changing historical conditions. In this regard, the contrast between Hegel's dialectical model of political philosophy—his political cosmology, as it were—and both idealizing theories of politics and positive historicism will come to the fore.

Hegel's Concept of the World—In Kant's Aftermath

It is one of the most famous, most quoted and discussed passages of Hegel's *corpus*, dated June 25, 1820 (later misattributed to 1821). At issue is the fundamental relation between philosophical thinking and the "contemporary world" (*gegenwärtige Welt*). Hegel sets out to define the task and content of his "philosophy of right" as a treatise on "*Staatswissenschaft.*" As a genuinely philosophical enterprise, he argues, such a treatise is an attempt at conceptually comprehending and presenting the state in its full actuality. *Begreifen* and *Darstellen* are the philosophical tasks at hand, which can be jointly executed precisely because and insofar as the state is considered "as an entity in itself rational" (*als ein in sich Vernünftiges*). On this basis, Hegel sets his work against two different intellectual programs or types of theory of the political. The aim of the philosophy of right, he explains, is neither to "construct a state how it ought to be," i.e., an ideal (or utopian) state, nor to "instruct" the (existing) state as to "how it ought to be." If a normative "ought" is entailed in the philosopher's work, it is rather the one contained in the question of how "the ethical universe [*das sittliche Universum*] ought to be cognized."

And herein the specific task of a philosophy of right broadens into what, for Hegel, is the more general and fundamental task of philosophical thinking at such. The question is how philosophical thinking should relate to its object or content. Indeed, the "ethical universe" or, more broadly, the "world" is the touchstone for philosophy itself: "*Hic* Rhodus, *hic* saltus" (here [is] Rhodes, jump here), says Hegel concisely, referring to Aesop's fable (TW 7, 26). Herein (*hic*)—in the world or the universe in its ethical dimension—lies the test of philosophy's capacity of rational comprehension: not in the construction of an ideal; not in the instruction imparted to those in power or, directly (and naively), to the world itself (TW 7, 27). Indeed, as suggested by the reference to Aesop, it is "here," in the comprehension of the "ethical universe," that the relation that binds philosophy to the actual world—or the "universe" as such—is tested. The task of philosophy is the conceptual comprehension of "what is," of what is actual and present, because, Hegel insists, "what is actual is reason" (TW 7, 26). Since the world is the totality of what is, it encompasses the order of rationality. In this regard, philosophy and the world belong to the same order. This is a cosmological order, as it were. Installed within the "ethical universe," the *philosophy* of right embraces a crucial dimension of such an order.

The "ethical universe" displays a fundamental temporal dimension as well. The world is actual—*wirklich*—as the "*contemporary* world." Thus, the world that philosophy thematizes and to which philosophy belongs is, specifically, the "*gegenwärtige Welt.*" Accordingly, philosophy is, most generally, the rational comprehension of the contemporary world or, in Hegel's famous formulation, "philosophy is its own time apprehended in thoughts" (TW 7, 26).

While an extensive literature almost exclusively concentrates on the connection that Hegel's formulation establishes between philosophy and the present time (hence history), I want to emphasize the connection between philosophy and the "world" as the totality in which philosophy is always and necessarily inscribed. Indeed, Hegel's *Weltbegriff* of philosophy is at stake here: not so much the concept of the world produced by philosophical speculation as that of the world in which philosophy necessarily operates as the conceptual comprehension of its contents. Philosophy is *in its own world*, and is in the present time because the present is a constitutive feature of the world. Philosophy is, more precisely, an immanent dimension of that very world and time, namely, the dimension of rational (self-) comprehension of the world itself.

The "contemporary world" includes its own philosophical comprehension. Reason is the common basis that joins the world and its philosophical comprehension. The world is neither a construction of reason (it is not a mere ideal lacking actuality) nor does it await instruction from reason as to what it "ought to be" (and is not: TW 7, 27). The world is the *actual* dimension of reason itself. To this extent, the world cannot be transcended, just as the dimension of the present cannot be transcended.

The world is the ultimate test of the powers of philosophical rationality—the intimation to actually perform, here and now, that winning "jump" in Aesop's fable. In requiring practice (or actual performance) as the only sign of truth, the world is, ultimately, the proof of truth itself; no other promises, witnesses, and additional conditions are required. Again, "*Hic* Rhodus, *hic* saltus." Properly, however, no "leaping" beyond the world, just as no leaping beyond one's time, is possible. Like knowledge itself, any such activity is possible only within the world and its presence (or *Gegenwart*). The world, like reason or the order of rationality, is the totality that cannot be transcended: only the position of immanence within it is warranted. Hence, Hegel completes the thought elicited by Aesop's quote with this: "It is just as foolish to imagine that any philosophy can transcend its contemporary world as that an individual can overleap its own time, or leap over Rhodes" (TW 7, 26).

In fact, that philosophy cannot transcend the actual world is less intuitively clear than the impossibility for the individual to overcome the time she lives in. Hasn't Plato (along with many, perhaps most philosophers) attempted precisely that, namely, to paint a world other than, and alternative to, the actual? Is this not a possibility (maybe even a *desideratum*) of philosophical thinking—particularly, perhaps, in its practical dimension, where it imagines worlds other (and indeed better) than the actual one? Why should philosophy be confined to the real world; why should it be placed under its condition?

Hegel denies philosophy the privilege of being free from the constraints of the actual world because, first, what is exercised in philosophy—and in the activity of philosophizing concerning spirit's practical world—is reason, not mere opinion or imagination or individual subjective belief and feeling;[9] and second, because unlike mere opinion, which most often is not rooted in the real (and not checked by it), reason is precisely that which animates actuality (*Wirklichkeit*), that which makes reality or the world *actual* and *present*. If a philosophical "theory does indeed transcend [its] own time, if it builds itself a world as it ought to be, then it certainly has an existence (*existiert sie wohl*), but only within his [i.e., the individual's] opinions—a pliant medium in which the imagination can construct anything it pleases" (TW 7, 26). An imagined, merely private world made up by individual opinion and feeling is properly not a "world," hence is not the actual and present world; it is not the shared and public ethical world and it is not the historical world. It is not the world inhabited by philosophy. It is a world that has no presence (*Gegenwart*) and no actuality (*Wirklichkeit*), and to this extent is not the topic of philosophical comprehension. Accordingly, the retreat into allegedly private, alternative, merely possible (non-) "worlds" appears to sanction philosophy's renunciation of the actual and present world along with the renunciation of its own peculiar cognitive task. Ultimately, it signals that the commitment to rationality is being abandoned. Philosophy is then thought to concern, instead, how the world or more specifically "the ethical universe ought to be cognized" (TW 7, 26). Herein we have Hegel's first lesson for the current pandemic age—indeed, for the crisis of our contemporary world.[10]

Plato's construction of an ideal or utopian state is famously the explicit target of this well-known passage in the preface to the *Philosophy of Right*. Hegel's point is that even utopian or ideal constructions of alternatives to the real world depend on the real world and are inescapably determined and oriented by it. The escape from the world is a leap over Rhodes: it is not possible even in fiction, the imagination, or empty speculation. But it is Kant's more recent critical reflection on the concept of the "world" that at this juncture adds a new dimension to Hegel's idea of the "ethical universe" and its relation to philosophy.

Kant's *Critique of Pure Reason* offers two seemingly incompatible concepts of the world or *Weltbegriffe*, which, in turn, in their connection with philosophy, yield a twofold concept of philosophy itself. The first concept of the world emerges in the antinomies of the Transcendental Dialectic, where Kant criticizes speculative reason's flight from the empirical reality of nature towards the cosmological idea of the world of dogmatic metaphysics.[11] This is the concept made up by philosophy as a "scholastic" discipline. In the Architectonic of the Transcendental Doctrine of Method we are presented with Kant's second *Weltbegriff*. In laying out the crucial concept of "system" in its relation to rational knowledge, Kant foregrounds the connection between the "idea" of philosophy and the concept of the world—a concept that now differs significantly from the one that accounts for reason's antinomies. The constellation Kant develops in this conclusive step of the *Critique*—the notion of system, that of reason, the idea of philosophy itself—becomes central for Hegel. Curiously, however, although Kant's *Weltbegriff* of philosophy has attracted the attention of interpreters as hardly any other concept of the first *Critique*, its relation to Hegel is underexplored.

In the Doctrine of Method, Kant describes the task of the first *Critique* as that of "outlining the architectonic of all cognitions from pure reason" (B863/A835). With regard to the form of cognition (or "subjectively"), Kant opposes "historical" to "rational" cognition (B864/A836). Philosophical cognition is "rational" insofar as it is "cognition from concepts." Surprisingly, Kant claims that one cannot learn philosophy ("except historically") because there is no actual philosophy to be learned. Philosophy is the "mere idea of a possible science" never given *in concreto*. Thus, Kant asks, "where is it?"—where is philosophy in actuality? (B866/A838). In its ideality, philosophy—let alone the system of philosophy—does not seem to belong to the actual world. It is nowhere to be found *in concreto*, allegedly inhabiting a merely speculative ideal realm. However, Kant suggests that one can learn the *activity of philosophizing*, which is the exercise of the "talent of reason" in following its general principles. Unlike (the idea of) philosophy, philosophizing is an open-ended process taking place in the world and aiming at the idea of that possible science. It is the activity practiced by philosophers in the world. At this point, Kant introduces the distinction between the *Schulbegriff* (scholastic concept) and the *Weltbegriff* (world concept) of philosophy—a distinction that is placed in the specific time frame of the present, setting to the present a specific task. "*Until now*," Kant maintains, "the concept of philosophy has only been a *Schulbegriff*, namely, that of a system of cognition," the end of which is nothing more than "the systematic unity of this knowledge, hence only the logical perfection" and completeness of cognition. "But there is also a *Weltbegriff* (*conceptus cosmicus*) of philosophy that has always grounded this term, especially when it is, as it were, personified and represented as an archetype in the ideal of the philosopher" (B866f./A838f.). The *Weltbegriff* of philosophy is somehow more original and foundational than the *Schulbegriff*, and shows this originality "especially" in the personification and individualization the idea of philosophy receives in the "ideal of the philosopher." Somehow, in the philosopher (as ideal), philosophy comes closer to the world joining its *conceptus cosmicus*, which needs now to be retrieved by the critical and transcendental standpoint beyond its dominant scholastic notion. The *Weltbegriff*, Kant argues, sets "all cognition in relation to the essential ends of human reason." In this perspective, the philosopher is not a "*Vernunftkünstler*" (an artist of reason) occupied with building a logically consistent system (as are the mathematician, the natural scientist, and the logician). In referring all cognition to the "essential ends" of reason, the philosopher is rather "the legislator of human reason."

The world is at issue in this latter, legislative task but is absent in the former. The concept of the world is related to reason's highest and most essential ends—ends in which every human being has a necessary "interest" (B867/A839)—and is also related to a different kind of rational systematicity. These are the ends that shape the activity of philosophizing within the "world." Accordingly, the world is the expanded sphere of a rationality that is fundamentally intersubjective or collective.

The duality of Kant's *Weltbegriff*, namely, the world in *sensu scholastico* and the world in *sensu cosmico,* or rather *cosmopolitico,* becomes relevant when philosophy's connection to the world is at stake: its presence, as it were, within the world as well as its capacity to shape its own world.[12] At issue is the difference between the world as a cosmological and indeed scholastic concept produced by philosophy (in its *Schulbegriff*); and the concept of the world as the totality in which philosophy (and reason) as activity is itself thematized and on which philosophy is dependent in its most essential ends.[13] The latter is the world to which philosophy originally belongs, quite in the sense Hegel puts at the center of his definition of the philosophy of right. The *Schulbegriff* of the world is the metaphysical concept that gives rise to reason's cosmological antinomies —the conflicts that ultimately disintegrate the world (in its speculative ideality). Such a concept, although an inevitable (indeed, a "natural") possession of reason bound to posit to it necessary and unavoidable questions, is not one of its "essential ends."

The world in which the philosopher is active, and in which reason's highest and most essential ends are inscribed, is neither nature nor the cosmos of speculative cosmology but the public ethical world. The public dimension of reason is a sphere or a "world," as it were, determined not by contingent and arbitrary empirical aims but by what "essentially" and "necessarily" interests and concerns all human beings. This is the moral sphere of reason, which seems to correspond to

Hegel's "ethical universe." In setting the "essential ends" of human reason in relation to the highest end, Kant presents the latter as "*die ganze Bestimmung des Menschen*" (the whole determination/vocation of man). Insofar as philosophy is concerned with it, he emphasizes, it is called "moral philosophy" (B868/A840).[14] At stake is the necessary connection between philosophy in its *Weltbegriff* (or *cosmopolitical* concept) and the "world" as the realm of reason's moral activity; the connection between philosophy as ongoing rational practice and the intersubjective public world of human action. The world is the totality, the broader whole, in which our human destination or vocation is essentially inscribed and ought to be recognized and enacted. The world is the sphere encompassing those ends that necessarily concern everyone. Reason is practically legislative within *this* world. Kant claims that philosophy's task is to produce "*Kenntnis der Welt*"—"knowledge of the world"—capable of orienting our "life" in it by disclosing our essential human ends, and, ultimately, the highest end that is our human vocation—*Bestimmung*.[15] Such "cognition of the world" informs, in its turn, the moral world in which such vocation is embedded. The "world" at issue here is the world as the necessary basis of moral philosophy, ethics, anthropology, and history; not the cosmos; not nature.

Indeed, moving from the Transcendental Dialectic to the Architectonic, Kant clearly severs the link between the cosmological and the moral concept of the world. This duality parallels—but is not identical with—the separation between nature and freedom. It is on the latter, moral concept of the world and its relation to philosophy (i.e., on the *Weltbegriff* of philosophy) that Kant and Hegel find common ground—Kant's "*Kenntnis der Welt*" (AA 2, 443) echoed by Hegel's definition of philosophy as "*Gedanke der Welt*" (TW 7, 28). At the center, in both cases, is the power of reason. Common to them is the idea of a rationality that is legislative over a public, intersubjective sphere structured as a "world." Yet there are important differences. First and foremost, the relationship between the cosmological and the moral concept of the world is conceived of differently, with their separation endorsed by Kant and rejected by Hegel. Moreover, Hegel makes no mention of our human *Bestimmung* or of the highest end of human reason. For him, the rational comprehension that defines philosophy is measured, directly, against the *actuality* of the ethical world, not the ideal deferment of a moral "ought to."

A fundamental optimism underlies Kant's cosmopolitical concept of philosophy. For him, this concept offers an empowering insight that shapes the world according to our human vocation precisely because the moral world is separated from and opposed to the speculative, cosmological idea of the world. The latter concept depicts the world as inherently fragile—even more so after having gone through reason's dialectical antinomy and criticism. The cosmos-world is a whole that poses to speculative reason an insoluble problem of beginning or origin—as well as a problem of end and disintegration. It is a whole that constantly risks losing its unity and scattering into its possibly irreducible atomistic parts; it is a world in which freedom is paralyzed, as its presence can neither be proven nor denied. In this perspective, there is no human determination or vocation inscribed in and supported by the structure of the world of which reason can have knowledge. Only Kant's second *Weltbegriff*, the cosmopolitical concept, allows him to tie philosophy to the world on the ground of philosophy's own practical validity. There is no way to *know* that the moral world is, objectively, a unitary cosmos that makes human sense and supports our human vocation. However, providing such knowledge is not philosophy's task. The moral world is not open to reason's *knowledge*; it is instead the sphere of reason's free action. Reason (and philosophy) must act *as if* the world were amenable to moral and free action, *as if* the world made human sense.[16] This condition separates the moral world from its empirical and historical actuality, the ideal from the real.

It is this condition, and the consequent split in the concept of the world, that Hegel sets out to remove. On Hegel's view, there is, in fact, a question of knowledge that the ethical universe poses to philosophy in contrast to common sense, opinion, and feeling. This is the problem that interests Hegel. Indeed, the broader question of the *Philosophy of Right* concerns how "the ethical universe ought to be cognized" (TW 7, 26). However, as far as philosophical cognition is concerned, the ethical universe is not a different world than the natural world.

Hegel installs philosophy within the *actual* world of which, in turn, both the metaphysical cosmos, nature, and the moral or cosmopolitical world are integral parts. There is only one (actual) world. *Wirklichkeit* is one, although this implies neither the homogeneity nor the uniformity and unidirectionality of its process. In fact, the totality that is the actual world dialectically encompasses and conjoins nature, the cosmos, and the cosmopolis. In the passage of the preface to the *Philosophy of Right* examined above, Hegel seems to present the task of philosophy *vis à vis* the world in humble and diminutive terms when compared to Kant. At stake, he maintains, can only be the conceptual comprehension of the actual, i.e., of the contemporary world—not its ideal construction, not philosophy's legislation over it (the philosopher is not meant to be king). This is indeed the "limit" of the philosophical science of right (PR §3 Remark, TW 7, 35). It is no longer an issue of human ends nor of human *Bestimmung*—ethical and cosmopolitical. At issue is the conceptual knowledge of actuality, because the core of actuality is reason itself.

This apparently straightforward argument, which rejects Kant's division of the *Weltbegriff* (along with the usually underlined separation of nature and freedom), placing philosophy's activity at the core of the world's actuality, has as its backdrop Hegel's more complex dialectical transformation of the concept of the world, initiated in the Logic and introduced in its general outline in the opening sections of the *Encyclopedia*. These sections (in the 1830 edition of the manual) explicitly take up and clarify the argument first proposed in the preface to the *Philosophy of Right*.

In the *Encyclopedia*, in presenting the Positions of Thought Toward Objectivity that introduce the Logic, Hegel confronts the concepts of the world theorized by metaphysics and by what he considers Kant's critical version of empiricism—the first and second positions of thought. On Hegel's view, the "positions of thought" do not merely designate historical theories (or, in Kant's rendering, philosophy in its *Schulbegriff*). They are instead "always-present" fundamental attitudes of thinking toward objectivity. They indicate, as it were, thinking in its *Weltbegriff*.[17] Accordingly, in these sections, Hegel articulates his own *Weltbegriff* of philosophy. He does so by tackling the problem of how to dialectically and speculatively think of the world so as to overcome the shortcomings of both dogmatic metaphysics and Kant's criticism, while at the same time capitalizing on their respective gains. In sum, Hegel's claim is that the "world" is not a given object of thought. It is neither an "object" (*Gegenstand*) nor an "already given" and fully constituted object (Enz. §30). Rather, the world is thinking itself in its objectivity—"*objektiver Gedanke*" (Enz. §25). The idea of "objective spirit," topic of the philosophy of right, is the full systematic development and embodiment of this claim. Objective spirit is the world in its practical and poietic dimension. It is the world in the process of its spiritual (self-) constitution.

Furthermore, the world (like the other metaphysical "objects," namely, the soul and god) is not a *fixed* object that, in its fixity, can serve as an anchor for thinking in its activity. Metaphysics takes the world as a fixed point (or object) where thinking can rest, finding "*ein fester Halt*" (a firm foothold) on which to hang its static predicates (Enz. §31). Empirical thinking, for its part, finds in the immediate presence and givenness of the world the anchor ("*der feste Halt*": Enz. §38) to which empirical cognition owes its own certainty. For Hegel, however, far from being a fixed and concluded object (a metaphysical whole or an empirical given), the world is *one dynamically ongoing and interconnected process*. It is a process at one with thinking's own process of (self) determination and (self) apprehension. In its pure form, this process is staged by the Logic. In its concrete, specific determination in actuality, the world-process constitutes the world of nature (or *the world as nature*) and the world of spirit (or *the world as spirit*). Ultimately, in the process of the world we meet philosophy's systematicity: the system of philosophy is the ongoing process that in actuality constitutes and reconstitutes the manifold and differentiated system of the world.

In a famous programmatic formulation of the *Phenomenology of Spirit*, Hegel expresses the task of his dialectic-speculative method as the task of "bringing fluidity to fixed thoughts" or, alternatively, of "realizing and spiritualizing the universal [*das Allgemeine zu verwirklichen und zu begeistern*] by overcoming fixed ... thoughts" (TW 3, 37). On Hegel's view, fixed thoughts and fixed objects, such as the concept of the world, characterize both the logic and metaphysics of the tradition and Kant's transcendental logic. The fulfillment of Hegel's Heraclitean task is identical with the transformation of "pure thoughts" into the speculative concept, but its fulfillment also implies the act of bringing those determinations into actuality, their *Verwirklichung* (actualization), as it were. Accordingly, the dialectic-speculative concept of the world arises as the fixity of the world-object is set in motion and converted into the fluidity of a process, a process that is now, for the first time, truly real in the sense of being actual and spiritual.

Central to this operation is the work of contradiction. To be sure, Kant's critical approach to the metaphysical concept of the world already begins its dialectical transformation. Ultimately, however, just as metaphysical cosmology is dominated—and indeed paralyzed—by "absolute oppositions" (Enz. §35 Remark), in Kant's critical cosmology reason is paralyzed by the antinomies offered to it by the world taken as an "unconditioned" object (Enz. §48). Indeed, on Hegel's view, Kant's alleged "solution" of reason's cosmological problem consists merely in shifting the burden of the contradiction from the world as object to reason as subject. In this way, however, Kant forecloses the possibility of seeing the objective force of contradiction at work in shaping the world itself in its actuality, and, with the world, in shaping reason, which immanently inhabits the actual world. Kant rejects the possibility that the "worldly essence may be in itself tarnished by contradiction" and accordingly puts its burden "*only* on thinking reason, on the essence of spirit" (Enz. §48 Remark). In other words, Kant refuses to set the world-object in motion—an inconceivable possibility for Kantian reason, which, unable to cope with the destabilizing force of contradiction, cannot run the risk of losing its "*fester Halt*." Indeed, to set the world in motion means, for Kantian reason, utterly to dissolve it as object, and consequently to lose its bearings and orientation, to become impotent as "empty, indeterminate thinking." As reason loses its object (or the world), it also loses its determination and mission—its *Bestimmung*, as it were, which does not exist in a vacuum but is fundamentally tied to the world. Having lost its world, Kantian reason is ultimately a "thinking of nothing," thinking suspended in the ideality of a void (Enz. §48 Remark). As much as Kant attempted to separate them, the cosmological and cosmopolitical concepts of both philosophy (or reason) and the world inexorably imply each other, according to Hegel. The crucial point, for him, is to recognize that the world has contradiction immanently and objectively at work within itself. The world is itself the actual display of contradiction objectively at work. For it is contradiction that sets the fixity of the cosmological object in motion, shaping the world as a process that embraces reason and spirit within itself. In fact, reason and spirit are not separated from the world taken as a *Gegen-stand* (an object, literally: a "standing against"); they are immanently involved in the process whereby the world is progressively constituted and made actual.

In *Encyclopedia* §6, harkening back to the passage in the preface to the *Philosophy of Right* discussed above, Hegel offers his *Weltbegriff* of philosophy—the concept that the *Rechtsphilosophie* more directly instantiates. He posits that philosophy's "content" (*Inhalt*) is the "*Gehalt* that has originally been produced and reproduces itself in the sphere of the living spirit, a *content turned into a world* [*zur Welt . . . gemachte Gehalt*]." This "world" is then further determined as the "inner and outer world of consciousness" or, directly, as "actuality" (*Wirklichkeit*) (Enz. §6—my emphasis). The world is not an already constituted object. It is an activity in progress—a living activity (the *Wirken* in *Wirklichkeit*)[18] of spiritual production, re-production, and ultimately self-production of a content that is then shaped into the totality of the world. Hegel maintains that "the closest consciousness of this content," which is the world, is "experience." Philosophy is its conceptual comprehension. Accordingly, the world, experience, and philosophical thinking constitute aspects of the same process that is the production (*Hervorbringen*) of the world in its actuality—*Wirklichkeit*. Their distinction is only a distinction of "form."

Consistently with the passage from the preface to the *Philosophy of Right*, Hegel insists that philosophy must be "in agreement" (*Übereinstimmung*) with both experience and actuality. Philosophical thinking cannot escape from the world and its experience: it cannot be about something else; it cannot produce something outside or beyond the world. Whatever "ideal" (or vocation) philosophy pursues, it must be immanent in the world, must constitute the world in its actuality, and should be able to become conscious experience. In fact, philosophy's ideal is always within the world, even when philosophers deny it (as Plato did). Indeed, agreement with the world, or actuality, should be taken as the "external test" (*Prüfstein*) of the truth of philosophy itself (Enz. §6). As Hegel insists, "*Hic* Rhodus, *hic* saltus." The world is the touchstone of philosophy's truth, its Rhodes. Hegel now carries this point a step further by turning it into the defining task of philosophy in its *Weltbegriff*. "It must be regarded as the highest and final goal of science to bring about through the cognition of this agreement [i.e., the agreement of actuality and experience] the reconciliation [*Versöhnung*] of reason that is self-conscious [*selbstbewusste Vernunft*] with reason that *exists* [*seiende Vernunft*], namely, with actuality" (Enz. §6). "Self-conscious reason" is present and at work, subjectively, in the experience of the world as well as in the production (and self-production) that is the world itself. But reason is also, objectively, the deeper rational dimension of actuality—of *Wirklichkeit* insofar as actuality is the existent form assumed by reason as "*seiende Vernunft*." Ultimately, the actuality of reason is the world itself.

Moreover, the convergence—which is both correspondence and reconciliation, *Übereinstimmung* and *Versöhnung*—that Hegel indicates with this program is also the convergence of the theoretical and the practical function of philosophy. The cosmological and cosmopolitical concepts of the world, necessarily separated in Kant's critical philosophy, converge in Hegel's program. Science, like truth, is a rational activity in which the theoretical and the practical dimensions of reason converge: to recognize and to know that actuality and experience constitute a unity, to recognize and to know that reason is one and the same reason in its self-conscious and objective worldly manifestations, is to produce or "to bring about" the "reconciliation" of the two sides, to bring into existence a new and higher—indeed a reconciled—form of actuality, a new "world." *Wirklichkeit* indicates precisely this multi-layered, constructed convergence. *Wirklichkeit* is the manifest sediment or objectivization of reason's own activity, the solid yet always dynamic reality assumed by an "activity" (*Wirken*) that has shown and continues to show its enduring *efficacy* (*Wirksamkeit*) in the world precisely by constituting and re-constituting the world as the world of the living spirit, the experienced, inner and outer world of consciousness.

The Making of Spirit's World—A Problem of Method

Given the backdrop of Hegel's transformation of the concept of the world, the *Philosophy of Right* offers the closest instantiation—or, properly, actualization—of the *Weltbegriff* of philosophy and is framed, accordingly, as the project of what I call a "political cosmology" carried out on the basis of the dialectic-speculative method. We now have to see how this method is responsible for the type of political theory Hegel advances in contrast both to idealizations that ultimately amount to a flight from the real world, and to historicist positions that ultimately distort actuality by offering an intellectual justification of contingent, merely historical political and juridical reality.

The crucial point is that in the case of both of these un-dialectical types of theories, the necessary change that animates the making of spirit's objective world cannot be comprehended and is consequently blocked. On these views, spirit's world falls back into the static essentialist object of non-dialectical thinking proper of the understanding (proper, historically, to dogmatic metaphysics and Kant's critical philosophy as well as previous social contract theories).

The world is the dialectical process whereby spirit's actuality is self-constituted through the movement of contradiction. Spirit's world is a complex dynamic system made up of relatively independent yet interconnected dimensions or processes, each moving at its own speed, each fulfilling different tasks and needs, each subject to a justification and a right of its own, yet all ultimately conjoined and interdependent within the totality that is the actual world. The task of the dialectic-speculative method is to bring to light the emergence of such dimensions in the totality of the world.

Ultimately, this is the condition for the theoretical understanding and, at once, the practical implementation of change. Ontologically, however, the world is not just actuality. It is the dynamic system that embraces and articulates the differential relationship of *Wirklichkeit* and *Existenz*. This relationship may be a harmonious correspondence or, more often, an oppositional and contradictory strife. Epistemologically, on the other hand, spirit's objective world is the layered interconnection of *Begriff* and *Gestaltung* (concept and figuration). We shall now see how Hegel argues for the relevance of these distinctions in the program of the philosophy of right.

Spirit's World: Wirklichkeit *and* Existenz; Begriff *and* Gestaltung

In the preface to the *Philosophy of Right*, Hegel argues that the rationality of actuality, hence reason's embeddedness in the actual world, is the ground of both common consciousness and the philosophical standpoint. That standpoint, however, assumes the rationality of actuality as the explicit starting point of its investigation of both "the *spiritual* and the *natural* universe." Kant's dualism within the concept of the world is already overcome in the unified or rather stratified dimension of the world's actuality: the natural and spiritual universes go hand in hand in their constitution.

Hegel's contention is that while "subjective consciousness"—the philosophical stance projected toward an ideality always set beyond the present—may regard the present (the present *world*) with disdain, considering it "futile" (*eitel*) and presuming a superior knowledge beyond it, consciousness and philosophical reflection can themselves claim "actuality," hence relevance, only in the dimension of the present world. Placed outside of the world (in their disdain for it, given an alleged superior "beyond"), they are positions condemned to irrelevance and indeed to utter futility. In other words, the world in its undeniable presence and solid actuality already entails the refutation of all stances claiming to lead outside of it.

The world implies and entails its *Weltanschauung* (PR §129) and is, ultimately, the judge of the validity and relevance of the views (indeed, often, of the ideologies) subjectively articulated within it. Truly, there is no way to avoid the judgment of the world—the *Weltgericht*, as it were. The world is thinking's inescapable Rhodes. Hegel's position, then, is that philosophy deals with actuality *but also* with the "idea," because the idea is what is supremely "actual." In short, "nothing is actual except the idea" (TW 7, 25). To deny actuality to the idea is to reduce it to the whim of subjective opinion. Herein, the position that reduces actuality to futile and vain existence with the illusory promise of a better reality beyond it converges with the view that reduces the idea to merely subjective opinion. Hegel's realism, by contrast, is a *realism of the idea*. To be rooted in the real-actual world through the idea is necessary if philosophy in general—and a philosophy of right in particular—wants to avoid the illusion of false truths, the absolutization of one-sided subjective standpoints, and the dismissal of the rationality that lies at the core of the actual. This is the case because the present world, as spirit's ongoing changing process, is not ontologically homogeneous.

Here we meet the epistemological task of philosophically apprehending spirit's world. "What matters," Hegel argues, "is to recognize in the semblance (*Schein*) of the temporal and transient the substance which is immanent and the eternal which is present." Since *Wirklichkeit*, which as the actualization of the rational "is synonym with the idea," manifests itself by entering into "external existence," actuality is not homogeneous but is a dynamic composite process. In entering into external existence, the rational "emerges in an infinite wealth of forms, appearances, and figures, and surrounds its core with a brightly colored covering in which consciousness at first resides, but which only the concept can penetrate in order to find the inner pulse, and detect its continued beat even within the external figures" (TW 7, 25). The world of spirit, hence the broader sphere of "right," is such a composite process, in which the rational core of actuality is enveloped by a multiform layer of appearances. Consciousness inhabits the outer layers of appearance and existence and either rejects them in an ideal projection beyond reality or dwells satisfied in them, often by taking them as an "absolute" not to be transcended—*das Bekannte* of the *Phenomenology*, or what Gramsci calls the "natural absolutism of the present."[19] Philosophical insight, by contrast, is able to connect external existence with its rational core, to recognize the necessity for rationality to manifest itself as a manifold of outer appearances; but also, most importantly, is able to hold fast to the rational core of actuality without being lost in "the infinite material" of external existence, in its various relations and organizations. This is, for Hegel, the problem of the dialectic-speculative method as method of the philosophy of right.

While it may seem self-explanatory that philosophy is (or should be) concerned with reason and rationality, an important source of philosophical deception, an obstacle to the attainment of truth, is the fact that rationality is actualized by entering the manifold forms of external existence and its organization.[20] This is the deceptive trap that external existence sets to the political philosopher—the trap into which Plato and Fichte, Hegel argues, have fallen: the former by making recommendations to nurses as to how to put children to sleep, the latter by getting lost in the details of passport regulations for suspect people (TW 7, 25). Philosophy does not show its practical concern with actuality—both descriptively and normatively—in holding fast to the manifold contingent details of historical existence and pretending to make recommendations in this regard or that. Philosophy's task is instead, famously and in a much-commented-upon claim, rife with subtle referents, to recognize "reason as the rose in the cross of the present" (TW 7, 26): to bring to light the ways in which the outer appearances of institutions, customs, and ways of life are connected to and reveal the inner rational core that is (the idea of) freedom in its complex actualization-process. This is the condition for all social, political, historical change.

When *political* actuality or the actuality of the state is at issue, the philosophical consideration can only be the "idea" of the state or the "state as an inherently rational entity," not the state in its contingent, historical forms of existence (TW 7, 26). While the idea is certainly bound to manifest itself in a manifold of external and historical appearances, it is not this that constitutes the topic of political philosophy. On this point, Hegel's dialectical approach to political actuality diverges methodologically from historicist positions. It is not, however, immediately clear how philosophy should thread the balance between the recognition of the rational core proper of the "state" (in its idea) and its appreciation of the fact that the external existence in which such idea enters, while still being valued as the appearance of the idea of the state, should not be the ultimate reality to which philosophy appeals. Again, quite generally, Hegel rejects Plato's and, more recently, Kant's dualistic separation of actuality and existence from the idea. Yet while historical existence does not constitute the topic of the philosophical account of right, it cannot be ignored and should not be discarded. How, then, is historical existence integrated in the consideration of the rationality of the political world? This is the crucial issue that Hegel invokes in the opening section of the *Philosophy of Right*.

Consistently with what we have heretofore seen, Hegel maintains that "the *philosophical science of right* [*Rechtswissenschaft*] has the *idea of right*" as its object. Now, however, on the basis of the Logic as the first sphere of the philosophical system,[21] he spells out the double dimension or the double track that belongs to that "idea" in its development. The idea of right implies both the "concept of right" and its "actualization" or *Verwirklichung*. Hegel insists that the dialectic-speculative concept (hence not the non-dialectical "determination of the understanding") involves actuality insofar as "it gives actuality to itself" (PR §1). *Wirklichkeit* is self-produced reality. It denotes the way in which the "concept of right" makes itself an integral part of the real world, affirming itself *in* the world and *as* spirit's own world. To this extent, "actualization" already implies the activity of freedom (as self-production). This specification is now the criterion that discriminates between actuality and merely contingent existence. Indeed, "everything other than this actuality posited through the concept itself, is impermanent existence, external contingency, opinion, inessential appearance, un-truth, deception, etc." (PR §1 Remark).[22] But external appearance, as appearance *of the concept*, cannot be utterly discarded. It is, instead, to be recognized and valued to the extent that it is the peculiar *Gestaltung* (figuration) of the concept, i.e., the way in which the concept enters existence and *gives itself* determinate shape and figure. The objective world is the self-production of spirit *both* in its pure rationality *and* in its *Gestaltung*.

The process of "figuration" is essential to the movement of actualization. Thus, Hegel explains, "the *figuration* [*Gestaltung*] that the concept gives to itself in its actualization [*Verwirklichung*] is the other, essential moment of the idea, essential to the cognition of the *concept* and distinct from its *form* of being only as concept" (PR §1 Remark). In this way, Hegel destabilizes the dualistic, un-dialectical opposition between what is essential and necessary and what is inessential and merely contingent, what is true and what is un-true, and reconfigures it as the composite, multi-track process in which, by giving itself actuality, the concept enters a process of figuration.

Verwirklichung and *Gestaltung* go hand in hand but are not identical. They are both necessary processes; they are both self-produced by spirit in its core rationality (the concept), yet the latter engages the concept in external, contingent existence. Here Hegel underscores the chief difference between the logical consideration of the world and its ethical-social-political apprehension—*Erkenntnis*, as it were. The movement of *Gestaltung* is, in the latter case, unavoidable and indispensable to a philosophical science of right. The question, then, clearly concerns the nature of that *Gestaltung*.[23] Figuration and the concept's "figure" are distinct from the pure "form" of "being only as concept," but as self-production of the concept they are also connected to it in a vital and essential way that is not proper to merely contingent existence (such as passport regulations and nurses' behavior). Figures are historical and are crystallized, epistemologically, in individual and collective representations, in language, habits, and customs. The latter are themselves integral parts of the social and political world.

My suggestion is that it is precisely in this figurative side of the movement of actualization, the figurative side of spirit's objective world in its constitutive relation to the concept (as its self-production), that Hegel's realism of the idea differs radically both from ideal theories of the political and from historicist and positivist ones.

A Provisional Conclusion

I shall now outline a brief answer to the question of where this analysis, and with it this interpretive framing of Hegel's *Philosophy of Right*, may lead us.

The backdrop of my discussion is the global, expanding crisis of our own present world. We live immersed in it—no critical distance seemingly separating us and our lives from our thematic object. We are unavoidably placed in what I called the "position of immanence": we live, think, act, inescapably, within the world. As much as such a position seems to defy the possibility of critically appraising and practically intervening in our present, Hegel teaches us that learning how to live, know, and act in this predicament is precisely what constitutes the philosophical—and properly the *dialectical*—stance of reason. "It is just as foolish to imagine that any philosophy can transcend its contemporary world as that an individual can overleap its own time, or leap over Rhodes"

(TW 7, 26). So here are three suggestions that the *Philosophy of Right* can offer to us today.[24]

First, we should pay more attention to the figurative movement of the concept and value it as such, namely, neither as an absolute reality able to speak for itself without being animated by the concept, nor as a fleeting, immaterial individuality or particularization unworthy of philosophical attention in the face of the concept's universality. "Figures"—or historical ways of life—have deep roots in the rationality of the idea but are also concretely embodied in our collective representations, language, and customs. At stake is the question of whether and how our ways of collective life correspond or do not correspond to the rationality that has once animated them—the question of whether such ways of life are, in fact, fostering freedom or rather suppressing it. This question is certainly at the forefront for us today, in a world that has been deeply shaken, at all levels, by the global pandemic.

Figures are no "absolutes." Rather, they may have to undergo change lest they become what Hegel calls the "dead positive." How, then, and to what extent are we to persevere in or, alternatively, abandon and radically change our ways of interacting—physically and virtually—our ways of collectively participating in the public and political world, in the social and economic sphere, in the world of culture, the arts and sciences?

Second, we should learn how to think "cosmologically," as it were, about the matters concerning our social and political world but also our environment and nature as such. Freedom, after all, is for Kant a cosmological idea before becoming a practical one. As Hegel overcomes the Kantian need to separate the cosmos from the moral world, freedom is squarely installed within the world. The world is not only the inescapable thematic object of our theoretical consideration. The world is ourselves, our self. The world, most importantly, is our Rhodes. We cannot think smaller than the world. But we cannot think any bigger than the world—not, at least, without leaving the order of philosophical rationality. Moreover, there is only one world—whether we want it or not. The world is, at once, the interconnectedness of nature and freedom, the interconnectedness of all of us, the *ordo et connectio* of all its parts. We are responsible for our world but also, we are what we are in and on the ground of the world.

Third, what is at stake is, again, the issue of change—social and political change, change in our forms of collective life, change in the world-earth-environment. Herein the suggestion is to bring the two previous points together. Change is a "cosmological" matter and is, first and foremost, a matter of freedom and responsibility. It takes place at different levels and occurs with differential times—but all levels and times are interconnected and interdependent. Change takes place at the deeper structural level of the concept as well as at the level of the concept's figurations—but also in utterly contingent and external forms of existence.

The first task of our philosophical comprehension is certainly to get these levels—ontological, epistemological, practical—sorted out in the right way. We may think, for example, that we accomplish something momentous in changing our individual or collective habits. But then we may leave the underlying structures and institutions unchanged. Not much is, in this case, accomplished. The obsolescence—or positivity, as it were—of those structures will catch up to us soon enough. This predicament should resonate with us today and constitute a lesson for our not-yet post-pandemic world.

NOTES

1. This is, famously, Kant's claim about human reason with regard to metaphysics in the opening of the 1781 preface to the *Critique of Pure Reason* (Avii).
2. See, for example, TW 6, 550ff; TW 3, 11, 13, 44, *et passim*.
3. Hegel aims to transform "*das Bekannte*" into "*das Erkannte*" (TW 3, 18).
4. See PR §§341-360; Enz. §§548-552.
5. See Enz. §§79-82.
6. See, famously, Hegel's claims against the view of the method as *Werkzeug* in the introduction to the *Phenomenology of Spirit*, TW 3, 68f.
7. See my extensive development of this point in Nuzzo 2018a, Appendix.
8. I develop this point more extensively in a forthcoming companion essay.
9. The pretension impugned by these positions is "vanity" or *Eitelkeit* (TW 7, 25).
10. I have developed this point in Nuzzo 2020.
11. See KrV B446/A418 for the terminological distinction between "*Welt*" and "*Natur.*" In addition, following Hegel's assessment of Plato's ideal state, we could add that speculative reason's flight toward the metaphysical idea of the cosmos is not just an eternal "natural" tendency or "fate" of human reason, but in turn betrays reason's predicament in the actual world.
12. See for example *Logik Pölitz* (AA 28. 2,1, 532f.). Accordingly, Hinske suggests that in this passage of the *Critique* Kant means "*sensus cosmicus*" as "*sensus cosmopoliticus*" (Hinske 2013, 270f.). Kant's added parenthesis intends to differentiate the scholastic concept at stake in the antinomies from the concept of the world of the Architectonic.
13. See Hinske 2013, 271.
14. Kant's contemporaries, from Spalding to Mendelssohn to Fichte later on, shared with him the use of the influential expression "*Bestimmung des Menschen*" to indicate the same problematic constellation.

15. See AA 2, 443: *Vorlesungsankündigung* for the Summer semester 1775; also see Kant's letter to Marcus Herz at the end of 1773: AA 10, 146.
16. See, for a broader discussion of this point, Geuss 2013.
17. Enz. §27 with regard to metaphysics. But my suggestion is that this is true for all the positions of thought examined in these introductory sections of the *Encyclopedia.*
18. See Nuzzo 2018b.
19. Gramsci 1975; Quaderno 14, 1932-33, 1727. See Nuzzo 2018a, Appendix for a discussion of this passage.
20. This latter, crucial point is rarely stressed by the interpreters.
21. See PR §2 and the end of the Remark (TW 7, 32).
22. Interestingly, this passage echoes a passage that opens the last chapter of the Logic, dedicated to the absolute idea as absolute method: TW 6, 549; see Nuzzo 2005.
23. I cannot address this issue here but I have done so at length in Nuzzo 2018a, chapter 3.
24. I further elaborate on these points in the companion essay to this.

REFERENCES

Geuss, Raymond. 2013. "The Wisdom of Oedipus and the Idea of a Moral Cosmos." *Arion, A Journal of Humanities and the Classics* 20(3): 59-89.

Gramsci, Antonio. 1975. *Quaderni dal carcere*, ed. V. Gerratana. Torino: Einaudi.

Hegel, G.W.F. [1817] 1830. *Enzyklopädie der philosophischen Wissenschaften*, in TW vols. 8–10. (=Enz.).

Hegel, G.W.F. [1820] 1821. *Grundlinien der Philosophie des Rechts*, in TW vol. 7. (=PR).

Hegel, G.W.F. 1986. *Werke in zwanzig Bände*, Hrsg. v. E. Moldenhauer and H. M. Michel. Frankfurt a.M.: Surhkamp (=TW).

Hinske, Norbert. 2013. "Kants Verankerung der Kritik im Weltbegriff." In *Kant and Philosophy in a Cosmopolitical Sense*. Akten des XI Kant-Kongress, ed. S. Bacin, A. Ferrarin, and M. Ruffing. Berlin: De Gruyter.

Kant, Immanuel. 1910ff. *Kants gesammelte Schriften*, Hrsg. v. Der Preußischen Akademie der Wissenschaften. Berlin: De Gruyter (=AA).

Nuzzo, Angelica. 2020. "Philosophy and the World at the End—Hegelian Reflections." *Argumenta Philosophica* 20(2): 123-146.

Nuzzo, Angelica. 2018a. *Approaching Hegel's Logic, Obliquely: Melville, Molière, Beckett.* Albany: SUNY Press.

Nuzzo, Angelica. 2018b. "*Wirklichkeit* and *Wirken*: Hegel's Logic of Action." In *Wirklichkeit. Beiträge zu einem Schlüsselbegriff der hegelschen Philosophie*, ed. L. Illetterati and F. Menegoni. Frankfurt a.M.: Kostermann.

Nuzzo, Angelica. 2005. "The End of Hegel's Logic: Absolute Idea as Absolute Method." In *Hegel's Theory of the Subject*, ed. David G. Carlson. London: Palgrave Macmillan.

Alan Patten

HEGEL'S ALTERNATIVE TO NATIONALISM

ABSTRACT: *All of the major German Idealists perceived a gap between ideals and social reality. Kant sought to bridge this gap through an institutional design that forced self-interest to track the public good. Fichte embraced cultural nationalism, according to which, to overcome the gap between ideals and reality, a nation must revive and strengthen its original culture. Hegel's solution, in contrast, rests on the idea of ethical habituation. For Hegel, the institutions of a well-designed social order encourage the habits and virtues needed for the successful reproduction of that order. The article reflects on the implications of these contrasts for the prospects of liberal democracy.*

The fifty-year period from the publication of Kant's First *Critique* (1781) to the death of Hegel (1831) was a remarkable one in the history of political philosophy. The major works of the German Idealists were written against the backdrop of the French Revolution, the expansion of commercial society, the consolidation of the modern state, and the rise of nationalism. Even works of theoretical philosophy in this era were filled with references to normative and political ideas, such as freedom, recognition, history, and revolution.

While German thinkers of the period were confident about the revolutionary importance of their ideas, they were also painfully aware of a gap between the exhilarating ideals they announced and the reality of their contemporary world. They all drew attention to this gap, even if they were frequently guarded, for political reasons, about elaborating their criticisms of the status quo. At the same time, they wrestled with the more or less practical problem of how their ideals might be realized and sustained.

In the context of his political philosophy, Kant drew attention to the gap very explicitly in a famous passage of his 1795 essay, "Toward Perpetual Peace: A Philosophical Project." After laying out three "articles" for perpetual peace, Kant turned to the question of what could serve as a "guarantee of perpetual peace" (Kant [1795] 1996, 331). How does nature ensure, Kant asked, that human beings in fact do what their own reason commands them freely to do (ibid., 334)? The problem seems particularly pressing in the context of the republican form of government favored by Kant, which is said to be especially difficult to establish and preserve: "many assert it would have to be a state of *angels* because human beings, with their self-seeking inclinations, would not be capable of such a sublime form of constitution" (ibid., 335).

Kant's view was that the problem and its solution could be found in the same place. The problem is selfishness, or what he called "self-seeking inclinations" (*selbstsüchtige Neigungen*), but these same inclinations also point to the solution:

> But now nature comes to the aid of the general will grounded in reason, revered but impotent in practice, and does so precisely through those self-seeking inclinations, so that it is a matter only of a good organization of a state (which is certainly within the capacity of human beings), of arranging those forces of nature in opposition to one another in such a way that one checks the destructive effect of the other or cancels it, so that the result for reason turns out as if neither of them existed at all and the human being is constrained to become a good citizen even if not a morally good human being. (Ibid.)

Kant drew here on a well-established eighteenth-century doctrine of political theory embraced by Mandeville, Montesquieu, Hume, Adam Smith, and James Madison, among others. Through clever institutional design, the selfishly pursued power of one political actor could be made to check and contain the equally selfish power of another. Though everyone is acting on the basis of their own selfish interest, the public good emerges. Thus, Kant thought it possible to organize a good state "even for a nation of devils." The solution consists in establishing a constitution in such a way that, "although in their private dispositions they strive against one another, these yet so check one another that in their public conduct the result is the same as if they had no such evil dispositions" (ibid.). This solution requires not "the moral improvement of human beings" but a comprehension of what Kant calls the "mechanism of nature," a mechanism that does not depend on "inner morality" but rather works "through self-seeking inclinations that naturally counteract one another" (ibid., 335-36).

In this article, I consider the views of two of the leading philosophers of the period who rejected Kant's 1795 position on this problem. Fichte and Hegel agreed with Kant that correct institutional design is a *part* of the solution. This was a position held by almost every political thinker of the period. Kant's theory of a good will notwithstanding, nobody expected individuals to in fact follow the dictates of morality simply because they are right, and without any intervention or motivation by institutions. Moreover, Hegel recognized a sphere of human activity—civil society—in which "the selfish end" (*der selbstsüchtige Zweck*) "establishes a system of all-round interdependence" that aligns the welfare of the individual with "the subsistence, welfare, and rights of all" (Hegel [1821] 1991, para. 183). However, as a general solution to the problem, both Fichte and Hegel rejected Kant's "invisible-hand" theory that well-designed institutions could be made to direct and channel selfishly motivated actions so that their combined, unintended result is to produce the public good.

Fichte and Hegel departed from Kant's solution for several reasons. First, as Fichte explained most fully, the invisible-hand solution seems importantly incomplete (Fichte [1808] 2008, 88-90). No system of checks and balances is self-creating or completely self-maintaining. "What compels your final part," Fichte wondered, "in which all compulsion in the machine originates?" How "do you mean to set this mainspring in motion and compel it to see and will what is right without exception?" It seems that an invisible-hand solution faces a dilemma. Either it is unreliable or it is incomplete. It is unreliable insofar as the officials who establish and oversee the institutions that constitute it, and ensure that they continue to direct and channel selfish activity in the appropriate way, are assumed to be selfishly motivated. If they are selfishly motivated, then it is a matter of pure contingency whether these officials will fulfil their responsibilities as required. Alternatively, the assumption could be that officials are motivated in some other way, with a moral purpose that directs them to fulfill their responsibilities. But then the solution is incomplete. It does not give an account of how officials develop the assumed moral sensibilities.

A second objection to Kant's solution is that it conflicts with freedom. Although Kant characterized his solution as being "without prejudice to ... freedom" (Kant [1795] 1996, 334), Fichte and Hegel believed otherwise. The solution works only to the extent that institutions constrain individuals to direct their selfish energies in publicly beneficial ways. Each individual must, as Fichte put it, be "compelled ... against his wish and will, to promote the general good" (Fichte [1808] 2008, 88). For Hegel, as noted above, civil society is the sphere in which "the principle of particularity passes over into *universality*." But the unity between these principles in civil society, he insisted, "is not present as freedom" (Hegel [1821] 1991, para. 186). For both Fichte and Hegel, full political freedom consists, in part, in individuals spontaneously embracing the public good as their own end.

Although these objections could be explored further, I mainly want to devote the present article to exploring two alternative solutions presented by Fichte and Hegel for bridging the gap between political ideals and social reality. These solutions are importantly different. The one I will attribute to Fichte embraces *cultural nationalism* as its central component. To bridge the gap between ideals and social reality, a nation must have an appropriate form of background culture, and it must actively encourage individuals to embrace this culture, express it, and preserve it. By contrast, Hegel's solution is built around the idea of *ethical habituation*. On Hegel's view, the institutions of a well-designed social order will tend to encourage the formation of the habits, dispositions, and virtues needed for the success and reproduction of that order. For Hegel, the key to bridging the gap between ideals and social reality is to recognize that modern societies already have, in their existing "ethical life," many of the elements they need to support well-ordered freedom. Bridging the gap, then, is not a matter of looking for, or contriving, some wholly new source of motivation. Rather, it means nourishing and supporting the ethical tendencies that are already latent in existing practices and institutions, while avoiding the entrenchment of highly subjective and/or individualistic normative principles that corrode those practices and institutions.

The disagreement between these two approaches is relevant to several important contemporary debates.

One concerns nationalism. The suggestion that attachment to culture and nation can provide a source of trust and solidarity needed for the success of modern states is an enduring one, often repeated by today's philosophical defenders of nationalism (e.g., Miller 1995, 90-99; idem 2000, ch. 4). Fichte articulates an early formulation of this claim, while Hegel points to an alternative.

A second, related debate is about the universality of the political ideals — liberty, equality, fraternity—associated with the French Revolution. As we shall see, Fichte's argument seems to imply that the realization of these ideals is only possible for some peoples: those with the appropriate cultural background. While Hegel seemed to think that Europeans were in the vanguard of realizing freedom, and while he held chauvinistic and, indeed, racist views about the character of non-European peoples, his theory of ethical habituation implies that, in principle at least, any people can establish self-sustaining institutions of freedom.

Finally, a third debate concerns the fate of modern liberalism. Conservatives have long argued that liberalism, with its emphasis on freedom and markets, fails to guarantee the social conditions of its own persistence.[1] According to many conservatives, liberals are disdainful towards religion, which is in fact the bedrock guarantor of a stable set of protections for personal freedom. Fichte's account of nationalism—another object of liberal skepticism—is similar: by criticizing nationalist politics, liberals risk sawing off the very branch they are sitting on. The implications of Hegel's position are rather different. From a Hegelian perspective, liberalism can take an extreme individualist form, which pays insufficient attention to the role that institutions, practices, and communities play in ethical habituation. But taking seriously this role does not require liberals to abandon their values and principles. There is, then, a second, "social" version of liberalism (as I shall call it) that fosters ethical habituation without sacrificing freedom.

Fichte's Cultural Nationalism

Born in 1762, Fichte was a fairly young man at the moment of the French Revolution. Enthused by the events in France, he published a book, *Contribution to the Rectification of the Public's Judgment of the French Revolution*, that helped to establish his reputation as a political radical. He developed his political theory further in *Foundations of Natural Right* (1796-97), which drew on his Idealist philosophical system to argue for a republican, egalitarian, and activist view of the ideal state. In the early years of the 1800s he extended his philosophical system into an account of the philosophy of history. He argued that the present age was characterized by a willingness to question external authority, but still fell short of history's final destination, which would consist in a fully justified social order.

The Fichte text that I want to focus on here, the *Addresses to the German Nation*, elaborates a very specific account of how the German people might lead humanity into this final era. The *Addresses* were presented and published in Berlin in 1807-1808, while the city was under occupation by Napoleonic France. The opening pages capture the mood of despair and catastrophe shared by Fichte and his Berlin audience and readers. Under the present circumstances, Fichte proclaimed, "only the glory of obedience is left" (Fichte [1808] 2008, 10). Germans, he added, "face the downfall of [their] nation" unless they can "avoid giving themselves over entirely to the feeling of pain at the loss they have suffered" (ibid., 11).

Fichte described Germany's predicament as arising from one of the characteristic impulses of the age, which, echoing Kant, he called "selfishness" (*die Selbstsucht*) (ibid., 9). Selfishness has developed itself to its "highest degree" when, "after it has captured, with only a few exceptions, the totality of those ruled, it then takes possession of the rulers also and becomes their sole impulse in life." Without loyalty, duty, honor, or courage, "the commonwealth goes under with the first serious attack launched against it" (ibid., 14).

For "such a sunken nation ... to be able to save itself," Fichte then went on to argue, there must be "the creation of an entirely new order of things" (ibid., 15). The new order imagined by Fichte must be a new *moral* order. Germans must be shaken out of their selfish degradation and made to embrace and love the good for its own sake. In this way, a "completely new self" (ibid., 17) must be cultivated that is attached to morality and the commonwealth for their own sakes. A new form of education is needed that will succeed in "making its vision of a moral world so vivid that the pupil is seized by ardent love and longing for it." As Fichte added a little later on, "We must therefore replace this self-love, which can no longer be connected with anything that is good for us, with another kind of love, one that aims directly at the good, simply as such and for its own sake, and plant it in the minds of all those whom we wish to reckon among our nation" (ibid., 25).

If the general direction of Fichte's thinking is familiar here, the next move in his argument is not. He argued that, despite its present predicament, the German people are peculiarly well-suited for this moral transformation. The reason lies in the linguistic and cultural character of the Germans. The distinctive trait of the Germans, according to Fichte, is that they retained their *original* language. This means that a crucial resource for moral regeneration remains close at hand. Other peoples —such as the French—borrowed heavily from a foreign language (Latin) and thereby cut themselves off from their own original language, and so from an important source of moral transformation.

Influenced by Herder, but contrary to the received wisdom, Fichte did not think of language as a pattern of arbitrary conventions. Instead he claimed that "there exists ... a fundamental law according to which each concept is expressed by this sound and no other through the human speech organs" (ibid., 49). Linguistic diversity is not evidence of the conventional nature of language but of the ways in which the one original language of humanity was formed and modified by the varying environmental and historical conditions facing different groups of language users. Indeed, a distinct nation or people (*Volk*), for Fichte, is not understood in ethnic or racial terms, but as a group of people, extended through time, who live together, who develop in continuous communication, and whose speech is subject to the same external influences (ibid., 50).[2]

The non-arbitrary character of language, as Fichte saw it, has great moral significance. The original language of a people is an immediate expression of its common life. It designates objects in a way that is directly influenced by the senses, and that expresses the moral and aesthetic reactions of the language community. As an original language builds up an abstract (or what Fichte terms "supersensuous" [ibid., 51]) vocabulary, it relies on the "sensuous" part of the language—the language used to designate objects of the senses. The moral terminology of a people that has retained its original language thus has the immediate, evocative power and clarity of lived experience. As Fichte put it,

> since language is not the product of arbitrary arrangement but breaks forth as an immediate force of nature from rational life, a language that has continued to develop without interruption ... also has the power to intervene

> directly in life and stimulate it. As things immediately present to man move him, so too must the words of such a language move him who understands it, for they also are things and by no means arbitrary contrivances. (Ibid., 53)

In this way, peoples that retain their original language—peoples in the "higher sense of the word"—can be said to produce themselves (i.e. their rational and moral nature) out of themselves (i.e. their original formative sphere of intuitions and experiences) (ibid., 103).

Contrast this with a people that ends up borrowing its abstract vocabulary from another, higher-status language and culture. Fichte was especially thinking of the French here, who borrowed extensively from Latin, but the pattern is true of many European languages. The systematic borrowing of supersensuous vocabulary introduces a rupture between the language of sense and immediate experience, on the one hand, and the language of thought and moral action, on the other. The discourse of morality becomes little more than a lifeless language game. "The most they can do is have the symbol and its spiritual meaning explained to them, whereby they receive only the flat and lifeless history of an alien culture but not a culture of their own, and get images which for them are neither immediately clear nor a vital stimulus, but which must seem to them as entirely arbitrary" (ibid., 54). While this abstract language was living and meaningful for the people that originally formed it—e.g., the Romans in the case of Latin—when borrowed by a later people, it is little more than "an incoherent collection of arbitrary and utterly inexplicable signs of equally arbitrary concepts; and nothing else can be done with either sign or concept beyond simply learning them" (ibid., 57). A borrowed language with this character requires blind trust in experts and authorities, and leads to class inequality between those who have and have not mastered the appropriate language games (ibid., 65-66).

Fichte's argument was most clearly directed at his fellow Germans. Long dominated by an aristocratic class infatuated with French culture and language, Fichte's recipe for moral regeneration called on Germans to reject the cultural domination of the French and to revive and re-energize their own cultural heritage. Although not without foreign borrowings, Fichte believed that German remained enough of an original, "living" language that, with concerted effort from a national education program, it could build a national culture rooted in its original language.

Ultimately, then, Fichte's solution to the gap between moral ideals and social reality is a nationalist program of reviving, developing, and celebrating the original language and culture of the people. Fichte was confident that a return to its cultural and linguistic roots would bring out the earthy morality of simplicity, loyalty, earnestness, and spirituality he associated with the German common people. Upon that solid foundation, Fichte thought that the German Idealist philosophy of freedom could articulate and sustain a rational state that realizes something like the principles of the French Revolution that he admired.

Hegel's Alternative

Born in 1770, Hegel was also an ardent enthusiast for the French Revolution, in his case from the safe distance of his student quarters in Tübingen (Pinkard 2000, 22-26). Although never a radical political thinker like Fichte, Hegel remained committed to the principles of the Revolution throughout his life, once telling a contemporary that he annually drank a toast to the storming of the Bastille on its July 14th anniversary (ibid., 451). Hegel was certainly conservative in many respects, but his political theory never rejects or seeks to replace "the right of *subjective freedom*," which he characterized as "the pivotal and focal point in the difference between *antiquity* and the *modern* age" (Hegel [1821] 1991, para. 124). Instead, the central concern of his political philosophy is with how to *consolidate* a political order defined around the value of freedom. Regimes committed to freedom risk descending into anarchy—as happened in France's Terror—or giving way to an authoritarian like Bonaparte. Hegel thought that the central problem of political philosophy was how to articulate a social order that was at once hospitable to freedom *and* stable and self-reproducing.

This consolidation problem is at the heart of Hegel's main work of social and political philosophy, *The Philosophy of Right*. Most of the book is devoted to elaborating an account of "objective right," which is Hegel's term for the institutions, practices, and conditions that are needed for freedom to be "actualized"—that is, to be given an effective social reality. In this respect, Hegel's political philosophy is centrally concerned with overcoming the gap identified by Kant between normative principles and social reality. Adding to the difficulty of Hegel's account, this task of identifying the conditions that actualize freedom also involves an exposition of what freedom is. For Hegel, the true nature of freedom is best discovered in the very process of working out the conditions that realize freedom effectively in the social world.

Like all of Hegel's arguments, his account of the conditions that actualize freedom proceeds in a dialectical fashion.[3] He starts with an extremely minimal conception of what freedom is and of which objective conditions would need to be present in order for freedom in that sense to be realized in the world. Any plausible conception of freedom would need to include this initial minimal element, and in that sense it is indispensable. But Hegel then goes on to argue that the minimal conception, together with the objective conditions that realize it, are self-undermining. The successful exercise of freedom, understood in this minimal way, works eventually to undermine the objective conditions that are necessary for freedom's continued realization. Hegel thus characterizes this initial, minimal structure of freedom as lacking "self-sufficiency" and "independence" (e.g., Hegel [1821] 1991, para. 32A).

If freedom is to be actualized, then a richer conception of freedom and its conditions is needed, one that supersedes without completely cancelling the initial minimal conception. This richer conception is then subjected to the same dialectical examination. Hegel argues that its very success will bring about its own downfall, so some further enrichment is needed. And so on. The result, if Hegel can carry it out, is a rich and highly differentiated conception both of what freedom is and of the world of social institutions and practices that are needed to give it social reality. In contrast with the early abstract stages, which lack self-sufficiency, the final result is compared with a living organism that is able to reproduce itself continuously (ibid., paras. 146, 267–69). The ongoing reproduction of a social order is never guaranteed, but a healthy organism does not actively encourage its own demise and instead is able to withstand a range of shocks and setbacks.

A crucial thing to appreciate about Hegel's project in the *Philosophy of Right*, then, is how thoroughly it is committed to bridging the gap between normative ideal and social reality. What makes the initial conception of freedom considered at the outset insufficient is that it cannot form part of a stable and self-reproducing social order. An adequate account of freedom is one that does not merely announce an attractive ideal but also demonstrates how that ideal can form part of an organic, self-supporting social structure.

The first step in this complex argument is laid out in Part I of the *Philosophy of Right*, "Abstract Right." Here Hegel starts with a very minimal notion of free agency, which he terms "personality." To be a free person, very roughly, is to recognize that one is confronted with a given set of circumstances but, at the same time, that one is independent of those circumstances, that they do not necessarily prescribe a specific action or way of being. It is, in effect, to think of oneself as a maker of choices, capable of imposing one's own will onto a given situation.

Hegel argues that the institutions of private property and contract are needed to realize this minimal conception in the world. Through property, individuals develop and solidify a sense of themselves as agents whose choices make a difference in the world. And through contract they express their recognition of one another as possessing this capacity. But as the account of Abstract Right progresses, Hegel brings out a contradiction lurking in the initial attempt to characterize freedom and its actualization (ibid., paras. 81-82). On the one hand, the institutions needed to realize the minimal conception of freedom—property and contract—rely for their success on a general respect for property, a disposition to keep contracts, and so on. On the other hand, the bare idea of agents as choosers does not say anything about the particular *content* of their choices. As choosers, they might act in ways that support property and contract, but just as possibly they might not. The minimal world of Abstract Right fails to guarantee the conditions of its own success and stability.

There is much more that could be said about this first step in Hegel's argument, but already we can see Hegel's concern with bridging the gap between the ideal and the social reality of freedom. Hegel's concern is that a system that merely encourages independent personality has potentially destabilizing consequences for established institutions and practices, including the very institutions and practices that are needed to develop and express the capacity for personality itself. This is a problem that Hegel thinks was first encountered by the ancient Greeks. He describes the pre-Socratic Greeks as enjoying a harmonious social existence in which they habitually fulfilled the tasks and functions that protected their social order and caused it to reproduce itself. It was only when the Sophists introduced the principle of independent thought, and this principle gradually permeated Greek culture, that the reproduction of the social order was jeopardized (ibid., 20, para. 185). When individuals began to consult their own convictions about what to do rather than reflexively following the customs and conventions of their community, their willingness to take on the burdens and sacrifices needed for the community's continuation could no longer be relied on. Hegel read Plato's *Republic* somewhat idiosyncratically as a profoundly conservative attempt to describe what a community would have to do (among other things, ban private property, occupational choice, and the family) in order to re-establish a stable community by *fending off* the emergence of the principle of free personality.

Hegel's own project, however, was not to find ways of stifling individuality and free personality. Plato's attempt to "exclude particularity" and the "inherently infinite personality of the individual" was "of no help" because it "contradict[ed] the infinite right of the Idea to allow particularity its freedom," a right whose discovery Hegel credits to Christianity (ibid., paras. 185, 185A). Instead, Hegel was concerned to identify the features of the modern world that allow for a stable and self-sustaining realization of individual personality and subjectivity. It is possible to read the remainder of the *Philosophy of Right* as an attempt to develop a solution to the contradiction set up by property and contract. Property and contract are necessary moments in the development of freedom, but on their own they are self-undermining, and so some further articulation of the nature and conditions of freedom is needed.

One way of preventing personal choices from undermining property and contract would be to punish coercively those who make such choices. Hegel is sympathetic to such a response. Punishment protects the validity of right by negating the negation implicit in the wrongdoer's actions (ibid., para. 97A). But Hegel did not think that punishment and coercion are sufficient, on their own, to stabilize the structure of freedom depicted in "Abstract Right." Who would be the judge of wrongdoing or of the appropriate punishment to be applied to those identified as wrongdoers? Without a convincing answer, there is nothing to distinguish legitimate retribution from revenge (ibid., para. 102). Judgments about wrongdoing should be made by somebody with integrity, impartiality, and fair-mindedness: they require "a justice freed from subjective interest … and from the contingency of power" (ibid., para. 103). But these concepts are alien to the limited world of Abstract Right. Agents in Abstract Right are assumed to be free persons, and not necessarily to possess the inner depths of someone who acts for certain kinds of reasons and refuses to act for others. The sphere of right is characterized by "immediacy," meaning that an agent's choices are not mediated by reflection or moral reasoning. "Justice is therefore altogether contingent" (ibid., para. 102).

Implicit in this argument is a rebuke of the political theories developed by both Kant and Fichte in the 1790s. These theories were geared around the protection of free and independent persons who set and pursue their own ends. Kant and Fichte recognized the need for coercion and, indeed, for a public authority that settles disputes, resolves indeterminacies, and protects the vulnerable. But they failed to explain how a public authority could successfully fulfil these functions if it is controlled by officials and citizens who are nothing more than free and independent persons. Kant believed that clever institutional design could offer a way around the need for morally motivated officials and citizens, but as we have seen there are problems with this solution.

Part II of the *Philosophy of Right*, "Morality," is the book's first main attempt to identify conditions that would consolidate the initial progress made in Abstract Right. Hegel's proposal is that the problem of stabilizing the freedom introduced in Abstract Right could be solved if agents possess not just personality—the capacity for choice—but also subjectivity. The subject wills ends that are distinctively his own. He has purposes, intentions, and a conscience, and he is free only to the extent that his actions reflect and express these commitments. Hegel's thought is that, if the fundamental self-understanding and disposition of individuals is not just one of free personhood but also revolves around willing certain specific ends, or having certain motives, then the contradiction afflicting Abstract Right can be resolved. Again, this is compatible with the observation that what is needed at the end of Abstract Right is a judge of some sort who has integrity, impartiality, and so on.

By the end of Morality, however, Hegel has concluded that while morality and subjectivity are a necessary part of the resolution to the contradiction, they are not the complete solution. Morality fails to guarantee that individuals will find in their consciences the commitments that are needed to stabilize the structure of Abstract Right. They may or may not. Likewise, morality cannot guarantee that individuals will be disposed to follow their consciences rather than pursuing their own personal interests and satisfaction. So morality faces both a problem of content and a problem of motivation. There is no guarantee that moral reasoning will leave subjects with the right ends, and even if they have the right ends there is nothing inherent in morality that explains why they would be motivated to follow them. In morality, as in Abstract Right, it is entirely contingent whether individuals will have the ends and motives needed to secure the development of freedom. For this reason,

Hegel describes morality as "the indeterminate which *ought* to be determined" (ibid., para. 141). Morality is no more able to bridge the gap between ideal and social reality than Abstract Right.

Hegel's argument for these claims only becomes apparent in Part III of the *Philosophy of Right*, "Ethical Life." At this stage, agents are conceived of not simply as persons and subjects, but also as *members* of certain social institutions: the family, civil society, and the state. These institutions impose certain duties on those who occupy the roles they define: the duties, for instance, of parents, of colleagues and association members, and of citizens and public officials. They also habituate and socialize their members into having the subjective dispositions to support and affirm these duties. Ethical Life is a sphere of virtue because ethical institutions impose duties on their members (thus, defining content for ethical action) *and* imbue in them an inclination to perform those duties.

Returning, then, to morality, it is apparent that underlying Hegel's critique is the assumption that individuals' deepest convictions, values, and motives are shaped by the social practices and institutions in which they participate. The implication of Ethical Life is that, given the "right" social environment, individuals will find the "right" ends in their consciences and the motivation to follow those ends. The problem, however, is that morality, as Hegel understands it, makes no assumptions at all about social practices and institutions (except for property and contract in the background, which introduced the problem in the first place). Morality is, in effect, an attempt to solve the contradiction in an individualistic way that makes no reference to practices or institutions of community with others. For this reason, Hegel claims, morality is bound to fail. Unless certain practices and institutions are in place, which make certain ends salient and habituate people to value them, there is no reason to expect that individuals searching their consciences and considering their motives will end up acting in ways that stabilize the institutional structure established by the argument so far.

The details of Hegel's accounts of family, civil society, and the state are too complex to explore here. The important general point is that each set of institutions generates a form of *social unity* or *integration* among those who participate: through habituation and socialization, they each encourage their participants to act for the sake of others. The family does so through bonds of love and affection; civil society through relationships of mutual dependency as well as honor, comaraderie, and collegiality;

and the state through participation in, and subjection to, a common framework of deliberation, law, and political action.

The upshot is that Abstract Right and morality describe ideas and institutions that are necessary for freedom but that cannot, by themselves, guarantee their own stability over time. Ethical Life provides the resolution to this contradiction. It describes the social environment in which individuals can safely be left to enjoy the freedoms of personality and subjectivity that are characteristic of the modern world, because that environment reliably habituates individuals into developing other-regarding ends and dispositions. Shaped by the right social environment, individuals can be expected to freely accept the burdens and sacrifices presupposed by a self-reproducing social order that is hospitable to personality and subjectivity. Thus, Hegel bridges the gap between ideal and social reality identified by Kant, but not mainly through a mechanism that aligns self-interest with the public good. That idea does figure in Hegel's account of the "System of Needs" (a subsection of Civil Society), but it is not the general form of Hegel's solution. Rather, Hegel's proposal is to embed the ideal of individual freedom, which he shares with Kant and Fichte, in a supportive social structure that shapes individual ends and motivations in ways that conduce to the common good.

Unlike conservatives who emphasize the destabilizing effects of subjectivity, then, Hegel's conclusion is that a social order *can* tolerate a high degree of independent personality and subjectivity, but *only* if a crucial condition is met. Its citizens must be members of ethical institutions that habituate them into possessing those goals, values, convictions, and so forth, that—when they consult their own opinions and consciences about what to do—lead them to arrive at answers that reinforce that order rather than tearing it apart, as happened (in Hegel's view) in the French Revolution.

Discussion

There are deep dangers in the nationalist approach. Fichte's attitude towards the French was resentful and chauvinistic, while his discussion of the Germans tended towards the nostalgic and uncritical. Although Fichte borrowed many of his ideas from an earlier German thinker, J. G. Herder (1744-1803), there is much less emphasis in Fichte than in Herder on the ways in which peoples learn and benefit from one another.[4] Altogether, Fichte's nationalism anticipated many of the dangerous and troubling tendencies of nineteenth- and twentieth-century nationalist movements.

Hegel's views on non-European peoples were racist and contemptuous,[5] and his conception of history as culminating in the free societies of Europe was comfortably aligned with discourses of European imperialism that became ascendant in the nineteenth century. Unlike Fichte, however, Hegel was not sympathetic with the nationalist movements of his own day. He remained a Francophile throughout his adult life, and associated nationalism with the subjectivist philosophy and anti-Semitic outlook of his rival Jakob Friedrich Fries.[6] More importantly, there is a strand of argument in Hegel's political philosophy—which I have sought to expound here—that represents an interesting alternative to both Fichtean nationalism and Kant's faith in institutional mechanisms.

If Fichte's view is unappealing, Hegel's can seem a bit too good to be true. For Hegel, the key to bridging the gap between ideals and social reality is to recognize that modern societies already have, in their existing "ethical life," many of the elements they need to support well-ordered freedom. Bridging the gap, then, is not about contriving a new source of motivation, but nourishing and supporting the ethical tendencies that are already latent in existing practices and institutions. No great act of statesmanship or leadership is needed to bring about conditions of freedom. This is one meaning of Hegel's famous—for some, notorious—dictum, in the Preface to the *Philosophy of Right,* that "what is rational is actual and what is actual is rational."

But Hegel's account has some critical bite, and it also points to an agenda for political reformers. Negatively, Hegel meant to warn his readers against political theories that are overly simplistic and abstract. He had in mind the indiscriminate appeals to passion and feeling made by some of his Romantic contemporaries, as well as the reductionist formulas he associated with theorists of the social contract. Positively, Hegel's approach recommends vigilance and care for institutions like the family and the associational life of civil society; and attention to ways in which the political realm of the state integrates all citizens together and sets a tone for the whole society. Isolation and atomism are serious evils for a Hegelian, and belonging, civic virtue, and public service are key values. There is also a critical standard implicit in Hegel's supposition that what matters is not stability *tout court*, but the stability of a social order that is hospitable to modern forms of freedom. Stabilizing the institutions of reactionary monarchy, or of

Napoleonic authoritarianism, would not actualize freedom as Hegel understood it. That would be to bridge the gap between ideals and social reality by giving up on the ideals.

It is true that Fichtean nationalism may have considerable appeal in certain contexts. Societies that have long been dominated by colonial or foreign powers have experienced various forms of cultural imperialism. It is tempting to think that what these societies really need in order to flourish is to rediscover and reassert their authentic, original cultures. But the experience of nationalism in Europe should be a cautionary tale. The construction of an authentic national culture often magnifies and reifies longstanding forms of difference in a society. These constructions lead to forms of exclusion and marginalization that end up threatening the very freedom that the nationalist solution is meant to secure.

Moreover, an apparent implication of Fichte's argument is that some societies can *never* hope to realize freedom. Fichte tries to suggest otherwise. Germans should "inaugurate the new age, as pioneers and exemplars for the rest of humanity" (Fichte [1808] 2008, 43), implying that others might follow in their path. But it is not clear that he is entitled to universalize his argument in this way. Some peoples, such as the French, have given up much of their original language, so if Fichte's argument is correct they will never be able to morally reinvigorate themselves in the way that is needed for freedom. In contrast, the Hegelian model of social liberalism looks capable of traveling to other societies and contexts. It does not emphasize unalterable facts about the background culture, but looks for ways in which the existing institutions and practices of a society work to integrate people and orient them ethically so that leaving space for freedom does not lead to social breakdown.

Finally, we might wonder whether the Hegelian model has anything to say concerning the viability and future of liberalism. As I have suggested, Hegel's model sets itself against overly individualist and reductivist understandings of the values of liberalism. A Hegelian liberalism is one that guards against isolation, atomism, and the breakdown of families and communities. Without sacrificing its core values, this social liberalism might offer distinctive positions on issues like trade, immigration, the decline of unions, and technological innovation, which threaten to disrupt existing communities in ways that leave individuals vulnerable and isolated. In the abstract, it is hard to say whether social liberalism is viable over time, but Hegel's vision remains as relevant as any to the challenges we face today.

NOTES

1. For discussion, and references to the conservative literature, see Bowles 2011.
2. Arash Abizadeh (2005, 351-52) argues for the "crypto-ethnic" character of Fichte's nationalism. Abizadeh acknowledges Fichte's explicit denial that the distinguishing characteristic of the German people is its ethnic purity (see Fichte [1808] 2008, 49). But he insists that Fichte's repeated use of the genealogical language of "descent" (*Abstammung, Abknunft*) shows that Fichte was committed after all to an ethnic conception of peoplehood. Abizadeh's account is impressive, but ultimately I find it unconvincing. A more plausible reading is that Fichte employed the language of ancestry and descent in a sociological rather than a biological sense. Biological ancestry refers to a lineage of biological reproduction, while sociological ancestry refers to a lineage of socialization relations, where earlier generations socialize the next generation, which socializes the next generation, and so on. (For further discussion of this distinction, see Patten 2014, 51-52, 58-59). For Fichte, this sociological lineage is centrally focused on language, and thus he says that the distinguishing characteristic of the German people is not "the prior ancestry of those who continue to speak an original language, but only the fact that this language continues to be spoken without interruption, for men are formed by language far more than language is by men" (Fichte [1808] 2008, 49).
3. The overview of the structure of Hegel's argument in the *Philosophy of Right* that I offer here and in the next few paragraphs draws on a fuller discussion in Patten 1999, 176-90.
4. For discussion of Herder's brand of nationalism, see Patten 2010.
5. See, for instance, Hegel [1830] 2007, paras. 393, 393A; and Hegel 1975 Appendix 1, 152-208.
6. For discussion, see Avineri 1962 and Allen Wood's editor's notes to Hegel [1821] 1991, 385-86.

REFERENCES

Abizadeh, Arash. 2005. "Was Fichte an Ethnic Nationalist? Cultural Nationalism and Its Double." *History of Political Thought* 26(2): 334-59.

Avineri, Shlomo. 1962. "Hegel and Nationalism." *Review of Politics* 24(4): 461-84.

Bowles, Samuel. 2011. "Is Liberal Society a Parasite on Tradition?" *Philosophy & Public Affairs* 39(1): 46-81.

Fichte, J. G. [1808] 2008. *Addresses to the German Nation*, ed. Gregory Moore. Cambridge: Cambridge University Press.

Hegel, G.W.F. 1975. *Lectures on the Philosophy of World History: Introduction*, trans. H. B. Nisbet. Cambridge: Cambridge University Press.

Hegel, G.W.F. [1821] 1991. *Elements of the Philosophy of Right*, ed. Allen W. Wood, trans. H. B. Nisbet. Cambridge: Cambridge University Press.

Hegel, G.W.F. [1830] 2007. *Philosophy of Mind*, trans. W. Wallace and A. V. Miller. Oxford: Oxford University Press.

Kant, Immanuel. [1795] 1996. "Toward Perpetual Peace." In idem, *Practical Philosophy*, ed. and trans. Mary Gregor. Cambridge: Cambridge University Press.

Miller, David. 1995. *On Nationality*. Oxford: Oxford University Press.

Miller, David. 2000. *Citizenship and National Identity*. Cambridge: Polity Press.

Patten, Alan. 1999. *Hegel's Idea of Freedom*. Oxford: Oxford University Press.

Patten, Alan. 2010. "'The Most Natural State': Herder and Nationalism." *History of Political Thought* 31(4): 657–89.

Patten, Alan. 2014. *Equal Recognition: The Moral Foundations of Minority Rights*. Princeton: Princeton University Press.

Pinkard, Terry. 2000. *Hegel: A Biography*. Cambridge: Cambridge University Press.

Terry Pinkard

HEGEL'S OWN TIME GRASPED IN OUR THOUGHTS AFTER TWO HUNDRED YEARS

ABSTRACT: *Hegel viewed the task of philosophy as not to direct the present but to grasp its fundamental commitments by uncovering its animating baselines. This led him to depict the antinomies of modern life as manifestations of the same baseline: equal freedom. By grasping equal freedom as a progressive principle of modern life, Hegel was able to criticize the conservatives of his day for treating natural inequalities as unalterable. Hegel's alternative was a holist account according to which the oppositions contained in modern society, such as that between nature and freedom, are gradually worked out in forms of life that aim to realize the baseline modern commitment to equal freedom.*

When Hegel published his "baselines" —the *Grundlinien* in the title—for his philosophy of "the right," he noted in the preface that in his view, philosophy was only its own time grasped in thoughts. By that, he did not mean anything like, say, a snapshot of either public opinion or elite opinion, nor did he mean simply a view of emerging trends (the favorite of pundits and of the bogus discipline of futurology). Rather, a philosophy of "right" had to do with the extended present: where it came from (its history), how it came to be in the state in which it finds itself, and what are the matters still to be settled that are on the horizon. He explicitly disavowed any role for philosophy in predicting where or in what form those settlements were going to be, and he explicitly foreswore the idea that philosophy was to teach the world what it really ought to be.

His reason was straightforward: Philosophy should not aspire to the task of teaching the world a moral lesson because philosophy simply cannot do that, and it cannot do that by virtue of what it, as philosophy, is. This is not merely a limitation of philosophy that we might hope to overcome—as if Hegel were saying that philosophy cannot do this because of some temporary or contingent fact (say, because people on the whole do not pay attention to it). It is rather a limit such that when one violates it, one is not on the other side of the limit but more like nowhere. Violating the limit means one is no longer making sense. As he put it, "philosophy has to start from concepts, and even if it establishes little, still one must be satisfied with it" (EN §270, p. 106). When philosophy turns into futurology, it simply ceases to be philosophy.

What it can do, however, is lay out the basic concepts that are fundamentally at play in the current time. These fundamental concepts are the absolute commitments of a time, the matters of which entertaining their absence would seem more or less nonsensical to the people inhabiting that time. Yet it seemed clear to Hegel that he was living at a time when those absolute commitments at various moments seemed to be by and large up for grabs. The French Revolution had upended the old assumptions about privilege, the Napoleonic wars had redrawn the map of Europe and brought the revolutionary ideas of government to new places, and the Congress of Vienna, in its settlement of the Napoleonic era, had mostly failed to do what the old order of things had hoped it would do, namely, turn back the clock to pre-1789 days. Reform and restructuring were in the air, calls for more representation (although mostly not yet for full democracy) were reverberating around the continent, and the forces of the *ancien régime* were, although shaken, still hoping to hold their ground. The idea of fundamental reform, top to bottom, was on the horizon—especially in Prussia, under the reform program led by Stein and Hardenberg—and nobody could think of where they were without thinking of where things would be going. The indeterminate future was the major temporal phase of the present.

This is part of the reason why Hegel elected to call his book a set of "baselines" for law and ethics. It could not predict where things were going to end up, nor could it prescribe exactly what institutions and practices needed to be put into place, but it could, so he thought, lay down, as it were, the lines that may not be crossed—a bit like the lines on a football field or a tennis court.

Where does that leave us, two hundred years later? Hegel was looking ahead to a fairly indeterminate future (and through the fog that the future always holds). But us? Looking back with our historical 20/20 hindsight, what do we make of the *Grundlinien*?

It would be naturally tempting to start by noting all the things that Hegel got wrong. He did declare that war between European states would now be so irrational that it was henceforth impossible. (Wrong.) He did not think there was any basis for German unification. (Maybe.) He thought the early modern estates and corporate bodies could be extended into the new reformed order. (They couldn't.) He thought that capitalism, at that point still in its still infant form in Germany, could be steered away from its worst possible consequences by enlightened bureaucratic regulation. (The jury is still out on that one.) The list could be continued, but going on would be a bit churlish. It is better to ask why he thought his proposals really were the baselines. This involves looking at why he thought his own dialectical philosophical program had something special to recommend it.

Equal Freedom as the Modern Baseline

Hegel thought his speculative philosophy had a particular advantage because—even before the denouement of the Congress of Vienna in 1815—he had developed a view of history as inexorably moving from a conception of ethical communities as resting on natural or divinely inspired hierarchies, where only some are free, all the way to the modern comprehension that all are free and that nobody, by natural fact alone (such as birth), has commanding authority over others. That, more than anything else, established "the" baseline for all the post-1815 projects of reform. Any insinuation that, say, serfdom might be reestablished would be simply out of bounds.

It was not, of course, as if he thought that the principle of equal freedom would lead immediately to a social and political order of equals, but rather that it expressed a way of agents thinking of themselves that, in turn, had to have long-term practical consequences. If people's self-conceptions (a component of their self-consciousness, as Hegel would phrase it) had still been tied into some kind of naturally or divinely legitimated hierarchy (such as the natural and divine authority of aristocrats over commoners), the options for what the settlements in the social and political order might be would be constrained by these self-conceptions. Once they no longer see themselves as so constrained, however, people become, so to speak, different versions of themselves than they had been, and make different demands on each other, and on the social and political order, than they did before.

In itself, the principle of equal freedom, stated as an isolated proposition, does not specify much of anything. But it does set into relief what philosophy actually can do, which is to deal with the antinomies (Kant's term, which Hegel picked up) at work in what will turn out to be the areas where the future settlements will take place, particularly with regard to freedom. These antinomies will take the shape of what look like very basic contradictions and incompatibilities between opposing views, each of which is itself generated out of other baselines of the social and political order that is in the process of forming itself. Speculative philosophy, as Hegel called his dialectical approach, does not seek to resolve an antinomy by showing one or the other side to be false, but by showing how both sides are in fact not really incompatible but are essential components of a comprehensive conception, for which Hegel adopted, as a technical term (again, partly following Kant), the ordinary German *Idee* (Idea). What may look like fundamental, ground-level contradictions in the order of the day may in fact not be so contradictory at all, but something more like fundamental components of a more comprehensive view of things.

Hegel identified several elements in post-1815 European life where such antinomies surface. To readers of Hegel and students of political theory, they are very well known. There is, first, the familiar Lockean triumvirate of basic rights to life, liberty and property, which generates a whole set of such philosophical problems (such as the natural right to property versus the legally established right to property, as that antinomy appears in the differing accounts offered by, among others, Locke and Hobbes). Second, there is the modern conception of morality as imposing universal obligations on all people versus the kinds of obligations that only come with one's station in life, along with the competing demands of happiness versus duty. There is, third, an institutional sphere, for which Hegel again takes an ordinary German word, *Sittlichkeit*—nowadays rendered in English as "ethical life," but perhaps more accurately as "moral ethos"—to identify the modern institutional orders of family, civil society, and the state. Taken separately or as a jumble, these antinomies all seem to present what at best looks like an unsurveyable patchwork of competing philosophical and metaphysical puzzles. But taken together (that is, speculatively), in the proper comprehensive conception of their respective roles, they embody the baselines within which Hegel's own time was developing, but without, in principle, predicting in which precise direction it would in fact go or what the crucial political and personal details would look like.

Hegel did, however, use the baselines of each of these spheres to illustrate when he thought the places he knew the most about (such as the German states, France, England, and the Netherlands) were going in the right direction or else were heading along a course that looked like it would inevitably generate conflicts with the established baselines that would not be resolvable speculatively or practically (but which, for all that, may be inevitable given certain social forces at work). That is not a mere empirical detail, as philosophers like to sniff, but a reflection on how best to realize the baselines that also does not pretend to be an a priori demand for the way the world is supposed to be.

Hegel against Conservatism

Strikingly, however, Hegel also maintained that for anything like this kind of philosophical project to be possible, it must be that a form of life—a *Gestalt des Lebens*—has already formed itself completely enough so that baselines can be discerned in it. It must be a "form of life that has grown old," and thus may be either fully formed and ready for centuries of stabilization, or else reaching the end of its days and about to become transformed and left behind, as so many others have been before it. Hegel was cagey enough not to say which is his preferred view, and from the very day of its publication, his book was variously seen as the ideology of the ruling regime or as a glimpse into a proto-revolutionary future.

In its most crucial form, however, the book was, as many of its contemporary critics often saw, firmly anti-conservative.

Conservatives of all stripes share at least one thing in common, which is the desire – usually intensely and passionately held—to hold onto some kind of a hierarchical order of authority and obedience or, if not that, to restore such an order that has been toppled. (Or, in the odd cases of conservative revolutionaries, to create a new hierarchical order of command

and obedience to replace what they see as an ineffective, usually effete, hierarchy that they think is no longer capable of defending itself.) In this sense, Hegel's ground-level baseline for the emerging order was not only not conservative, but profoundly anti-conservative. The equal standing of each, and the universal self-conception that all are free, means that all natural or divine hierarchies are illegitimate at the outset, and that whatever hierarchies of command there have to be will have to be rationally justified. Of course, what will count as rational justification, to whom such justifications will be addressed, and who will be making the justifications, are some of the issues to be addressed in the realization of a social order based on freedom and equality.

It is fair to say that Hegel himself did not clearly see just how far others might take his own professed views, nor how far and how radical the new self-conception of freedom would go; nor did he clearly grasp the vehemence of the rejection of this new equality among those attached and attracted to hierarchical modes of life. Even worse, he could not bring himself to draw some conclusions that seemed to follow directly from what he said. Even as he committed himself in print to the proposition that racial descent "affords no ground for granting or denying freedom and dominion to human beings," and that this implies the "futility of a rigid distinction between races which have rights and those which have none" (EG §393Z), he continued to espouse profoundly racist views in his lectures (particularly in the infamous lectures on the lack of a place for Africa in world history). Even though he thought of his views on bourgeois family life as exhibiting the moral and institutional equality of women and men, what he had to say in print and in lectures about the role of women actually resembled something more like a dark parody of patriarchal sexism. (But it was not parody; he meant it seriously.)

Hegel also thought that his form of "speculative thought" required a version of post-Kantian Idealism, namely, one according to which the absolute could only be adequately apprehended in thought and not, with full adequacy, in any kind of direct experience of it. The "absolute" – the name he and Schelling adopted early on as their own replacement for Kant's terminology of the "unconditioned"—is the whole, beyond which is nothing. The absolute has no other further conditions. It is the world itself, all that there is, and to ask what the further conditions of the world are—to ask what more is there in addition to all there is —is to ask a nonsensical question that only has the semblance of making sense. One can always ask where any finite being comes from, and thus it might seem sensible to ask of the world as a whole where it came from, but that question presupposes that one can occupy a position outside the world as a whole, which makes no sense.

The temptation to look for the conditions of the world as a whole, as if the person doing so were some godlike figure outside of it, was diagnosed by Hegel in terms of a modified version of the Kantian distinction between reason and the "understanding"—*der Verstand*, the intellect—in which the "understanding" looks to both individual finite things and collections of such finite things and is led to ask for their further conditions. "Reason" (*die Vernunft*), on the other hand, seeks the unconditioned, the whole, the "absolute" of all those finite things. When the "understanding" tries to grasp the whole, it is often erroneously led by its own nature to ask where the whole comes from. The problem with the very idea of such a godlike figure outside of the whole is that this figure would be just one more finite thing, leading naturally enough to the question where it came from, ad infinitum. (Hegel also tends to identify the standpoint of the "understanding" with that of "consciousness" as awareness of objects independent of oneself, or as having some kind of status independently of oneself.)

The "understanding" thus always deals with such infinities and infinite regresses in terms of what Hegel called the "bad infinite." The bad infinite is symbolized by a straight line that extends out to infinity so that no matter how much you follow that line, you never reach the end. The "true infinite" (the object of "reason") is symbolized by a circle. If you start at a point on the circumference and begin traveling, you will return to that point, and although you can do that an infinite number of times, you will still be going around the same circle. Hegel thus described his own philosophy in some places as a "circle of circles" that, in turn, make up the whole that is "reason's" concern (EL §15). (Even those who have only a passing knowledge of Spinoza will see its echoes in Hegel's statement of his views.) This constitutes the playing field for Idealism, with its provocative thesis that "the concept" is the absolute.

The *Grundlinien* itself is written from the standpoint of "reason," that is, from that of the "absolute" as a comprehensive *rational* grasp of the whole. In particular, it is guided by the semblance of opposition between freedom and nature which, if itself taken to be the absolute, means that the whole is, for us, unknowable—i.e., that we must merely presume that we are free, but with no way of placing that freedom (or for that matter, the normative in general) in any kind of natural context.[1] If this uneasy contradiction were simply allowed to stay in place, much of what Hegel takes to be fundamental to the *Grundlinien* would be up in the air, since the way would be open—especially in Hegel's own time, as the transitional phase it was—to all those who would argue against freedom and equality as violating the natural status of humans, contending that the natural status of humans is inequality of all kinds of different assets. It is thus no surprise that large portions of the text are devoted to attacking various attempts at asserting this, views that were very much alive in Hegel's day and that he felt it important to demolish.

Hegel's Holism

However, attacking his opponents on this point also required the positive construction of the whole in which the conservative opposition is, in Hegel's term, sublated (*aufgehoben*), that is, gathered up into the unity in which both sides of the opposition have their respective places. (They are, as the German term suggests, both canceled and preserved.) Recent work on Hegel's philosophy of nature shows that we must think of organisms—of "life" as such—as inherently purposive, not in the sense that it was designed for a particular purpose by a master fabricator, but in the sense that it functions on its own as purposive. Organs play the role they do in the organism because of the functions they provide: hearts pump the blood, kidneys clean the blood of toxins, and so on. Self-conscious life, in turn, has its own functions, which are not simply those of organic life in general but require the performance of a new set of functions if it is to find satisfaction with itself.

Specifically, self-conscious life aims at freedom. Freedom, in Hegel's succinct definition, is being "with oneself" or "at one with oneself" (*bei sich*, in Hegel's German). By that he means that freedom in its most abstract sense consists in acting and thinking in terms that are constitutive of agency as self-conscious life. In his 1807 *Phenomenology*, he accuses Stoicism of being the philosophy that identifies concrete freedom with this abstract conception, thus leading the Stoic to conclude (erroneously) that it is only in his own internal thinking that he is free (PhG ¶197). In the *Grundlinien*, he identifies concrete freedom as, more specifically, being at one with oneself in an other—that is, as acting in terms that are constitutive of agency in its full social realization.

Unlike more Kantian-inspired approaches, Hegel does not attempt to derive specific norms or values from this constitutive function. Kant might seem to do this when he argues that to be an agent is to be committed to the categorical imperative, from which all kinds of very determinate duties are supposed to be derivable by means of a type of procedure about which Kantians and anti-Kantians have argued ever since. (Some contemporary expositors of Kant even hold that the constitutive function of agency implies commitment to a certain value, that of rational nature as an end in itself.) In contrast, Hegel's point is that agency, even at its most abstract (in activities like contractual exchanges of property), manifests the fact that the "relation of will to will is the distinctive and true basis in which freedom has its existence" (RP §71). Rather than trying to derive determinate duties and prohibitions, as one might from a legal code—as if philosophers were the a priori lawyers and judges of morality—we should instead look to see how the baselines are rooted in a kind of agency that has the specific shape it does in part because of where it historically came from, and to see, as well, that these norms can be objective (as giving reality to the aims of agency) yet also not thereby alien to us. On the Hegelian view, in drawing out the commitments of freedom, we are not trying to maximize some abstract sense of "the good," as the classical consequentialists had it, nor are we trying to derive practical norms from more general norms, as an author of a legal code would have it. Instead, so he proposes, we should give an account of why certain norms can be compelling to us by virtue of who we are—the kinds of agents we have become—and whether the whole of such norms can itself make a claim to being rational.

That is why he speaks of a form of life—a *Gestalt des Lebens*—rather than a set of imperatives that stand in relations of derivation to each other. He knew that this was rubbing up against the grain of much of the political philosophy that was current in his own time, and he also was clear that he was self-consciously appropriating large parts of Aristotle's philosophy into his own views. A form of life in general is a set of what we nowadays call practices, which involve habits, dispositions, and the like but are informed by the concepts we bring to the practices. Unlike a lot of contemporary philosophy, which has been much taken with the model of games and rules to make sense of practices, Hegel modeled his conception of practices on the idea of a concept (or set of concepts) seeking actualization, making such rules ancillary to this idea of a practice.

On the other hand, Hegel was also not an early precursor to the philosophers of "the lifeworld"—with their insistence on the primary and originary element of the world as it is experienced and lived by types of organisms in their own irreducible way—but more of a precursor of sorts to Wittgenstein's Tractarian idea of logic as the form of the world which, as such a form, shows itself in linguistic practices (and which the Wittgenstein of the *Tractatus* thought could not therefore be "said"). The form of life manifests itself in the practices of the members who, in turn, exhibit the practices without therefore being instances of a general set of rules. And in that way, Hegel is also a kind of very attenuated precursor to the later Wittgenstein's idea of viewing philosophical issues as manifesting the logic of a form of life, *Lebensform*. The practices of a "We" show themselves in the acts of the individual agent (an "I"). This neither reduces the "We" to a mere collection of individuals nor dissolves the many "I's" into some kind of super-social entity. It is, as Hegel famously put it, an "I that is a We and a We that is an I." Hegel's triad of abstract right, morality, and moral ethos expresses the way in which more abstract logical forms build up to the more concrete logical forms of the practices of his own time (as grasped in thoughts). Not the lifeworld but the logic of the lifeworld was Hegel's concern, which underlay his idea of drawing up the baselines for that form of life.

This was also part and parcel of Hegel's version of idealism. The true is the whole as grasped by pure thinking, but the whole consists of apparent oppositions (such as that between free agency and nature, especially the nature construed by the natural sciences) that must be viewed in terms of a comprehensive conception of how that whole holds together. Although Hegel famously held that the true is the whole, he did not hold that the whole is always the true. In the ancient slave-owning societies of Greece and Rome, for example, slavery was part of the very logic of their form of life (so he thought), but that did not make it right. Slavery occurred in a world where, he said, "a wrong is still right." This is more powerful in the original German, where, in the classical world, "*ein Unrecht Recht ist*"—a "wrong" is nonetheless legally right, and thus confusedly also seen as morally right.

The *Grundlinien* of the ancient slave-owning world were therefore fundamentally irrational. It is part of the idea of progress in history that, so Hegel thought, whatever other shortcomings our own world might and surely does have, there is no way in it for such a wrong as slavery to be right, period. Attempted justifications of slavery in our world must appear as material nonsense or bordering on such. The madhouse atmosphere of the Confederate states in the American Civil War is only another example of how the sheer irrationality of the attempt to justify slavery in modern times comes to light as nonsense or ruthless madness.

It is completely consistent with Hegel's view, then, that much indeed could be wrong with some of the institutional arrangements that he took to be the way in which the form of life that emerged abstractly after 1789, as well as in its more nearly full form after 1815, a form of life that manifested itself in the different practices of the different and differently affected European countries. However, none of these arrangements could contradict the baseline of the other baselines, the view that "all are free," and still make any claim to rationality. Any existing society would almost surely fall short in various areas, but that would not be an argument against the baseline of freedom and equality, merely an argument that those societies failed to be perfect realizations of that to which we (and they) are most deeply committed. As Hegel put it, "Who would not have enough good sense to see much around him that is indeed not as it should be?" (EG §15).

It would be a mistake to think, then, that because our own society is unjust, justice in it is a false ideal or not really one of its baselines. It might be tempting, similarly, to argue that the shortcomings in Hegel's triadic structure of family, civil society, and state can be gingerly overlooked as evidence that he was being blinkered by his own time, such that, in some dreamy state, one could entertain the happy thought that if somehow, one could strap oneself into a time machine and go back to explain those shortcomings to him, he would happily endorse our corrections of his views on gender equality, racism, authoritarianism, war, wages, etc., many of which run the gamut from embarrassing to appalling. But that is just fantasy, and Hegel himself knew it. The obvious shortcomings of Hegel's own views on the family, civil society, and the state are not just historically blinkered views. He thought they followed logically from some key provisions in his philosophy about what would be necessary to institutionalize abstract rights and morality.

The Organic Metaphor

Hegel's way of combining freedom and nature relied on the idea of life as having an internal purposiveness that could be extended to and modified to understand self-conscious life, and he relied heavily on the model of the organism for his understanding of how the baselines all fit together. Each is like an organ in a living organism with its own part to play, and when the fit is wrong, or one of them degenerates (becomes "ill," as it were), the whole is thrown off and various pathologies in the "body politic" (the apt metaphor here) appear. This organic model has many downsides, not the least of which is that social and political life are not living organisms but unities of self-conscious organisms. Many of those influenced by Hegel follow this out, seeing not an organism but a structural-functional unity of practices and institutions that, when not calibrated correctly, produces such "pathologies" or is thrown off by one of the organs or constellations of organs (for example, capitalism) acting like a cancer on the lifeworld of the organism and gradually strangling the lifeworld itself. While this has obvious attractions as a view, it is not clear that the organic view should be taken as anything more than a metaphor rather than a metaphysics. The basic and guiding idea for Hegel is that the "Idea" (in the way it works in the *Grundlinien*) is the unity of what seem at first glance to be fundamental oppositions at work in life (individual, social and political). The Idea is expressed in the ongoing project of coming to terms with those oppositions and readjusting ourselves accordingly. It is the whole in which these oppositions live, rise, and fall, and it is not clear that the concept of the organic is best suited to comprehending that conception of dealing with oppositions. For that, the better fit is that of a form of life (not a lifeworld) and the ways it can become alienated within itself rather than that of the model of "the organism" and its "pathologies."

Moreover, the concept of the organic also clearly has its misuses. Hegel relied on his philosophy of nature to import and underwrite his view that the difference of the sexes did not itself have a merely natural but also a deeper metaphysical and ethical significance (that of polarity in the universe at large) that, in turn, underwrote the domination of women in his conception of a civil society supposedly committed to the freedom and equality of all—a kind of metaphysical *vive la différence* that ended up with women confined to the status of bourgeois *Hausfrauen* both in terms of moral ethos and legal oversight. What Hegel got right about that was his view that a mere commitment to freedom and equality—when taken in a legalistic frame of mind—would be insufficient to address the real issues of what it takes to actualize this freedom in real practical and institutional ways. The abstractions of "life, liberty and property" (or "the pursuit of happiness," to give it the Jeffersonian twist) can obviously be taken in many different ways that conflict with each other. How it gets taken has to do with the development of a form of life and with the often conflicting conditions in which it works itself out.

More troubling for Hegel's view, the subordination of women, and the exploitation of the vulnerable in order to produce surplus value for the privileged, may be not merely extraneous features of a world where "much around is indeed not as it should be," but more fundamental examples of how freedom necessarily fails to be actualized in terms of the deeper embeddedness in types of relations established within the form of life itself—in terms of what is constitutive of a type of agency as seen in a more holistic context, which includes the relations of power at work in that form of life. If the settlements of Hegel's time were inadequate as realizations of freedom, this does not show that freedom as a baseline should be abandoned. It shows that Hegel failed to grasp his own time in thoughts in the terms he laid down for himself.

* * *

To make one final remark about Hegel's system in the retrospect of two hundred years. Hegel invented an entirely new terminology for his system in order to secure its status as a rigorous theory – as a *Wissenschaft*. Even in his own day, it was famous for its obscurity, and that particular part of Hegel's fame (or infamy) has never gone away. Moreover, since his own day, the various expositors of Hegel have tried a variety of ways to tame the ferocity of Hegel's idiom, but none of those attempts have stuck. Hegel continues to be read, new expositions appear (and typically with their own version of a Hegel Rosetta Stone), but Hegel abides, his vocabulary intact, indicating perhaps that there really is something vital to the system in the way he chose to put it. That is one thing nobody could have predicted two hundred years ago.

NOTE

1. See the discussion in RP §57.

REFERENCES

EL Hegel, G.W.F. [1830] 1969a. *Enzyklopädie der philosophischen Wissenschaften I. Die Wissenschaft der Logik*, in TWA vol. 8.

EN Hegel, G.W.F. [1830] 1969. *Enzyklopädie der philosophischen Wissenschaften II. Die Naturphilosophie*, in TWA vol. 9.

EPG Hegel, G.W.F. [1830] 1969. *Enzyklopädie der philosophischen Wissenschaften III. Die Philosophie des Geistes*, in TWA vol. 10.

RP Hegel, G.W.F. [1821] 1969. *Grundlinien der Philosophie des Rechts*, in TWA vol. 7.

PhG Hegel, G.W.F. [1807] 1969. *Phänomenologie des Geistes*, in TWA vol. 3.

TWA Hegel, G.W.F. 1969-1979. *Werke. Theorie-Werkausgabe*, 20 vols., ed. E. Moldenhauer and K. M. Michel.

Paul Rosenberg

HEGEL'S POLITICAL PHILOSOPHY

ABSTRACT: The Philosophy of Right *presents us with a vision of bureaucratic paternalism that is designed to check the excesses of free markets set in motion by the triumph of natural-law thinking, which abstracted the principles of private property and subjective freedom from the institutions that had tamed them and situated them in a stable context. Against these excesses Hegel pits the agricultural estate, which has not succumbed to natural-law thinking; and a "universal estate" of bureaucrats who are educated in Hegel's philosophy itself, freeing them of the natural-law conflation of human needs with arbitrary and endlessly expanding preferences. Taught by Hegel to look after the needs of the organic whole that is society rather than the gratification of their own preferences, the task of the bureaucrats of the universal estate is to curb the tendency of free markets to produce the social preconditions for an alienated "rabble" to bring down the system.*

The revival of scholarly interest in Hegel's political thought that has taken place in recent decades has presented political theorists with a growing paradox.

On the one hand, the dominant impression one receives from reading the *Philosophy of Right* is that Hegel is modern liberalism's most ambitious and most philosophically sophisticated critic. Hegel believed that his conception of modern *Sittlichkeit* represented a reconciliation, a higher synthesis, of the liberal ideal of individual freedom and the classical Hellenic ideal of all-encompassing community. As Hegel's generation of German intellectuals had thought of the classical polis as the embodiment of everything good that had been lost in the transition to modernity, the promise of a reconciliation between liberal freedom and ancient *Sittlichkeit* meant nothing less than a final reconciliation of all human goods, a stopping point in the historical process. Hegel's critique of liberalism has served as the inspiration or the legitimation for many of the myriad forms of anti-liberalism that have developed since his death, from Marxism to American academic communitarianism.

The other side of the paradox is the ease with which the *Philosophy of Right* can be interpreted as a philosophically sophisticated *vindication* of liberalism. Most of Hegel's more prominent recent interpreters in the English-speaking world have argued that Hegel is essentially a liberal. These interpreters do not take the naive view that all of the major and minor positions taken in the *Philosophy of Right* are compatible with liberalism, but the more sophisticated view that the more systematic arguments of the *Philosophy of Right* point to a form of welfare-state liberalism. This view, whose best-known representatives are Shlomo Avineri (1972), Paul Franco (1999), Frederick Neuhouser (2000), Z. A. Pelczynski (1964), Terry Pinkard (2000), Robert Pippin (1997), Steven B. Smith (1989), and Allen Wood (1990), has dominated Hegel scholarship since the 1960s.

The first aim of this paper is to outline an interpretation of Hegel's political thought that will go some way toward explaining this paradox. The key to my explanation is the following idea: that there is a substantial overlap, though by no means an identity, between the essential normative conclusions of the *Philosophy of Right* and the beliefs of contemporary welfare-state liberals. It is this overlap that explains the possibility of a selective reading of the *Philosophy of Right* that dilutes Hegel's notion of *Sittlichkeit* and brings Hegel quite close to present-day academic liberalism. But interpreting Hegel in this way abstracts away from a series of assumptions that Hegel made about the overall system of norms and institutions that liberal civil society needs to be embedded in if the liberal value of individual freedom is to be preserved. These additional norms and institutions were not, for Hegel, simply instrumental to the project of maintaining a form of welfare-state liberalism: he thought that liberal goals were ultimately intelligible only as a subordinate part of a larger system of social ideals.

Hegel's assumptions about what is required for a viable form of a modern society are more obscure, more controversial, and much more bound to the context of Hegel's milieu and time than is his underlying endorsement of modernity itself. But it is these assumptions that must be excavated if we are to understand how Hegel thought of modern *Sittlichkeit* as a reconciliation of classical *Sittlichkeit* and modern individual freedom. Hegel assumed that any stable form of modern society requires the integrating values of shared participation in an economic division of labor. He also assumed that this division of labor requires distinct socio-economic estates, with a clean separation between a market-oriented "mercantile" estate that is exceedingly narrow in its education and outlook, and a social welfare-oriented "universal" estate that receives an esoteric, philosophical education. Hegel also thought that modern *Sittlichkeit* requires bureaucratic paternalism rather than representative democracy; and state promotion of a single hierarchy of ideals of the good life rather than pluralism or governmental neutrality about the good life.

There is an additional insight that I believe is useful for explaining the paradox of Hegel's dual attitude toward liberalism. Hegel's belief in the pedagogic, character-forming, "perfectionistic" tasks of *Sittlichkeit* seems very foreign to our contemporary understanding of what a liberal society is about, but this foreignness is partly explained by the distorted view of present-day liberal societies found in much academic political philosophy. The social-contractarian systems that dominated academic political philosophy at the end of the twentieth century were generally meant to be normative rather than descriptive, but they led political theorists, liberals and communitarians alike, to an exaggeratedly atomistic picture of modern society. Once this picture is corrected so that we recognize the more *sittlich* aspects of welfare-liberal societies, the distance between Hegel's conception of modern *Sittlichkeit* and the practical reality of welfare-liberal societies becomes smaller. However, I cannot develop this thought here.

The picture of Hegel's political philosophy that emerges from my reconstruction has the following major features. Hegel was a modernizer who substantially accepted the atomizing, leveling effects of the Enlightenment liberal revolution taking place in his time, but was also critical of the self-understanding of this revolution. Enlightenment liberalism could not be generated out of the ahistorical, proceduralist premises of social contract theory or "natural law." Even though the Enlightenment liberal revolution was worldwide in its implications, its moral premises were rooted in the customary practices of the particular societies of early modern Europe. This insight was crucial not because the Enlightenment liberal destruction of the *ancien régime* needed to be reversed or slowed down, but because this revolution had the indirect consequence of unleashing the dynamic of the laissez-faire market, a dynamic that, if left unchecked, would end in the destruction of all ethical traditions. The unchallenged belief in the natural-law foundations of Enlightenment liberalism would allow this destruction to proceed. This Hegelian insight was meant to lead to a new system of institutions—largely those of a bureaucratic, paternalistic welfare state—that would contain and stabilize the market system, preserving the modern achievement of individual freedom by situating the institutions that sustained it within a larger framework that was self-consciously character-forming or pedagogic, hence "classical" rather than "modern."

Even this brief summary of my argument makes clear that I am proposing to disregard one of Hegel's clearest and most emphatic—though also most controversial and most frequently challenged—stipulations about his political thought: that, as he unambivalently states in the "Preface" to the *Philosophy of Right,* his book is a rational reconstruction and *ex post facto* justification of the modern rational state, not a program for social and political activism (PR 21). His claim is incompatible with what I take to be the "deep structure" of Hegel's thought. The reconstruction I give in what follows, of an activist, socially transformative Hegel, *is* my argument that the best understanding of Hegel's political theory is an activist one. To avoid any ambiguity, however, I will state at the outset my conception of how Hegel's thought should be interpreted as socially and politically activist:

1. *The Philosophy of Right* is not an *ex post facto* justification of institutions or institutional tendencies that already exist.
2. *The Philosophy of Right* requires Hegel's entire ontological system for its proper understanding. Thus, the entire philosophical system should be thought of as activist rather than contemplative.
3. *The Philosophy of Right* is not an ahistorical utopia: it is meant to be an intervention in the very specific historical situation of post-Napoleonic Europe, where Hegel's "agrarian" and "mercantile" estates already exist but the "universal" estate does not.

4. *The Philosophy of Right,* and Hegel's philosophical system more generally, are a pedagogy for students at the newly reformed German universities, aimed at the creation of a universal estate of civil servants.

I. *SITTLICHKEIT*, NATURAL LAW, AND ABSTRACT RIGHT

Hegel's great claim in the *Philosophy of Right* is that the modern achievement of individual subjective freedom can be compromised—forced to limit itself for the sake of higher values—without being entirely negated.

Hegel can make this claim because he takes a more complex view of what is essential to individual subjective freedom than is found in many of its defenders. A simplistic but, at the same time, very powerful and widespread interpretation of individual subjective freedom holds that the only justification for the coercive limitation of an individual's freedom is the need to respect the equal freedom of all other individuals. This view makes no provision for the possibility of distinguishing between more and less valuable exercises of individual freedom. Hegel's very different understanding of what is essential in modern individual freedom, while elusive and difficult to define, seems to me to have the following components: (1) Freedom requires that at least *some* individuals have the option of choosing between substantively differing ways of life. (2) Freedom requires that *all* individuals have the option of choosing between ways of life that *they subjectively perceive* as embodying substantive differences. (3) All individuals must have at least one way of life open to them that does *not* exemplify any of the great classical or Christian virtues of heroism, saintliness, moral or intellectual perfection: one way of life that exemplifies only ordinary, unheroic, relatively undemanding forms of virtue. (4) All individuals have duties to society that go beyond the minimal liberal duty of not harming or coercing others; but there is a presumption that, except for the occasional public emergency, these duties can be fulfilled in ways that individuals experience as self-realizing: as utilizing what they themselves perceive to be their highest talents and capacities.

Hegel's belief is that modern rational *Sittlichkeit* can respect these requirements of individual subjective freedom while at the same time working toward goals that are reminiscent of classical political thought: the moral and intellectual improvement of individual character, and the primacy of collective ends over those that are merely individual.

Perhaps counterintuitively, modern rational *Sittlichkeit* is capable of achieving these goals only because the meaning of its essential norms and institutions is not equally accessible and transparent to all of its members. It is a requirement of *Sittlichkeit* that it be divided into the three social groups Hegel calls the agrarian, mercantile, and universal estates: groups characterized by sharply differing norms, cultural traditions, and "forms of consciousness." The members of the agrarian estate have only an unreflective feeling of loyalty and trust toward society's laws and institutions, a feeling very similar to the unreflecting trust children are supposed to have in their parents and other authority figures. The members of the mercantile estate lack any such feeling of unreflecting trust. Their way of life requires that they have a conscious, explicit rationale for making their decisions. But their way of life also requires that their attention is very narrowly focused on the decisions they must make as businessmen, workers, and consumers; and that they pay little attention to the larger sphere of institutions that constrain their activities and set the parameters within which they can act as rational economic agents. Their feeling toward *Sittlichkeit* as a whole is neither one of trust and oneness nor one of suspicion or antagonism; they simply pay it very little attention. Members of the mercantile estate attach great importance to rational action, but their notion of rationality only extends to what Hegel calls "the understanding" (*Verstand*), a form of rationality that is profoundly inadequate for grasping the meaning of *Sittlichkeit*. Finally there is the universal estate, whose members' way of life is based on the exercise of the higher, philosophical form of rationality that Hegel calls *Vernunft*, and who do grasp the meaning of *Sittlichkeit* as a whole. All three of these mental attitudes are necessary in a society if modern *Sittlichkeit* is to be maintained.

Because modern *Sittlicheit* requires that the social consciousness of its members be split into different levels, however, the process of *Sittlichkeit*'s self-reproduction is always accompanied by the tendency for some members of society—members of the mercantile estate—to relapse into a false self-understanding: the ideology of natural-law theory. It would be incorrect to claim that natural-law ideology is a constitutive feature of the everyday life or everyday consciousness of the members of the mercantile estate, as their everyday consciousness does not take the form of an explicit, worked-out ideological system. But the peculiarly narrow, constrained focus of attention of members of the mercantile estate gives them a strong predisposition to fall into ideological consciousness if they do engage in any kind of philosophical reflection.

I believe that the key to grasping why this natural-law ideology will constantly tend to re-emerge in modern *Sittlichkeit* is the complex relationship between it and what Hegel calls "abstract right."

By "natural law," I mean to refer only to the tradition of *modern* natural law, a tradition that Hegel thought of as beginning with Grotius or Hobbes and stretching until Kant and Fichte.[1] This tradition has two defining characteristics. All modern natural-law theories, liberal and illiberal, treat social relationships on the analogy of contractual relationships between individuals who are intrinsically free and equal, individuals with goals and desires that pre-exist their social relationships. And all modern natural law theories, "empirical" (Locke) and "formal" (Kant), hold that their essential premises can be generated out of an abstract, ahistorical, procedural type of rationality; that they are independent of any reliance on custom, tradition, or "positive" authority.

By "abstract right," Hegel means something even more abstract, but also narrower: a system of moral norms, and corresponding legal institutions, that give each of the members of some group of individuals the right to have "absolute" Roman-law type property rights over physical objects. Abstract right is not just the set of property rights these individuals happen to have in various physical objects: it is the right to have these rights. Individuals cannot actually have absolute property rights in physical objects unless they also enjoy certain rights that go with the legal status of *personhood*: not being a slave or a serf, having standing to defend one's property rights in court, etc. Hegel's "abstract right" is roughly the set of rights associated with the Roman law concept of personhood. His "motto" of abstract right is "be a person and respect others as persons" (PR §36).

It may seem that natural-law theory and the belief in abstract right are the same thing, but this is a conflation that reads far too much into Hegel's concept of abstract right. It is one thing for an individual to have legally enforceable rights of absolute property over various physical objects and to have the legal status of personhood needed to exercise these rights, as guaranteed by abstract right. It is a very different matter for an individual to have the broad spectrum of rights encompassed in natural-law freedom and equality.

Say that I have an absolute property right over some object such as a wooden table. The concept of an absolute property right actually consists of a bundle of distinct rights: the right to exclude others from any physical interaction with the table, to move or situate the table in any physical space that I have a right to be bodily present in, to use the table in any way I like, to destroy the table if I wish, and, finally, the right to contract with any other legal person to transfer this bundle of rights. The ability to exercise my absolute property right over the table requires that I also enjoy the rights of legal personality: I cannot be made a slave or a serf; no other individual or agency can arbitrarily take away my life or my physical mobility or cause me bodily injury; and I must have the right to procedural justice in the courts to defend all of these rights. Enjoying these rights of legal personality means that, if I think of my existence exclusively in terms of my relation to the objects over which I have absolute property rights, I can conceive my existence as that of *an absolutely free will.* There is no other agency that has a right to interfere with my exercise of this will.

There is, in contrast, a very wide range of freedoms entailed in natural law that are not implied in or required by the right of legal personality. These include, for example, freedom of conscience, the free exercise of religion, freedom of speech and assembly, and the free choice of marriage and vocation. And while abstract right is egalitarian to an extent, it is not as egalitarian as natural law. My legal personality puts me, in a very limited sense, on a basis of equality with others who enjoy legal personality. The poor man's property right over his donkey is just as absolute and just as legally sacrosanct as the rich man's right over his villa; and when the poor man and the rich man meet each other in the marketplace and contract to exchange goods, they do so as formal equals. But this strictly delimited relationship of equality is perfectly compatible with both parties being members of a wider society in which they are profoundly unequal because they belong to different estates, are subject to different codes of criminal law, and have unequal rights to exercise their religions, or vote, or enter certain vocations. In contrast, natural law holds that all individuals are equally free contractors.

If it is the case that the belief in abstract right and natural law theory are as different as I am claiming here, how should we conceive of their relationship?

Hegel claims that the abstract right to property is the "first existence of freedom" (PR §45R). This claim implies two things: that the freedom individuals can possess in holding an abstract right to property is only the beginning of the full liberal freedom and equality of modern civil society; and also that the limited freedom of abstract right is somehow basic, structurally fundamental, for all other liberal freedoms. In the following section I will outline a way in which the full natural law ideology of freedom and equality could have developed from a basis provided by a system of abstract right.

II. THE CONTRADICTION IN NATURAL LAW

Natural-law theory is a revolutionary view of society, a radical, leveling critique of almost all the institutions of the *ancien régime*. But it is a revolutionary project that takes its start from a particular historical context: an *ancien régime* that has only a subset of individuals who are legally recognized in a system of abstract right, each of whom owns property under the rules of this system and can form contractual relationships with each other under these rules. Natural-law theory constructs its contractual image of a society of free and equal individuals through a process of abstraction and generalization from this starting point in the abstract right sanctioned by the *ancien régime*. We can form a picture of how this process might take place if we envisage the following sequence of mental operations:

1. Begin by ignoring all members of society who do not hold any absolute property rights and thus are not defined as persons under the existing system of abstract right. With the individuals who remain, imagine that the only legal rights they have are their abstract rights: the rights they have *qua* persons to their abstract property accompanied by the additional rights they require to have freedom of action as persons. Imagine further that the only duties toward them on the part of other individuals or the government are duties to respect these abstract rights. Correspondingly, the individuals with these rights have no other obligations to anyone else.

2. Imagine that these individuals can interact with each other and enter into contracts under the protection of exactly those legal rules that, in the real historical context from which we are abstracting, already govern the contracts that individuals with abstract property rights can form with each other. The criminal penalties that apply to persons who injure the persons or abstract property of others are also carried over from this real historical context into our imaginary society.

3. We now make our imaginary contractual society more realistic by bringing back into the picture all the other, non-absolute forms of property that were initially "abstracted out," but transforming them into the possessions of all, who are now treated as enjoying a universalized form of abstract right. All entities that in the real historical context were held as complex, legally encumbered or entangled, non-absolute forms of

property are now to be assigned to the absolute ownership of some individual legal person, or to state ownership, or perhaps to the status of "commons." There is no simple procedure for making this assignment: one must use the skills of legal reasoning to find the new pattern of ownership under absolute abstract-right rules of property that most closely approximates the older, more complex forms of ownership.

In effect, according to Hegel, what the natural-law theorist has done is construct a contractual image of society—society as envisaged by classical or bourgeois liberalism—by extracting from the *ancien régime* its skeleton or, more precisely, its joints and ligaments, the principles of abstract right, and discarding the rest. This enables us to make sense of one of his more interesting statements about natural-law theory. Hegel writes in the Introduction to the *Philosophy of Right* that it is important "to indicate the limits of philosophical right and at the same time to rule out any possible idea, let alone expectation, that its systematic development should give rise to a positive code of laws such as is required by an actual state. - Natural law or philosophical right is different from positive right, but it would be a grave misunderstanding to distort this difference into an opposition or antagonism; on the contrary, their relation is like that between Institutes and Pandects" (PR §3R). The reason it is impossible for philosophical right to generate a code of positive laws is not that the natural-law theorists were unable to write the necessary code books, but that in doing so they were not actually starting from purely philosophical premises. Natural-law theory was only a workable enterprise because its starting point was a surreptitious dependence on an already existing system of moral and legal rules that gave content to its notion of abstract right. These were the rules that describe what sort of objects can become property, how property is acquired, who counts as a legal person, how contracts are made between property owners, the additional rights that are required for the status of legal personhood, and the punishments for the violations of these rules.

Hegel's analysis sees in natural-law theory a peculiar dual structure. Natural-law theory is both tradition-dependent and revolutionary: it is both dependent for its content and moral plausibility on existing "positive" customs and moral intuitions *and* capable of abstracting and generalizing from its starting point so as to project a radical critique of society. This peculiar dual structure explains both the power of natural-law theory and why the theory must always be in false consciousness as to its own nature. Hegel's claim—the detailed validation of which I will examine in section IV below—is that natural-law theory is intrinsically dependent for its content on an existing system of abstract right. The conclusions of natural-law theory appear morally plausible not because they have actually been derived from abstract philosophical reasoning, but because they are in agreement with a particular set of existing moral and legal practices.

At the same time, natural-law theory needs its belief that its conclusions are grounded in abstract philosophical reasoning. The natural-law theorist can pass judgment on the institutions and moral traditions of the *ancien régime* only by denying that tradition as such is a source of legitimacy.[2] Accepting the authority of an existing system of abstract right as a means of denying the authority of all other moral traditions would be an exercise in arbitrariness. Natural-law theory was a revolutionary force because it was able to generalize an existing system of moral and legal norms into a full-fledged contractual image of society while at the same time hiding its implicit dependence on this system.

III. PROCEDURAL AND SUBSTANTIVE RATIONALITY

The relationship between natural law and abstract right that I have just sketched is, I believe, one of the two keys to understanding Hegel's analysis and critique of natural law. The other key is the relationship between the ideal of abstract, ahistorical rationality that was essential to the natural-law theorists—an ideal that Hegel calls "subjective rationality," and for which I will use the narrower, less confusing term "procedural rationality"—and the very different, substantive understanding of rationality that was rejected at the beginning of the modern era, which Hegel believes we must revive if we are to wrest free of the grip of natural-law ideology.[3]

The existence of a system of abstract right as one component of the moral and legal systems of early modern European society was a necessary, but by no means a sufficient, precondition for the rise of natural-law theory. The other factor was the development of the procedural understanding of rationality so prominent in Descartes, Hobbes, Locke, Hume, Kant, and most of post-Enlightenment Anglophone philosophy. The critique of this procedural understanding of rationality was at the very center of Hegel's philosophical enterprise.

Hegel saw the entrenchment of the procedural ideal in modern consciousness—an entrenchment that had grown far stronger through the triumph of the natural-law revolution—as having two historical roots. The first of these was the rejection of the older ideal of substantive rationality, the ideal that provides the most useful counter-concept to the idea of procedural rationality. The second root was the early-modern discovery of deep-seated moral and religious pluralism. I will examine each of these roots in turn.

The concept of procedural rationality is best understood in contrast to the older idea of substantive rationality, which was most fully exemplified in the metaphysical systems of Aristotle, Stoicism, Aquinas, and certain forms of Platonism. Substantive rationality is characterized by belief in what Charles Taylor has called "ontic logos": reason as a property of objectively existing beings in the world, and only secondarily and derivatively a property of human subjectivity. Three core beliefs characterize the notion of an ontic logos. First, as the ontic logos is the ultimate principle that structures and grounds reality, it cannot be other than it is. Aspects of reality may be contingent, but the ultimate laws that structure reality and govern how entities may behave are not and cannot be contingent. A residue of this notion still exists in the belief of certain modern philosophies of science that the orderliness of physical nature rests on fundamental laws or ultimate principles that could not be other than they are. Second, the ontic logos is not hidden or mysterious but self-revealing or self-manifesting. It is intrinsic to human beings that we are to some degree aware of it or attuned to it, much in the same way that it is intrinsic to human beings that we are aware of the design and position of our bodies.[4] Third, the ontic logos has normative power over us. To be aware of it is intrinsically to love it and to will to be in conformity with it.

In a series of developments that began with the nominalist theology of Ockham and his school and culminated in the mechanistic, "disenchanted" view of nature of the seventeenth-century Scientific Revolution, belief in substantive rationality came under increasingly influential attack. The idea of reason was transmuted into a very different, subjectivist form, giving rise to our familiar idea of procedural rationality. As with substantive rationality, the idea of procedural rationality can be defined through three essential beliefs. First, the orderliness and knowability of reality cannot simply be assumed. It is not *intrinsic* to the human mind that it has contact with reality; our ability to have knowledge of reality is something that must be proven, and belief about reality does not have the status of knowledge until its reliability has been proven. Second, it is possible to reflect on what knowledge is, on the nature of the human *faculty* for knowledge, independently of any assumptions as to the content of this knowledge. Third, rationality is not a property of the world, but a potentiality of our faculty of knowledge. We are rational when we make sure that this faculty is in good working order.

The second development in the culture of early modern Europe that motivated the rise of the procedural ideal was the discovery of intractable moral and religious pluralism, a consequence of the Reformation and the sixteenth-century rediscovery of ancient philosophical skepticism. To be aware of the fundamentally contested quality of one's most basic beliefs was a motivation for distrust: a motivation for looking carefully at the nature of our "cognitive faculty" and for putting all existing loyalties to institutions, and all received opinions, to the test. Cultures that did not have this awareness of moral and religious pluralism did not necessarily have the belief in substantive rationality or an ontic logos, but there is an obvious affinity between the rise of an awareness of moral and religious pluralism and the motivation to call any notion of an ontic logos into question. The realization that we should not trust even the core beliefs of our society, hence that we have a profound capacity for being deceived, calls into question the idea that the ultimate structure of reality is intrinsically manifest to human beings.

Somewhat less obviously, the belief in substantive rationality or an ontic logos works against the idea that we could ever have reason to radically distrust existing institutions and opinions. The ontic logos is reason that manifests itself or embodies itself in the structures of the world: reason that is itself a causal power. If we assume that the natural world is an embodiment of this ontic logos, we also have strong reason to presume that the social world, the world of human institutions, customs, norms, and beliefs, is to some degree an embodiment of the ontic logos as well. If awareness of the ontic logos is to some degree intrinsic to human beings, then this awareness must have been at work in the formation of human custom and belief from time immemorial. The idea that the individual philosopher has suddenly discovered that social custom and belief might be in need of radical revision requires an extraordinary megalomania on the part of the philosopher: the presumption that his contact with the ontic logos is of a drastically superior quality to that of any human being who preceded him.

IV. REASON AT WORK IN HISTORY

Hegel's most extensive discussion of the natural-law tradition does not take place in the *Philosophy of Right,* but in a lengthy essay that he published 20 years earlier, "On the Scientific Ways of Treating Natural Law." The essay divides natural-law theories into two types, empirical and formal. Empirical natural-law theories, best exemplified by Locke's *Two Treatises of Government,* are premised on the existence of a literal state of nature and a historically real social contract. The literal state of nature is somehow taken to be a guide to the moral rights and duties human beings should have in political society. The difficulty with arguments of this sort is that, even given the generous assumptions that a literal state of nature did exist and that we could know details about it, there are an indefinitely large number of possible ways to assess which features of this state of nature have permanent moral significance and which do not. Theories of an empirical social contract selectively highlight particular features of the imaginary state of nature so as to provide a justification for present-day moral "common sense" (Hegel [1802-3] 1999, 67-68).

Steven Smith (1989, 67-68) has usefully provided the following summary of Hegel's argument here:

> Hegel's objection to empirical theories of natural right turns not so much on their conclusions as on the method by which they purport to arrive at them. Empirical theorists like Hobbes and Locke claim to discover the most universal features of human beings by means of a kind of thought experiment, hypothetically stripping or peeling away everything man has acquired through the influences of history, custom, and tradition, in order to discover the state of nature and the natural man behind them. "If we think away," Hegel writes, "everything that someone's obscure inkling may reckon amongst the particular and transitory as belonging to particular manners, to history, to civilization, and even to the state, then what remains is man in the image of the bare state of nature, or the abstraction of man with his essential potentialities, and we have only to look in order to find what is necessary."
>
> The problem is that insofar as it aspires to be a theory of rights at all, empiricism cannot establish what it wants to prove. For if empiricism wants to be more than just a description of what rights we happen to enjoy, it must have some way of showing these rights to be necessary and universal. But, according to Hegel, this is just what empiricism is incapable of showing. For categories like "necessity" and "universality" are not given in experience or discoverable through observation but must be gleaned through other

> means. In Hegel's own language, empiricism is incapable of distinguishing between the necessary and the contingent. "Empiricism lacks all criteria for drawing the boundary between the accidental and the necessary; i.e., for determining what in the chaos of the state of nature or in the abstraction of man must remain and what must be discarded."

The apparent results of empirical social-contract theory are actually just ratifications of existing customs. Empirical natural law theory is "entangled in such concepts as have been fixed in the culture of the day as 'healthy common sense' and so seem to have been drawn directly from experience" (ibid., 69).

Hegel's second category of natural-law theory is the "formal" natural-law theory represented by Kant and Fichte. Hegel's discussions of formal natural-law theories are considerably more complex than his discussion of empirical natural-law theories and are scattered over a number of different places in his work. I will concentrate here only on the most famous of these discussions, the critique of Kant's "universalization" formula provided by Hegel in the *Philosophy of Right*. Hegel's charge is that Kant's best-known formulation of the Categorical Imperative, "Act only on that maxim through which you can at the same time will that it should become a universal law," is empty in that it actually leads to no determinate moral conclusions. Hegel writes:

> However essential it may be to emphasize the pure and unconditional self-determination of the will as the root of duty—for knowledge [*Erkenntnis*] of the will first gained a firm foundation and point of departure in the philosophy of Kant, through the thought of its infinite autonomy—to cling to a merely moral point of view without making the transition to the concept of ethics reduces this gain to an *empty formalism,* and moral science to an empty rhetoric of *duty for duty's sake.* From this point of view, no immanent theory of duties is possible. One may indeed bring in material from *outside* and thereby arrive at *particular* duties, but it is impossible to make the transition to the determination of particular duties from the above determination of duty as *absence of contradiction,* a formal *correspondence with itself* which is no different from the specification of abstract indeterminacy; and even if such a particular content for action is taken into consideration, there is no criterion within that principle for deciding whether or not this content is a duty. (PR §135R)

Hegel continues:

> Whereas we earlier emphasized that the point of view of Kant's philosophy is sublime inasmuch as it asserts the conformity of duty and reason, it must

> be pointed out here that this point of view is defective in that it lacks all articulation. For the proposition "Consider whether your maxim can be asserted as a universal principle" would be all very well if we already had determinate principles concerning how to act. In other words, if we demand of a principle that it should also be able to serve as the determinant of a universal legislation, this presupposes that it already has a content; and if this content were present, it would be easy to apply the principle. But in this case, the principle is not yet available, and the criterion that there should be no contradiction is non-productive—for where there is nothing, there can be no contradiction either. (PR §135A)

It is not difficult to see why Kant's universalization formula has the illusion of substance. Any complex society will have a great many moral concepts and practices that, because they are defined abstractly or without reference to particular individuals, are implicitly universal. Our concept of "property" is abstract, so that my right to a particular piece of property I happen to own is an instantiation of the general practice of respecting rights to property. Moral consistency requires that the attitude taken toward my particular property claim should be the same as the attitude toward any other such claim. The universalization formula is a making explicit of the implicit universalism of abstract moral concepts such as the right to property, but as such it is entirely dependent on the way that particular societies make use of abstract moral concepts. It can ratify these implicit moral practices but it cannot generate any system of moral practices *ex nihilo*. As Smith writes: "One cannot help but notice, then, that behind Kant's purely formal deduction of natural right there is presupposed the legitimacy of certain social and political institutions and practices. . . . Through a conceptual 'sleight of hand' the legitimacy of modern bourgeois liberalism is simply assumed" (Smith 1989, 75).

Hegel's critique of the natural-law tradition aims at undermining the core belief of this tradition, the belief that pure procedural rationality, wielded by the solitary individual, can provide an Archimedean standpoint from which one is entitled to legislate the historical process. Hegel's belief is that such a standpoint is an illusion: philosophy must rather begin from the idea that reason is a power already active in nature and the historical process and that we must, at the most fundamental level at least, have trust in this historical process.

It is crucial that Hegel's belief is that we must trust the historical *process*, and not simply any existing set of institutions and customs that this process has created. Hegel saw his critique of natural law as the product of a very particular set of historical circumstances, and as meant to influence the direction of social and political action only in those circumstances. He did not think that his critique of natural law could have been discovered under the circumstances of the *ancien régime,* and he did not think the critique should be regarded as applying "retroactively"—as an argument that the original advocates of natural law were doing the wrong thing in their destructive attack on the *ancien régime,* and that the results of this attack should be reversed. The inventive and the destructive application of natural-law theory were both aspects of a historical process Hegel thought of as being rational, necessary, and irreversible.

The above discussion presents us with an apparent paradox: Hegel was both a critic of natural-law ideology and a defender of the Enlightenment-liberal revolutions and reforms that emerged, largely, from natural-law ideology. Hegel in no way wanted his critique of procedural rationality and of the premises of the social-contractarian image of society to give aid and comfort to the conservatives and reactionaries of his time, who still defended the *ancien régime.* So what, if any, were the consequences for politics and public policy that Hegel thought would follow from his critique of natural-law theory?

The key to understanding Hegel's thought here, I believe, is the distinction between the direct and intentional and the indirect but inevitable consequences of the natural-law revolution. There were ethical and institutional traditions in the *ancien régime* that either the natural-law revolution never intended to destroy or that, because of their peculiarly implicit, non-theorized character, it never had the power to destroy. The direct and intentional consequences of the natural-law revolution never included the destruction of these traditions. But the natural-law revolution also had the indirect, unintended, but inevitable effect of setting loose the dynamic of the modern laissez-faire market, and it was Hegel's belief that this dynamic, if unchecked, would eventually destroy all the significant ethical traditions that had survived from the *ancien régime.* Natural-law theory did not consciously will this destruction, but it did have the consequence of standing in the way of the public-policy measures needed to save these ethical traditions by restraining the dynamic of the market.

Hegel's political project in the *Philosophy of Right* was built around conserving three major ethical traditions that, not being direct targets of the natural-law revolution, had survived from the *ancien régime,* but were threatened by the laissez-faire market.

The first of these traditions is the post-Protestant work ethic, the implicitly held view that work must be at the center of any realized human life. Hegel thought that this view was shared by a substantial and growing number of individuals in all Protestant societies and all societies that had significant cultural contact with Protestant societies.[5] The second tradition is the system of abstract right itself—considered as a "tradition," of course, because its power depended on its customary legitimacy and not on its (illusory) derivation from procedural rationality. The third tradition, and by far the oldest, was the traditionalist, non-individualistic orientation toward life, and especially toward earning and spending, of the rural or agricultural population. All three of these traditions had survived the liberal critique of the *ancien régime*. The first two traditions were in fact still spreading and strengthening in power: the European tradition of abstract right was being spread by Enlightenment liberalism itself, with or without the Napoleonic armies behind it; and the post-Protestant tradition of a work-oriented culture was spreading from the regions of its Protestant origins to all the other societies that the forces of the modern world were bringing into contact with those regions.

Hegel believed in the intrinsic goodness of each of these three traditions. His grounds for this belief were not abstract or purely philosophical. The evidence of the intrinsic goodness of the three traditions was provided by their ability to survive the natural-law critique of the *ancien régime,* and, in the first two cases, to continue to spread and entrench themselves in the modern world. It was, in fact, the persistence of the three traditions that provided the core motivation for Hegel's development of a teleological picture of human history, a picture that was to vindicate the idea that long-term historical convergence was an indication of goodness and truth.[6]

In the sections that follow I will look in some detail at the kinds of public-policy measures Hegel was advocating, and at why the natural-law tradition renders an endorsement of these measures impossible. My principal concern is with the measures Hegel thought necessary to stabilize the traditions of the work ethic and abstract right. Hegel's views on the agrarian estate will be discussed later in the paper, after my more general discussion of why Hegel believed in a system of estates.

V. SUSTAINING THE WORK ETHIC

In this section I will examine the first of the three ethical traditions that Hegel believed had survived the destruction of the *ancien régime* and that he wished to stabilize as a basis for modern *Sittlichkeit:* the first of Hegel's three motivations for his critique of natural-law theory. This is the tradition of the post-Protestant work ethic. Since the rise of modern secularism and the decline of the influence of the clergy and theology, the work ethic has gone without any explicit or theoretical basis, yet it has continued to strengthen its position in modern culture.

By "work" I mean disciplined, strenuous, full-time activity that contributes to meeting either the wants or, better still, the needs of others, or to providing for one's own sustenance. A life of work is both the moral basis for deserving a livelihood from society and, in general, the factual prerequisite for receiving such a livelihood. A life fully dedicated to work is a human life that is at least partly realized or successful. A life in which work is absent, at least in the context of modernity, can only count for Hegel as a failed life. Hegel's belief is that the future stability of the work ethic in the context of a market-oriented society will require an explicit, theoretical, perfectionist view of the value of work—a view that directly clashes with the anti-perfectionism of the natural-law tradition and the laissez-faire market to which it has given rise.

The unfettered development of the laissez-faire market threatens the stability of the culture of work in several ways. Market fluctuations can cause recessions with prolonged unemployment. Extremes of wealth and poverty can either remove individuals from the need to work or produce embitterment at the disparity between work and economic reward. And the unrestrained pursuit of individual self-interest can lead to isolation and the loss of the social reinforcement that individuals need if they are to feel pride in their work (PR §§236, 244, 253R). All of these conditions tend to disintegrate the strength of the work ethic and to draw individuals toward the "rabble" mentality that is Hegel's greatest fear for modern society.

Hegel advocates several policy measures that are either explicitly aimed at bolstering the work ethic or are aimed at preventing conditions he sees as potentially weakening it. These policies are the use of taxes, subsidies, and public provision to reduce extremes of inequality; government intervention to soften the business cycle and promote full employment; regulation of wages to ensure that work is adequately remunerated; taxation of luxury goods; and public education that teaches useful skills and upholds the value of work (PR §236). Hegel's discussion of welfare illustrates his preoccupation with the work ethic. Hegel thinks of individual welfare as a right, but thinks that to provide relief without the requirement of work is a direct assault on the ideal of work, the "principle of civil society and feeling of self-sufficiency and honour among its individual members" (PR §245). But subsidizing work for the poor will also fail: the extra goods that are produced will exacerbate the overproduction crisis that has created the condition of mass poverty in the first place (ibid.). Hegel throws up his hands at this point and declares that urban poverty is an intractable condition (ibid.). However, as commentators such as Paul Franco (1999, 268-75) have pointed out, Hegel's expression of pessimism here has no substantial basis in either his other reflections on socio-economic issues in the *Philosophy of Right* or in economic thought more generally. Hegel thought of individual welfare as a right due to any member of civil society and he had no *intrinsic* problem with tying welfare to useful work or with paternalistic government intervention in the lives of the poor.

The *Philosophy of Right*'s most famous and original idea for bolstering the work ethic was Hegel's proposal for the creation of a modern system of trade corporations. Both the need for the corporations and the possibility of their organization come from the specialization of the modern division of labor: "The work performed by civil society is divided into different branches according to its particular nature. Since the inherent likeness of such particulars, as the quality *common* to all of them, comes into existence in the *association,* the *selfish* end which preserves its own interest comprehends and expresses itself at the same time as a universal end; and the member of civil society, in accordance with his *particular skill,* is a member of a corporation whose end is therefore wholly *concrete,* and no wider in scope than the end inherent in the trade which is the corporation's proper business and interest" (PR §251). "By this definition," he continues, "the corporation has the right, under the supervision of the public authority, to look after its own interests within its enclosed sphere, to admit members in accordance with their objective qualification of skill and rectitude and in numbers determined by the universal context, to protect its members against particular contingencies, and to educate others so as to make them eligible for membership" (PR §252).

Hegel's corporations have some resemblance, of course, to the pre-capitalist guild system, which still had considerable importance in many of the German territories through the early nineteenth century. The guilds were in certain ways quite typical of the worst abuses of the *ancien régime:* membership was an hereditary privilege, and the guilds in general acted to protect the interests of their members at the expense of consumers and competitors without perceiving much of a need to justify their actions in terms of any notion of public good. Yet some guilds had an ideology of public service: maintaining high standards of quality, protecting consumers against shoddy goods, policing the ethical conduct of their members, and creating communal solidarity. In ideology if rarely in actual practice, certain aspects of the guild system anticipated and must have influenced Hegel's proposal for trade corporations.

VI. THE DISTINCTION BETWEEN WANTS AND NEEDS

The second of the three ethical traditions that Hegel found resistant to the leveling critique of natural-law theory, but threatened by the dynamic of laissez-faire market society that the natural law revolution had unleashed, was the tradition of abstract right itself.

The key to understanding Hegel's reasoning here is his concept of the "rabble" mentality:

> Particularity in itself, on the one hand indulging itself in all directions as it satisfies its needs, contingent arbitrariness, and subjective caprice, destroys itself and its substantial concept in the act of enjoyment; on the other hand, as infinitely agitated and continually dependent on external contingency and arbitrariness and at the same time limited by the power of universality, the satisfaction of both necessary and contingent needs is itself contingent. In these opposites and their complexity, civil society affords a spectacle of extravagance and misery as well as of the physical and ethical corruption common to both. (PR §185)

> Particularity in itself is boundless extravagance, and the forms of this extravagance are themselves boundless. . . . Deprivation and want are likewise boundless, and this confused situation can be restored to harmony only through the forcible intervention of the state. (PR §185A)

> When a large mass of people sinks below the level of a certain standard of living—which automatically regulates itself at the level necessary for a member of the society in question—that feeling of right, integrity [*Rechtlichkeit*], and honour which comes from supporting oneself by one's own activity and work is lost. This leads to the creation of a *rabble*, which in turn makes it easier for disproportionate wealth to be concentrated in a few hands. (PR §244)

It is crucially important that the condition of belonging to the "rabble" is not simply the condition of poverty, but a psychological and ethical disposition to which poverty strongly contributes. "Poverty in itself does not reduce people to a rabble; a rabble is created only by the disposition associated with poverty, by inward rebellion against the rich, against society, against government, etc. The rabble do not have sufficient honour to gain their livelihood through their own work, yet claim that they have a right to receive their livelihood" (PR §244A). Poverty contributes to the formation of a rabble mentality, but it is too simple to claim that poverty *causes* this formation in any mechanical sense. Hegel could not have accepted the more simplistic accounts of causal influences on human behavior that became common after his time with the rise of the positivistic social sciences, but neither did he accept a Kantian notion of the noumenal freedom of the will outside of the causal nexus of nature. The rabble mentality is a pathology to which individuals can *succumb*, not an ethical disposition that a rational individual would ever consciously or actively choose.

From the standpoint of the way in which we think about poverty, individual responsibility, and the social causation of behavior, it may seem difficult to grasp how Hegel could have thought that modern industrial poverty and the "rabble" mentality created any deep philosophical problem. But we must be careful to avoid slipping into anachronism by thinking that the explicit and implicit assumptions with which we approach social issues today were always shared by past cultures.

Our way of thinking about morality today is semi-consequentialist: we always consider the consequences of laws and social policies as at least one major factor in our evaluations. Hand in hand with semi-consequentialism is a strong tendency to think of behavior in terms of causal antecedents rather than individual free will, even as we recognize that causal influences on human behavior are almost always probabilistic rather than deterministic.In late twentieth-century debates about the "culture of poverty," the question was partly about the degree to which an environment of poverty can excuse anti-social or irresponsible behavior; and partly about whether measures to reduce poverty can produce attitudes of dependency that ultimately contribute to keeping people in poverty. By contrast, Hegel was trying to challenge an Enlightenment-liberal or natural-law view that had the following elements. First, there was no notion that it is a good thing to try to alleviate poverty on intrinsic or humanitarian grounds. Second, individuals were thought to be responsible only for the direct and foreseeable consequences of their actions. As individuals have freedom, their conduct cannot be considered to be foreseeable by another individual. The implication is that my responsibility for my action ends at exactly the point where the free decision-making power of another individual begins. Third, the anti-consequentialism of natural-law thinking went together with a tendency not to see individual action as the causal product of social circumstances. If the objection is made that an action of mine that leaves another individual in poverty increases the probability that this second individual will turn to lawlessness, the natural-law response is that probabilistic causation, if it is a coherent concept at all, is not equivalent to "real" causation. Only real causation counts in reckoning whether my action is moral or not.

This natural-law outlook had sweeping implications. It is not simply that there was no justification for policies that would limit the abstract-right freedom of individuals to dispose of their property so as to alleviate the poverty of other individuals. There were also no moral concepts available that could allow us to claim that an individual's existence in a state of poverty is an inherently or intrinsically bad thing. One might assume that individuals will rarely wish to exist in a state of poverty, but nothing in the natural-law tradition holds that it is a good thing for individual wishes or preferences to be realized. The welfarist-utilitarian tradition that has always shadowed natural-law theory does hold that it is a good thing that individual wishes or preferences be realized, but this tradition has always suffered from the problem of being tremendously inchoate: it must smuggle in forbidden assumptions from other moral traditions if it is to have any way of deciding which preferences of which individuals deserve priority.

There is an even further implication: the natural-law tradition, being anti-consequentialist, had no reason to be concerned about whether a society that adheres to natural-law principles is stable. If the creation of a polity based on natural-law principles had the consequence of generating social conditions that led to the alienation of most of society from these principles and the resulting collapse of the polity into chaos, this would reflect the unfortunate weakness of human nature, but would have no effect on the intrinsic validity of natural-law principles themselves. As Hegel describes the implications of Fichte's natural-law rigorism in an early essay, "*Fiat justitia, pereat mundus* is the law, and not even in the sense that Kant gave it: 'let right be done though all the scoundrels in the world perish.' But rather in this sense: right must be done, even though for its sake, all trust, all joy and love, all the potencies of a genuinely ethical [*sittlichen*] identity, must be eradicated root and branch" (quoted in Franco 1999, 28).

Hegel used his critique of the natural-law illusion that abstract right has pure procedural foundations as the basis for a critique of the rigorism and inflexibility of natural-law theory, a critique that results in recommendations for policy measures that would limit the principles of abstract right without by any means abolishing them.

The decision as to just how far abstract right should be recognized and how far it should be abrogated in any given social context can only be an *ad hoc* one. As one would expect, then, the *Philosophy of Right* gives a very general description of how welfare-redistributive institutions should operate, but does not give specific rules for determining such questions as the precise level of taxation or exactly how high the social minimum should be. Hegel explicitly warned against the expectation that philosophy can either prescribe or rationally reconstruct the details of social institutions or policy, a warning that he thought both Plato and Fichte egregiously violated (PR §23).

Some of the policy measures and institutions Hegel suggested for the stabilization of civil society are the same measures and institutions we have already discussed in the context of stabilizing the post-Protestant work ethic. Hegel was concerned with reducing the incidence of poverty without encouraging dependency, so he advocated measures to soften the business cycle to reduce and shorten unemployment, to regulate prices of basic necessities, and to publicly finance infrastructure projects (PR §236). Hegel's trade corporations were also meant to be welfare institutions in providing such benefits as unemployment insurance. Tying rights to welfare to membership in one of the corporations was also a way of lessening the humiliation of accepting an income one hasn't earned, and ensuring that permanent attitudes of dependency would not develop.

Hegel's concern with preventing the growth of the rabble mentality led him to propose measures that go beyond the conventional egalitarian ideal of transferring wealth from the rich to the poor, and throw an interesting light on the whole project of the modern welfare-redistributive state. Hegel wrote: "Society has the right and duty to act as guardian on behalf of those who destroy the security of their own and their families livelihood by their extravagance, and to implement their end and that of society in their place" (PR §240). For "on the one hand, it is true that every individual has an independent existence; but on the other, the individual is also a member of the system of civil society, and just as every human being has a right to demand a livelihood from society, so also must society protect him against himself. It is not just starvation which is at stake here; the wider viewpoint is the need to prevent a rabble from emerging. Since civil society is obliged to feed its members, it also has the right to urge them to provide for their own livelihood" (PR §240A). Hegel thus believed in the redistribution of wealth not just from the rich to the poor, but from the poor to themselves as well. This paternalistic understanding of redistribution is only intelligible if one accepts a substantial conception of needs as the commodities an individual *should* want, regardless of whatever it is that an individual actually happens to want. Hegel's paternalism here, together with the paternalism he endorsed in requiring paupers to do useful work, marked perhaps his most direct points of conflict with a natural-law, individualistic image of society, the points where he most directly asserted the priority of the social totality over the will of the individual. Hegel's assertion that the poor can and must be forced to look after their own needs and take part in the activity of civil society was an assertion that the freedom he defended *within* the institutions of *Sittlichkeit* did not extend to the freedom to be *outside* the institutions of *Sittlichkeit*.

Hegel's derivation of the notion of need from his critique of natural-law rigorism provides a useful focal point for thinking about his entire enterprise in the *Philosophy of Right*. All three of the ethical traditions that Hegel wished to preserve from the destructive force of the market can be seen as requiring a substantial notion of needs. A perfectionist view of the work ethic directly implies a concept of needs: if human life must be realized in work, then "needs" are the goods an individual must have access to in order to sustain the capacity for work. The agrarian estate's orientation to subsistence production and immunity from the temptations of the market, its self-limited view of its own economic activity, also requires an implicit understanding that there are needs as opposed to mere wants. The three ethical traditions provide separate, mutually reinforcing arguments for making a fundamental distinction between wants and needs, a distinction the natural-law tradition provided no basis for.

As individuals in the mercantile estate act for the satisfaction of wants —their own and, instrumentally, those of others—and have no articulated concept of needs; and as individuals in the universal estate renounce the consumption of luxuries and have as their task the articulation of a general distinction between wants and needs, the concept of need provides the clearest basis for thinking about Hegel's justification of the system of estates.

VII. THE THREE ESTATES AND THE ROLE OF THE BUREAUCRAT

It is useful to begin here by having a fuller picture of what Hegel meant by "estate" and how he envisaged the three estates that together compose the social world of modern *Sittlichkeit:*

> The infinitely varied means and their equally infinite and intertwined movements of reciprocal production and exchange *converge,* by virtue of the universality inherent in their content, and become *differentiated* into *universal masses.* In consequence, the whole complex evolves into *particular systems* of needs, with their corresponding means, varieties of work, modes of satisfaction, and theoretical and practical education—into systems to which individuals are separately assigned, i.e. into different *estates.* (PR §201)

> The estates are determined, in accordance with *the concept,* as the *substantial* or immediate estate, the reflecting or *formal* estate, and lastly, the *universal* estate. (PR §202)

Hegel divided his treatment of *Sittlichkeit* into three institutional levels: the three distinct spheres in which modern individuals are socialized, develop virtues and capacities, and engage in the activities that give meaning and content to their lives—the family, civil society, and the state.

Civil society is, strictly speaking, the institutional level of society that is divided or articulated into the system of estates. It is, first of all, the modern economic division of labor, the "system of needs" or of reciprocal economic interdependence. "Civil society" also carries the meaning of the sphere of activity that is the laissez-faire marketplace depicted and endorsed in classical political economy. This dual-purpose use of the term "civil society" carries the potential for significant confusion. The "system of needs" is emphatically *not* the laissez-faire marketplace. Hegel saw the division of labor that produces most goods and services as only in part organized through market transactions.

Hegel also made a double use of the term "state," which goes in tandem with his double use of "civil society." "Civil society," when used to mean the laissez-faire marketplace, has its antonym in Hegel's idiosyncratic use of the term "state" to mean *Sittlichkeit* as a whole, the ultimate locus of individual allegiance and the highest worldly vehicle of Absolute Spirit. "Civil society" used to mean the "system of needs" has an antonym of sorts in Hegel's more conventional use of the term "state" to mean "institutions of government." The system of needs is modern *Sittlichkeit* considered in its functioning as a division of labor. This includes the operations of the civil bureaucracy, but it leaves out the other formal institutions of state, such as the monarchy, the Estates Assembly, and the foreign-service bureaucracy, which Hegel discusses separately.

Hegel's "system of needs" is the institution that supplies all the goods and services that are not directly produced and consumed within the family, but this is only the first of its functions. The activity of participating in the system of needs, whether as a producer, a consumer, or a member of a corporation, is also the principal way that adult men develop and exercise their talents and capacities, find self-esteem and social identity, and realize themselves as human beings. Participation in the system of needs is also a pedagogic process in that it serves to inculcate in individuals those norms and attitudes that define modern *Sittlichkeit*. It inculcates both the aspiration to individual subjective freedom and the ability to see the limits of this form of freedom.

Hegel's three estates play both distinctive economic or productive roles and distinctive ethico-pedagogic roles within the system of needs. Why, however, did Hegel think that each of the three economic-productive functions must be carried out by a distinctive group of individuals who are *also* assigned a distinctive ethico-pedagogic function? In what follows I will examine how Hegel, starting with his essential distinction between wants and needs but also bringing in additional assumptions of varying degrees of plausibility, could derive or rationally reconstruct the necessity for the modern system of needs to have this functional division into estates. I will begin by looking at the mercantile and universal estates and their interrelationship, and afterwards consider the issue of Hegel's justification for the agrarian estate.

It is not that difficult to see how Hegel came to assume that there could be a distinct group of people who specialize in the direct production of goods and services to meet human wants or needs, people who take no interest in the activity of deciding on the content of needs. Hegel found this assumption ready-made in the social theory of classical political economy. Adam Smith and his followers shared the anti-perfectionist and anti-paternalist assumptions of the natural-law tradition, only they took these assumptions as descriptions of empirical behavior rather than as normative postulates. They believed that the economic activity of a modern society could be conducted by individuals who made decisions about work and investment based on maximizing individual self-interest in response to market demand, not on the basis of any normative ideals about what should be produced; and who similarly made personal decisions about consumption based on preferences, without the need for reliance on normative theories of what their preferences should be.

Hegel took classical political economy's social theory of "market man" as the model for his description of the way of life and characteristic activities of the mercantile estate. He did not hold that the market coordination of production and consumption is the only way in which the direct production of useful goods and services can be organized. We will see below that he thought the agrarian estate carried out its productive activity without relying on the market. But he did think that the realization of infinite subjective freedom required that modern *Sittlichkeit* carry out its production of non-agricultural goods and services through the mechanism of market incentives, and that the individuals responsible for this production have a specialized way of life that is uniquely oriented to market incentives.

Hegel's mercantile estate has two essential characteristics that are relevant here. The first is that its members have, at most, an inchoate sense that they have normative duties to society (or for that matter, to themselves) beyond law-abidingness or respect for the system of abstract right. Members of the mercantile estate may have feelings of charity or benevolence, but no more for Hegel than for Kant were such feelings equivalent to perceptions of duty. The second characteristic is that, while members of the mercantile estate derive a sense of pride, self-esteem, and social identity from their work and thus, in some sense, attach an intrinsic value to the process of work, they are nonetheless entirely guided in their decisions about what kind of work to do, and also in other economic decisions, such as how they should invest their money, by the extrinsic criterion of maximizing their income. Thus, members of the mercantile estate reliably make economic choices in response to market incentives.

Hegel's next assumption was that the agrarian and mercantile estates arrived on the historical scene first. The agrarian estate is age-old in its existence; the mercantile estate existed in an earlier form during the Roman Empire and has roots in its modern form going back to the medieval towns, but fully emerged only when the liberal-natural law revolution destroyed the *ancien régime*'s restrictions on commercial activity.

To fully grasp what the mercantile estate is we must see it not statically but in terms of an historical dynamic. Almost to the degree of Marx or Schumpeter, Hegel thought of the economy of the laissez-faire market as a force of creative destruction. The market breaks down all traditional restraints on the possibilities for both earning and spending money. It creates an unlimited horizon of opportunities for increasing the efficiency of production and an unlimited horizon of possible new wants and desires. This process weakens the authority of traditional institutions by constantly destabilizing local communities, and it also produces continually growing extremes of wealth and poverty. Both of these extremes place individuals in danger of succumbing to the rabble mentality. The wealthy are tempted by their money to buy themselves out of the ordinary restraints of law, morality, and the work ethic; and the poor are tempted to succumb to resentment against the unfairness of their situation. Hegel's philosophico-political project, and the universal estate of bureaucrats it is meant to educate, come into being as a response to this looming ethical and institutional crisis created by the laissez-faire market.

Members of the universal estate are selected meritocratically. They are individuals who would otherwise follow a standard path into membership in the mercantile estate, but who have been educated at one of the newly reformed German universities and have shown both intellectual aptitude for Hegelian thought and the requisite ethical disposition. They must be willing to sacrifice the opportunities for acquiring substantial wealth they might have had as members of the mercantile estate and to find personal fulfillment instead in working for the public good. The act of joining the universal estate must be purely intrinsic in its motivation: no one can be coerced into membership and the salary members receive must be sufficiently low that money will never be part of the incentive for individuals to join.

The purpose of the universal estate is to formulate and implement a systematic public policy based on the distinction between wants and needs, a policy that will stabilize market society and preserve the ethical traditions that survived the natural-law revolution. The universal estate does not abolish abstract right, private property, economic inequality, or market incentives. Instead it creates a system of taxes, regulations, subsidies, programs of welfare provision, and infrastructure projects within which market incentives function. The universal estate sets the parameters for the functioning of the market system. It does not own or manage any of the organizations that actually produce physical goods or provide day-to-day services; and it does not need to have the highly specialized knowledge required to manage such organizations. The universal estate can achieve its public policy goals without having to engage in direct economic production because it can rely on the fact that there is already a mercantile estate whose members are competent and eager to perform these tasks. The universal estate knows that the culture of Enlightenment civil society, a culture the mercantile estate both embodies and reproduces, effectively socializes individuals to respond to market incentives. The universal estate only needs to act to set up the right parameters to steer and constrain the functioning of the market system: it can depend on the mercantile estate (and in a sense on the agrarian estate as well) to do the rest.

It seems plausible that this division of labor could achieve what Hegel wanted—stability, efficiency, full employment, production for needs as well as wants, a widely shared "producerist" ethic—provided one could find people who have the character and motivation to be members of the universal estate. But why did Hegel think that these goals could *only* be accomplished in this way? Why didn't Hegel allow that individuals of all estates could act as *citizens* to establish a welfarist, needs-oriented social policy? And why didn't he think that individuals motivated to care about needs and collective welfare would not want to work to directly produce needful goods and services, or somehow to combine both policy work and the direct production of goods?

An answer to the first question is, of course, crucial both for understanding Hegel and for understanding the immense distance between the time and cultural milieu in which his assumptions about character and economic and political behavior could seem plausible and our way of thinking about these issues today. The question really amounts to asking: Why was Hegel a bureaucratic paternalist rather than a democrat?

Hegel's way of thinking about the universal estate involved assumptions that are obviously dramatically different from the assumptions we tend to make about these questions in present-day liberal-welfare states. In a wide variety of formal and informal, explicit and implicit ways, we do draw distinctions between needs and mere wants or preferences. But we are leery of assigning the power to decide how this distinction should be drawn to any one center of institutional power or any one subclass of individuals. The ideal of the professions as self-governing oligarchies, "above" market motivations and thus positioned to make such decisions, has rapidly faded. In the classical, late-nineteenth/early-twentieth-century formulations of this ideal, professionals were not merely people we *need* to trust because they have esoteric knowledge we are in no position to evaluate, as we now think of them, but also people we *should* trust because their professional education has somehow equipped them with the wisdom and virtues of character required to make paternalistic decisions about needs (Brint 1994, 36–37).

This image of the professions has obviously lost most of its currency since the 1960s. On the whole, we now tend to accept the sovereignty of consumers to decide where the distinction between wants and needs should be drawn as the *de facto* best solution to this problem—though it is a solution that is only really available where the needs of the middle class and the affluent are concerned. The diffusion of the power to make decisions about the content of needs has had the consequence that we do not tend to think very much about the kind of education or virtues of character that should go with making such decisions. In dramatic contrast, Hegel was very keen on the idea that the power to make decisions on the content of needs should be concentrated in the hands of a distinct class of individuals. To a certain extent, we might simply attribute this to the generally elitist, antidemocratic character of his milieu and time. Even the more liberal, reform-minded German intellectuals of the early nineteenth century were far from being democrats or even defenders of a bourgeois republic. The prestige of the German monarchies and the landed aristocracy was still very great; civil society and public-sphere institutions were not very developed; and German liberals tended to look to either Napoleonic France or the old Cameralist bureaucracies as the agents of reform. But Hegel also had a reason that was deeply rooted in his systematic philosophy for holding that the power to decide on the content of needs should be concentrated in a single subclass of individuals.

Simply stated, this reason was that, in the deep structure of his thought if obviously not in his notorious statements in the "Preface" to the

Philosophy of Right, Hegel was committed to an activist, politically interventionist view of both the *Philosophy of Right* and of his philosophical system as a whole. Considerations of space prevent me from giving this issue anything close to the attention it deserves, but it is possible to quickly list the following observations:

1. If it is the case, as I have argued, that the *Philosophy of Right* has at or near its center the critique of natural-law proceduralism, and that the adequate execution of this critique requires a rehabilitation of the idea of substantive rationality, then we have clear grounds for thinking that Hegel believed that the *Philosophy or Right* was dependent on his ontology and thus on his entire philosophical system.

2. Rejecting an activist interpretation of the *Philosophy of Right,* and holding that it was meant to be a rational reconstruction of an already existing system of modern *Sittlichkeit,* would leave Hegel's picture of modern *Sittlichkeit* with no account of either the educational curriculum that formed the universal estate or the theories or concepts by means of which the universal estate understood its own role.

3. It is well known that Hegel did not begin his career with the quietist or contemplative view of the role of his philosophy that he proclaimed at the end of it, but in fact turned to such a view only in 1807 or 1808, after he had published the *Phenomenology of Spirit.* Hegel's views on pretty much all of the major topics discussed in his philosophy, political theory included, had reached their mature form by 1808, and were elaborated but not fundamentally changed during the rest of his career (Forster 1998, 482-97). The implication is that Hegel himself, for much of his career, held to an activist rather than a contemplative interpretation of his mature philosophical system.

The possibility that Hegel's philosophy was meant to be activist rather than contemplative gives us the most plausible explanation of why he was a bureaucratic paternalist rather than a democrat and, indeed, why he took such a low view of modern public opinion (which, he said, "deserves to be respected as well as despised—despised for its concrete consciousness and expression, and respected for its essential basis, which appears in that concrete consciousness only in a more or less obscure manner"; PR §318). A strong element of Plato's *Republic* survives in the *Philosophy of Right,* as it does in a great many earlier and later thinkers influenced by German Idealism and neo-humanism. Hegel thought that good public policy in the context of a modern commercial society requires not just honesty and intelligence on the part of the civil bureaucracy but also a relatively esoteric form of knowledge. As this knowledge is ethical and not primarily technical, the bureaucracy must be an oligarchy that can be relied upon to police its own behavior, not a mere class of functionaries who work under the ultimate supervision of courts, parliaments, or citizens.

The second major assumption Hegel makes about the division of labor between social estates in modern *Sittlichkeit* involves the following question: why won't individuals who have been able to develop an altruistic, collective-welfare orientation want to engage in the direct production of needful goods and services? Why will they want to concentrate exclusively on the formulation of public policy? Hegel has several reasons—plausible, to some degree, in his time, but highly implausible today—for making this assumption. The first is simply the scarcity of the requisite motivation and talent. Hegel thought that Enlightenment-liberal civil society was the background out of which, against which, and in response to which the universal estate had to emerge. Each member of the universal estate had to go through what Hegel assumed was a painful existential transition: breaking away from a sense of identity or selfhood that had been formed by the culture and institutions of Enlightenment civil society—a sense of identity centered on the capacity for acting in response to market conditions in the quest to satisfy contingently given wants or desires. Hegel assumed that breaking with this form of identity in order to take up a new identity, in which the fulfillment of contingent wants and desires is subordinated to an ideal of self-realization through civic duty, is a strenuous and painful process, one that relatively few people would successfully complete. Hegel also assumed that the direct production of needful goods and services could be handled in its entirety by individuals who had not undergone this painful transition: individuals acting as self-interested agents responding to market incentives, inside the appropriate framework of taxes, regulations, and subsidies. For someone who had accomplished the transition to a "universal-estate" sense of personal identity, to engage in the direct production of goods and services rather than work at the formulation of public policy would simply be a wasteful use of scarce talent.

There is a final, somewhat less obvious reason why Hegel probably assumed that individuals with a "public-good" orientation would not want to engage in direct economic production. The universal estate of the *Philosophy of Right* does not act through piecemeal, disconnected policy measures. It forms a comprehensive view of the social, cultural, and economic condition of society and then formulates a comprehensive, unified program that distinguishes between needs and wants and uses the levers of public policy to steer the economic activity of society accordingly. The capacity of the universal estate to formulate and implement such a program depends on the reliability of the assumption that the economic actors it is trying to control are highly regular, and hence steerable, in their behavior. They are rational, self-interested actors who will make their decisions about investment, work, and consumption based on market incentives. If instead they were to adopt an altruistic, collective-welfarist orientation and make their economic decisions on the basis of their personal evaluations of collective needs, not on the basis of market incentives, we no longer have a single agency, the government, formulating a comprehensive social policy and being able to rely on predictable behavior from everyone else. We have a number of agents, acting without coordination, each trying to formulate a separate, personal vision of good social policy without being able to depend on the producer class responding predictably to the incentives that would otherwise be established by the policies set up by the universal, paternalistic class.

VIII. THE AGRARIAN ESTATE

Hegel's primary emphasis in his treatment of the agrarian estate is on its differences with the mercantile estate in attitudes toward earning and spending. "In our times," he writes,

> the [agricultural] economy, too, is run in a reflective manner, like a factory, and it accordingly takes on a character like that of the second [mercantile] estate and opposed to its own character of naturalness. Nevertheless, this first estate will always retain the patriarchal way of life and the substantial disposition associated with it. The human being reacts here with immediate feeling [*Empfindung*] as he accepts what he receives; he thanks God for it and lives in faith and confidence that this goodness will continue. What he receives is enough for him; he uses it up, for it will be replenished. This is a simple disposition which is not concerned with the acquisition of wealth; it may also be described as that of the *old nobility,* which consumed whatever it had. In this estate the main part is played by nature, and human industry is subordinate to it. In the second estate, however, it is the understanding itself which is essential, and products of nature can be regarded only as raw materials. (PR §203A)

The agrarian estate has a disposition that achieves in a unified, unreflective way the same thing that the mercantile and universal estates can only achieve by working together. The mercantile estate acts in pursuit of wants; the universal estate regulates the economic process to ensure that needs are taken care of first; the agrarian estate does not yet have an articulate distinction between needs and wants. The mercantile estate is engaged in direct economic production; the universal estate regulates and steers this production; the agrarian estate simultaneously produces and, through its passive acceptance of tradition, regulates and steers its own process of production.

Hegel's ground for believing in the intrinsic goodness of the way of life of the agrarian estate is the persistence of this way of life into liberal modernity. The natural-law revolution that destroyed feudal privilege, serfdom, and the guilds and created the emancipated attitudes of the modern individual did not change this culture. Liberal emancipation changed the legal structure of society, but the *mentalités* of the countryside were not dependent on this legal structure. The procedural rationality of the Enlightenment attacked and largely destroyed explicit systems of belief that were unable to pretend that they had proceduralist foundations, but the agrarian mindset was substantially independent of such systems of belief.

There was also a somewhat deeper reason for the immunity of rural culture to the liberal-Enlightenment onslaught. Natural-law theory and the procedural Enlightenment did everything they could to foster in individuals not merely the negative attitudes of skepticism and distrust of authority but also the positive attitudes of cosmopolitanism, curiosity, a thirst for knowledge and experience, and a desire to take an active part in the modern process of emancipation and revolution. All of these attitudes were of course profoundly antithetical to the way of life of the agrarian estate. But the Enlightenment, at least in the period before it gained control of state authority, did not have an automatic method of drawing the entire society into its project of emancipation and mobilization. The Enlightenment could only appeal to individuals who had already become detached, to some degree, from traditional institutions and ways of life and who were therefore open to its ideas. As long of the rural population led a self-contained existence, and didn't need to engage in frequent interaction with urban society or the literate middle classes, it was outside of the Enlightenment's reach.[7]

This cultural division between town and countryside would have had the potential to remain stable in the face of liberal modernity but for the fact that the natural-law revolution had the legal implication of turning all property into absolute, abstract property, a precondition for the commodification of land. Once land is no longer restricted to being passed down through inheritance and can be bought and sold on the market, the distinctive way of life of the agrarian estate is doomed. Agriculture becomes a branch of industry, nature is subordinated to the understanding, the individualistic, entrepreneurial, profit-maximizing attitude spreads to the countryside. If land is commodified, agricultural producers will no longer be able to maintain their traditionalist attitude toward earning and spending and will be subjected to the same unlimited striving for money and unlimited multiplication of arbitrary wants and desires that is both the freedom and the affliction of the mercantile estate.

Hegel's proposal is to prevent this transformation, which he saw as being already in process, by rejecting the natural-law requirement that all property should be in the form of abstract right and restoring the traditional custom of primogeniture in land (PR §306A). Restoring primogeniture has the effect of both closing the agrarian estate to entry by outsiders, so that anyone who owns land will necessarily have grown up inside the agrarian estate, and drastically diminishing the possibilities for either using land as a speculative instrument or treating agriculture as a capitalist, profit-maximizing business.

IX. THE AMBIVALENCE OF HEGEL'S POLITICAL PHILOSOPHY

Having presented my reconstruction of Hegel's theory of modern *Sittlichkeit,* I am now in a position to explain why his political philosophy can be so easily interpreted as a form of atomistic welfare-state liberalism, even while also being easily interpreted as nothing less than the reconciliation of classical *Sittlichkeit* with modern subjective freedom.

The first point that needs to be made here is that Hegel's system is far closer to the mainstream of modern liberal or social-democratic thought than are most of the alternatives to liberalism that political theorists have proposed over the past two centuries. Almost all the institutions of rational *Sittlichkeit* are in accordance with the meritocratic principle of careers open to talent: Hegel has no place for discrimination based on race and almost none for discrimination based on birth. The cultural unity of modern *Sittlichkeit* is one created by the distinctly modern institutions of the market, the corporations, the universities, and the bureaucracy: it does not require the existence of a unified ethnic or linguistic culture. Hegel allows the free exercise of religion. Hegel's system and its realization in modern *Sittlichkeit* is itself a new form of religion, but it is compatible with a modern society that is largely secular, in ordinary terms.

Somewhat less obviously, Hegel's political thought is also closer to modern liberal ideals than is the civic humanist or republican tradition. Hegel has far less of a problem than do the civic humanists with the modern expansion of production and consumption. His differentiated system of estates allows modern *Sittlichkeit* to promote classical (although not military or aristocratic) virtues, while at the same time allowing full scope to the distinctly modern, unheroic virtues of the bourgeoisie.

The second point to emphasize concerns Hegel's reasons for wanting to go beyond the natural-law, atomistic self-understanding of modernity. Hegel argued for constraining the liberal freedoms of modern civil society by embedding it inside a larger system of institutions that are paternalist, perfectionist, and collectivist. But his justification for these *sittlich* institutions always involved their necessity for the goal of preserving the core or essence of modern liberal freedom. Hegel was an internal rather than an external critic of liberalism. His position did involve a profound philosophical departure from liberalism in suggesting that the instability of a natural-law liberal society is intrinsic to it, and that it is only the core or essence of individual subjective freedom that should be preserved, not the unfettered subjective freedom of natural law. But his position is still essentially closer to liberalism than would be a philosophical critique that rejects modern liberalism on aesthetic grounds, because it destroys the warrior virtues of the aristocracy, or because it dilutes ethnic solidarity.

A final reason that the *Philosophy of Right* has appeared to most of its recent interpreters as an expression of a fairly conventional welfare-state liberalism involves the relatively limited ways in which Hegel departs from the liberal principle of antipaternalism. On the one hand, a limited form of paternalism is at the very core of the *Philosophy of Right:* the only reason that it is possible for Hegel to think of modern *Sittlichkeit* as a social totality analogous to the classical polis is that the cohesion of *Sittlichkeit* is ultimately a higher priority than the private freedom of individuals. The governmental institutions of *Sittlichkeit* act to ensure that its cohesion is preserved, and is not placed at the mercy of individuals making arbitrary choices. But the only really coercive measures that modern *Sittlichkeit* requires are those to ensure that all individuals are minimal participants in civil society: that all individuals are regularly engaged in work and that they make provisions to look after their own needs.

Thus, for present-day political philosophers whose primary interest is in liberal political thought, the justification of the welfare state, and questions such as the relationship between the rational justifiability of institutions and the freedom of the individuals who participate in those institutions, it is fully reasonable to concentrate on those features of the *Philosophy of Right* that bring it close to welfare-state liberalism, and to pay little attention to the other side of the *Philosophy of Right:* the controversial and context-bound assumptions that Hegel made about the norms and social institutions that had to exist if welfare-liberal goals were to be realized, and that he thought of as inextricably bound up with the preservation of any form of liberalism.

But for theorists with a broader interest in Hegel and his place in modern intellectual history, it is just these peculiar assumptions that make Hegel so interesting. Hegel thought that the natural-law belief in absolute rights to private property and in the antiperfectionist notion of nonrational human preferences were going to be persistent dangers in any modern society. He concluded from this premise that the success of modernity required a public philosophy that is explicitly perfectionist about the human good and is based on a systematic rehabilitation of a substantive, rather than a procedural, notion of rationality. Whether these conclusions justify Hegel's grand claim that modern *Sittlichkeit* should be thought of as a return on a higher level of the *Sittlichkeit* of the classical polis is of course a difficult question (and perhaps ultimately a question that is more semantic than real). But it is at least possible to understand how Hegel's idiosyncratic views about how modern *Sittlichkeit* have to function could have led him to the idea that, in his strange vision of a bureaucratic and paternalistic form of the liberal welfare state, the harmonious ethical life of the Greek city-state had somehow been reborn.

NOTES

1. It is important to avoid confusion with Stoic and Thomist natural law. The term "natural law" is used in contemporary political theory largely by such Thomist writers as John Finnis and Robert George.

2. The *Institutes* was a systematic textbook of Roman law. The *Pandects* was a collection of older sources on which the law was based. See Allen Wood's note to PR§ 393.
3. My terms "procedural" and "substantive" rationality are taken over from Charles Taylor, as is much of the content of the following discussion. A concise summary of some of Taylor's views on this subject can be found in his essay "Overcoming Epistemology" in Taylor 1995, 1-19.
4. In a seminar taught at the University of California, Berkeley, in 1983, Charles Taylor referred to such knowledge as "agent's knowledge."
5. See the discussion of the Reformation in Hegel [1830] 1999, 193.
6. Michael Forster (1998, 226-43) makes a convincing case for the conclusion that Hegel has an "enduring communal consensus" theory of truth.
7. The persistence of a profound divide between urban and rural cultures far into the nineteenth century is beautifully described in Weber 1976.

REFERENCES

Avineri, Shlomo. 1971. *Hegel's Theory of the Modern State*. Cambridge: Cambridge University Press.

Brint, Steven. 1994. *In an Age of Experts: The Changing Role of Professionals in Politics and Public Life*. Princeton: Princeton University Press.

Dickey, Laurence, ed. 1999. *Hegel's Political Writings*. Cambridge: Cambridge University Press.

Forster, Michael. 1998. *Hegel's Idea of a Phenomenology of Spirit*. Chicago: University of Chicago Press.

Franco, Paul. 1999. *Hegel's Philosophy of Freedom*. New Haven: Yale University Press.

Hegel, G.W.F. [1802-3] 1999. "On the Scientific Ways of Treating Natural Law." In Dickey 1999.

Hegel, G.W.F. [1821] 1991. *Elements of the Philosophy of Right*, ed. Allen W. Wood, tr. H. B. Nisbet. Cambridge: Cambridge University Press.

Hegel, G.W.F. [1830] 1999. "Address on the Tercentenary of the Submission of the Augsburg Confession." In Dickey 1999.

Neuhouser, Frederick. 2000. *Foundations of Hegel's Social Theory: Actualizing Freedom*. Cambridge, Mass.: Harvard University Press.

Pelcyzinski, Z. A., ed. 1964. *Hegel's Political Writings*. Oxford: Oxford University Press.

Pinkard, Terry. 2000. *Hegel: A Biography*. Cambridge: Cambridge University Press.

Pippin, Robert. 1997. *Idealism as Modernism*. Cambridge: Cambridge University Press.

Smith, Steven B. 1989. *Hegel's Critique of Liberalism: Rights in Context*. Chicago: University of Chicago Press.

Taylor, Charles. 1995. *Philosophical Arguments*. Cambridge, Mass.: Harvard University Press.

Weber, Eugen. 1976. *Peasants into Frenchmen*. Stanford: Stanford University Press.

Wood, Allen. 1990. *Hegel's Ethical Theory*. Cambridge: Cambridge University Press.

Jacob Roundtree

MARX'S DEMOCRATIZATION OF HEGEL'S *PHILOSOPHY OF RIGHT*

ABSTRACT: *In his famous critique of Hegel's* Philosophy of Right, *Marx criticized Hegel's contention that the general will can be achieved without popular sovereignty. Marx argued that Hegel's first error lay in his Idealist method, which mistook the realities of the family and civil society as mere emanations of the Idea. This methodological error, according to Marx, led Hegel to misunderstand the rational essence of the state as consisting in a "universal" will that is abstracted from the real will of the people itself, allowing Hegel to defend the pursuit of the good of the whole not by popular government but government by a special bureaucratic, "universal" estate, represented in government by civil servants. However, Marx failed to direct the same type of critique against Hegel's assertion that the bureaucracy would have the knowledge of the whole that it would need if it were to effectively regulate civil society in the universal interest.*

During Marx's tenure as the editor of the *Rheinische Zeitung* (1842-43), he believed that critical journalism could inspire state officials and the bourgeois elite of Germany to undertake the political reforms necessary to realize rational freedom, merely by exposing the irrationality of existing arrangements. In this effort he was following the lead of his fellow Young

Hegelians, who saw criticism as the primary way to effect social change. However, Marx eventually came to perceive this project as a dead end. Germany, he concluded, remained largely untouched by the modernization process that had so radically transformed British and French society. It was to this fact that he attributed the failure he and the other Young Hegelians had had in inspiring a transformation of German politics through the reformation of German consciousness. The turning point for Marx seems to have been the closing of the *Rheinische Zeitung* by the authorities. This signaled to Marx that critical journalism was relatively impotent vis-à-vis the political state, even as the political state was incapable of comprehending the necessity of social transformation merely by being exposed to the fact that it was irrational. Moreover, the German bourgeoisie—elements of which had funded the newspaper, drawn in by its initial defense of free trade—was incapable of being an agent of radical social change that would culminate in the reign of true freedom.

In an attempt to come to terms with what had gone wrong, Marx chose to move to Kreuznach shortly after his wedding to Jenny von Westphalen, where, over the course of five months, he undertook a systematic investigation of modern philosophy and the modern state. This marks the juncture at which he shifted from attempting to bring about the reformation of Germany's political conditions so as to raise it to the level of the modern states—England, France, and America—to critiquing the modern state itself, along with German philosophy. Thus, we find Marx developing thoughts about why the modern world had failed thus far to fulfill the ends of reason, what it would mean for modernity to be true to its rational essence, how such an end state could be brought about, why speculative philosophy in the hands of Hegel and the Young Hegelian critical critics had failed to solve the problem of modern irrationality, and how to forge a new program of social theory that could more adequately comprehend the problem of modernity and determine a solution to it. In his efforts to gain clear insight into these matters, Marx thought it necessary to go behind the ideas of Hegel to determine the actual significance of the master's sources and the essential characteristics of the modern state. This project entailed reflecting on a range of empirical research about the nature of the modern state, while exploring the political thought of such political theorists as Montesquieu, Rousseau, and Machiavelli.

One way to characterize the result of these efforts is as a democratization of Hegel's philosophical system that re-grounded German philosophy in the rational will of the people. The intended product of Marx's democratization of Hegel was a critical theory of modern society that both upheld the doctrine of rational freedom and liberated the method of immanent critique from the mystical framework of speculative philosophy. When the process was completed, Marx thought he had overcome the intrinsically ideological nature of German Idealism by turning it toward the analysis of an immanent (and imminent) proletarian social revolution, a revolution that would bring about a communist society in which the rational freedom of the people is realized.

In this paper, I consider the process by which Marx constructed this first version of critical social theory through the democratization of Hegel's philosophy of the modern state. I do so by analyzing Marx's early critique of the modern state in the "Contribution to the Critique of Hegel's Philosophy of Right." I begin with an account of Marx's critique of Hegel's method, move on to reviewing Marx's and Hegel's competing visions of the essence of the state, and discuss an epistemic lacuna in Marx's critique of Hegel's account of how the institutions of the modern state enable freedom to be realized.

I. MARX'S CRITIQUE OF HEGEL'S METHOD

It is necessary, Marx argued, to reflect critically upon the ideology of the modern state, which he believed was best expressed in the *Philosophy of Right:*

> The criticism of the German philosophy of state and law, which attained its most consistent, richest and final formulation through Hegel, is both a critical analysis of the modern state and of the reality connected with it, and the resolute negation of the whole German political and legal consciousness as practiced hitherto, the most distinguished, most universal expression of which, raised to the level of a science, is the speculative philosophy of law itself. If the speculative philosophy of law, that abstract extravagant thinking on the modern state, the reality of which remains a thing of the beyond, if only beyond the Rhine, was possible only in Germany, inversely the German thought-image of the modern state which disregards real man was possible only because and insofar as the modern state itself disregards real man or satisfies the whole of man only in imagination. In politics the Germans thought what other nations did. Germany was their theoretical consciousness. The abstraction and

> conceit of its thought always kept in step with the one-sidedness and stumpiness of its reality. If therefore the status quo of German statehood expresses the perfection of the *ancien régime*, the perfection of the thorn in the flesh of the modern state, the status quo of German political theory expresses the imperfection of the modern state, the defectiveness of its flesh itself. (Marx 1844 [1979], 181)

Marx interpreted the modern state as a form of life that proclaims itself to be the home of true freedom: a place where the people exercise rational control over their shared conditions of life in a way that enables each of them, and all of them, to systematically realize their authentically determined particular and general interests. On this score, Marx took Hegel's theory of freedom for granted and treated the *Philosophy of Right* as the most sophisticated statement not just of Hegel's own political thought, but of the normative self-understanding of the modern state itself. What he challenged was Hegel's methodological approach, and its metaphysical foundations, which had allowed him to claim that the modern state institutionally realizes the modern idea of freedom as a matter of empirical fact.

Thus, Marx criticizes Hegel for having produced a science of modern society by deducing it from the categories of the *Logic*—where Hegel had merely specified, philosophically, the meaning of true freedom. The consequence of this application of the *Logic* to existing actuality is that, of necessity, the status quo counts as a home for freedom because its institutional structure is the unfolding of "the Notion" *(der Begriff)*. For Marx, Hegel not only proceeded in a scientifically illegitimate fashion, but his procedure was necessarily an elitist, anti-democratic program of theory construction. Therefore, Marx created an alternative method of social theorizing that derived the normative meaning of institutional structures by determining the real content of the patterns of social interaction that they condition from the standpoint of the actual life of the people.

The Ideological Character of the Philosophy of Right

Marx begins his critique of the *Philosophy of Right* by exposing a fundamental tension in Hegel's conception of the relationship between the state and the sphere of private life, the latter consisting of civil society and family life. The primary task of Marx's text is to explain this fundamental tension as expressing the ideological character of Hegel's system and the pathological character of the modern state.

Thus, Marx quotes Hegel as conceiving of concrete freedom as the unity of the common good of the state with the particular interests of individuals (Marx [1843] 1979, 5). However he finds that Hegel describes this unity as the state being both the immanent end of the sphere of private life and as standing in a relation of external necessity to it, which Marx describes as an "unresolved antinomy" (ibid., 6). If an external relationship obtains between private life and the state, then individuals in private life have their wills heteronomously determined by the state, as they must unwillingly sacrifice their interests when they conflict with those of the state. But if an immanent relationship obtains, it must be the case that the state is fundamentally committed to advancing the particular and universal interests of individuals, requiring that it possesses the knowledge and power to do so. In this case, individuals fully actualize themselves as rationally *autonomous* beings by accepting the laws and institutions of the state as essential principles of their will and freely following them. In addition to this unresolved antinomy, Marx quotes Hegel as conceiving of the state as effecting its realization of itself in private life in a way that is determined by "circumstances, caprice, and the individual's own choice of vocation" (ibid., 7, quoting PR §262). For Marx, this conflicts with Hegel's view of the state as the universal substance that differentiates itself into the spheres of private life (civil society and the family) in a rationally necessary way so that it can return to itself as the concrete universal agent of the people. Instead of the state arising from the spheres of private life in a free and self-conscious way—such that it finds itself confirmed in the social processes determined there in accordance with what is necessary for its material reproduction—it would appear, Marx claims, that the "state arises from them in an unconscious and arbitrary fashion" (Marx [1843] 1979, 7).

The key to determining whether Hegel is justified in claiming that the state is the immanent end of interacting individuals in the sphere of private life depends, Marx notes, on whether he has succeeded in demonstrating that the state is a rational organism (ibid., 12). However, Marx accuses Hegel of failing to explain what the true essence of a state organism is, and of failing to show that the modern state is so constituted as to deserve being classified as a rational organism. Marx does applaud Hegel for having made "a great advance to treat the political state as an organism and therefore to look upon the variety of authorities no longer as something [in]organic, but as a living and rational differentiation" (ibid., 11). Hegel's great contribution to political thought consists in his having developed the conceptual resources to treat "the development of the state or the political constitution into distinct aspects" as an "organic development" (ibid., 12), which can be articulated in the following terms: the various aspects of the political constitution function as a rationally organic whole. The subject in this functionality is the "various aspects of the political constitution"; the "predicate is their characterization as organic" (ibid.). But to proclaim that the actual modern state fits this ideal would require a series of judgments about the operating logic of each sphere of the state and the pattern of effects they actually generate, as a consequence of how they are interrelated. These judgments, in turn, would rest on empirical research into their real internal relations. Given a proper definition of a rational organism, the research would show whether there is warrant for identifying the whole system of structures constituting the modern state as a rational organism.

According to Marx, Hegel did not follow this method. "The genuine thought is this: the development of the state or the political constitution into distinct aspects and their actuality is an organic development. The actual distinct aspects or various facets of the political constitution are the premise, the subject. The predicate is their characterisation as organic" (ibid.). But according to Marx, Hegel (1) deploys a conception of a generic organic entity that does not specify the essence of a political state; and (2) reconceptualizes the basic structures of the modern state, as they appear in empirical actuality, in accordance with the basic categories of absolute Idealism, such that the "Absolute Idea" functions as the subject that generates the institutions and social members out of itself, thus guaranteeing, a priori, that the modern state counts as a rationally integrated whole.

Let us consider what Marx says on the first point:

> By saying "this organism" (of the state, the political constitution) "is the development of the idea into its distinct aspects, etc.," I have said nothing at all about the specific idea of the political constitution; the same statement can be made with the same truth about the animal as about the political organism. By what, then, is the animal organism distinguished from the political? This cannot be deduced from this general definition. But an explanation which does not provide the differentia specifica is no explanation. At any rate, what he says holds good of every organism, and there is no predicate present which would justify the subject "this."

> The actual result he wants to attain is the description of the organism as the political constitution. But no bridge has been built whereby one could pass from the general idea of organism to the specific idea of the organism of the state or the political constitution, and no such bridge can ever be built. (Ibid.)

To say, as Hegel does, that "this organism" "is the development of the idea into its distinct aspects" holds true for any organism, because any organism is, by definition, an entity that actualizes its essential form through its constitutive parts. The proper question, then, is: What is the specific essence of the organic political state that distinguishes it from any other particular type of organism? Only by grasping the *specific* essence of the specifically political form of life would we know what it would mean for a political state to actualize itself through its distinct parts, and this would be critical to determining whether the modern state is true to its essence or is, instead, a pathological entity that must be transcended for it to become true to itself and thereby fully actual. When Marx says, then, that "no bridge has been built whereby one could pass from the general idea of organism to the specific idea of the organism of the state or the political constitution, and no such bridge can ever be built," the point he is making is that one must consider the specific nature of the entity in question to comprehend its essential concept.

Marx's second major objection is that Hegel does not show that the existing modern state functions in a way that warrants his description of it as a rational organism. In so describing it, Hegel has confused the categories of the *Logic*, which define the structure of any rational organic entity, for the actual, empirical agents and structures of the modern state. As Marx puts it:

> In truth, Hegel has done nothing but dissolve the "political constitution" into the general abstract idea of "organism"; but in appearance and in his own opinion he has evolved something determinate from the "general idea." He has turned the subject of the idea into a product, a predicate, of the idea. He does not develop his thinking from the object, but expounds the object in accordance with a thinking that is cut and dried —already formed and fixed in the abstract sphere of logic. It is not a question of evolving the specific idea of the political constitution, but of establishing a relationship of the political constitution to the abstract idea, of placing it as a phase in the life-history of the idea, a manifest piece of mystification. (Ibid., 14)

Hegel, then, provides no concrete investigation of the logic of the specific spheres of the modern state. Yet such an investigation is necessary to determine whether the state functions as a rational organism. Hegel merely organizes the totality of the basic facts pertaining to the really existing character of the modern state in accordance with the abstract categories of Absolute Idealism. By conceptualizing the concrete aspects of the modern state as predicates of the absolute idea, Hegel reaches the conclusion that the various aspects of the state operate as a rational and harmonious whole through a purely a priori procedure. Here lies the manifestly ideological character of Hegel's enterprise:

> Empirical actuality is thus accepted as it is. It is also expressed as rational, but it is not rational on account of its own reason, but because the empirical fact in its empirical existence has a different significance from it itself. The fact which is taken as a point of departure is not conceived as such, but as a mystical result. The actual becomes a phenomenon, but the idea has no other content than this phenomenon. Nor has the idea any other purpose than the logical one of being "explicitly infinite actual mind." (Ibid., 9)

Only by accepting empirical actuality as it is, and attributing a significance to it that he derives from the *Science of Logic*, can Hegel (according to Marx) describe the relationship of the state to the sphere of private life as actually functioning as a rationally integrated complex whole—even though, as Hegel acknowledges, the relationship appears to have an irrational character, in the sense of being heteronomously imposed.

Hegel's Dual Standpoints

Hegel, of course, offers an explanation for why the relationship of the state to the sphere of private life is bound to have this double meaning. It is all a matter of the standpoint from which one conceives of the relationship. From the standpoint of ordinary consciousness, located in the family and civil society, it would appear that the state is a force external to the will of the individuals—a force to which they must submit because of the state's overwhelming power. But from the standpoint of universal reason, as embodied in the highest domains of the state, the state is the essential end of society and its substantial basis. It functions as the ultimate horizon of meaning and the necessary material basis for, and agent of, the rational coordination of the totality of activities undertaken in "the spheres of civil law and private welfare, the spheres of the family and civil society" (PR §261). The state exercises this function through the laws and institutions it establishes and the mechanisms by which it translates the ideal content of the constitution into concrete determinations.

It appears that genuine knowledge of the state as the rational essence of all that is under its authority can be achieved only through acquaintance with Hegel's *Encyclopedia of the Philosophical Sciences*, of which the philosophy of law or right is an essential part. By contrast, the thought of the state as a form of external necessity (and thus as a mechanism of domination or heteronomous control) is a thought arrived at through reasoning at the level of common consciousness, which cannot grasp the absolute spirit that is the ground of all finite determinations. Thinking at this level, for Hegel, is a form of necessary false consciousness that has to be redeemed at the level of science, wherein the essential determinations underlying our unconsciously reached ordinary determinations are recovered and revealed in their truth.[1] At that point, the falseness of our ordinary determinations can be gleaned and their essential dependency on Absolute Spirit fully appreciated.

For Hegel "the difference between common conception [*Vorstellung*] and thought [*Gedanke*] is of special importance because philosophy may be said to do nothing but transform common conceptions into thoughts —though it works the further transformation of the mere thought into the notion, of course" (*Enz.* §20). What this means—in the theoretical domain of the science of right—is that people in the spheres of civil law and private welfare are inclined to think of themselves primarily as atomistic individuals who have the right to pursue the satisfaction of their particular interests, and who are only ever obligated to contribute to the welfare of non-family members if they voluntarily enter into a contract for mutual benefit with them. The system of civil law legitimates this self-understanding; the domain of activity it conditions provides a space for this self-conception to be successfully acted upon. However, this immediate conception of the self as a free-standing individual is dependent upon a more substantial form of the self as a universal being that is actualized through the institutions of the state, and which is itself the true foundation of the particular self and the domain of its actualization. In this way, just as "logic is the all-animating spirit of all the sciences" (*Enz.* §24), so, too, is the state the animating spirit of all the specialized spheres of social life.

Of special relevance to Marx is that without the state there are no property rights, no laws of contract, and therefore no stable system of complex market exchanges. And, ultimately, there is no division of labor and, therefore, no specialized labor. So when individuals think of the state as an external necessity, it is a consequence of their failure to reflect on their situation from a higher and deeper standpoint: higher in that it is a superior epistemological perspective (from which the inadequacies of one's abstract individual standpoint can be comprehended and cognitively overcome), as it articulates a true vision of the actual nature of social reality, one's place in it, and what is necessary for one to achieve one's finite ends; deeper in that it is internal to the self as a universal rational agent, which is a truer, more substantial aspect of the self than the particular standpoint from which the state is immediately and falsely seen as an external necessity (to which one feels the urge to resist but is compelled to submit because of its overwhelming power). For Hegel, individuals who saw themselves as dominated by the state would be suffering from pure subjective alienation owing to their own failure to recognize that the institutional structure of the modern state enables them to achieve actualization as rationally integrated self-conscious agents capable of participating in family life, an advanced economy, and (to a limited extent) government. [2]

Marx, however, saw Hegel's double standpoint as an ideological distortion of the true nature of the situation. He charged Hegel with offering "a double history, an esoteric and an exoteric. The content lies in the exoteric part. The interest of the esoteric part is always that of finding again in the state the history of the logical concept. It is on the exoteric side, however, that development proper takes place" (Marx [1843] 1979, 8). Marx is not denying that agents are composed of a universal rational essence and a particular character, with the latter being ultimately dependent on the former. He also does not wish to deny the ideological character of reasoning at the level of a particular self that fails to comprehend the collective determinants that make agency in the private sphere possible. However, agreeing with Hegel on these points does not commit Marx to endorse the thesis of dual standpoints on the modern state. Thus, Hegel has failed to demonstrate that it is mere illusion to see the state as an external authority; nor that the appearance of civil life as determined, in essence, by contingency and the arbitrary wills of its members is but a partial and thus untrue view of things, because the full truth is that the state is the universal rational agent of the people and exists as the immanent, substantial, and actually effective end of individuals in the spheres of family life and civil society. The state could very well establish the basic institutional conditions of social life and still relate to individuals as an external authority and fail to function as a site in which individuals are able to actualize their universal essence. In fact, Marx argues, this is the very issue that Hegel avoids addressing in a genuinely scientific way by viewing the state from the standpoint of the logic of the concept rather than the specific logic of the various spheres of social life constituting the modern state. Only using the latter method could he see whether their pattern of interactions, and the local and general consequences they generate, are such that we can know them to be rationally integrated in accordance with a coherent system of rules and institutions established by the state, on the basis of a comprehensive vision of the particular and general conditions and interests of each member and the whole order.

II. DEMOCRACY AS THE ESSENCE OF THE STATE

This general account of Marx's critique of Hegel leaves us with two questions to be investigated by Marx himself:

1. Is the state the immanent end of individuals engaged in social cooperation, as mediated by the structures of private life, or is the state, in actuality, a form of external necessity?
2. Does the state arise in a self-conscious, rational way from the domains of private life, or does it arise therefrom in an unconscious, arbitrary, and contingent way?

In order to answer these questions, Marx endeavors to do two things that he claims Hegel fails to do. First, he tries to explain the true essence of the political state, so that he can know what it would mean for the state to actualize its essential form and to be an organic entity that is true to that essence. Second, he investigates the principles that define the various domains of social life that constitute the modern bourgeois state, and the system of interactions conditioned by these principles. This will allow him to discern whether the whole system satisfies the criteria of a rationally integrated organism, with rationality defined by the true essence of the political community.

The Concept of the Will and the General Will

What, then, is the essence of the state? Although Marx claims that Hegel has failed to give a specific account of the essence of the state, it seems that his real criticism is that Hegel posits the "concept of the will" as the essence of the state, which leads him to produce a mystified portrait of the modern state that ultimately reflects his own will to see it as a home for freedom. For example, in the following passage we find Marx accusing Hegel of treating the various aspects of the social system as determinations issuing from the "essence of the will":

> It is the essence of the will which allegedly brings forth its attributes out of itself. The extant, various and disparate, empirical forms of existence of the state are looked upon as direct incarnations of one or other of these attributes. (Marx [1843] 1979, 42)

And in his discussion of Hegel's treatment of the role of the monarch, Marx reads Hegel as deducing the monarch's right to bear the sovereignty of the state from the concept of the will:

> Hegel converts all the attributes of the constitutional monarch in the Europe of today into the absolute self-determinations of the will. He does not say "the monarch's will is the final decision," but "the will's final decision is the monarch.". . . (Ibid., 25)

> The subject here is the pure self-determination of the will, the simple concept itself, it is the essence of the will as a mystical subject that makes decisions. It is not an actual, individual, conscious willing, it is the abstraction of volition which turns into a natural form of existence, the pure idea which embodies itself as one individual. (Ibid., 34)

Hegel, Marx claims, deduces the right of a single individual to bear the office of sovereign—i.e., the monarch—from the formal structure of his system of logic. Within Hegel's scheme, one moment of the will is the element of pure decision, hence the claimed necessity of a monarch. By proceeding in this way Hegel is able to ideologically legitimate the modern state and treat the conflict of the concrete wills of the various members of the state as moments in the unfolding of the concept of the will.

> The means is the absolute will and the word of the philosopher; the particular purpose is again the philosophizing subject's aim of constructing the

> hereditary monarch out of the pure idea. The realization of the purpose is simply an assertion by Hegel. (Ibid., 34–35)

Of course, Hegel would agree that he constructed his theory of the state through an immanent development of the logic of the concept of the will, but would contend that this is precisely what a truly scientific study of the state requires:

> The immanent development of a science, the derivation of its entire content from the simple concept—and without such a derivation it certainly does not deserve the name of a philosophical science—has the following distinctive feature. One and the same concept—in this case the will—which begins by being abstract (because it is itself the beginning), retains its character yet [at the same time] consolidates its determinations, again through its own exclusive agency, and thereby acquires a concrete content. (PR §279)

The real difference between Marx and Hegel on the essence of the state does not lie not in the fact that Marx has a specific account of the essence of the political organism while Hegel has none, but in the fact that the two thinkers have different conceptualizations of the idea of the *general* will.[3] Hegel congratulated Rousseau for putting the will forward as the principle of the state, but he faulted him for considering "the will only in the determinate form of the individual will," when he should have recognized that the universal will is the "the concept of the will," which is the "will's rationality in and for itself" (PR §258). The significance, for Hegel, of this difference is best captured in the following claim: "The universal will must really be the rational will, even if we are not conscious of the fact; the state is therefore not an association which is decreed by the arbitrary will of individuals" (Hegel [1825] 1995, 402).

This conception of the general will, as the rational will, entails that the people have no privileged right to determine the laws. What is rational in and for itself transcends the subjective will of any particular agent or class of agents; whereas for Rousseau it is absolutely necessary that the people themselves have a direct say in determining the fundamental terms of their social life. It is this view that, I believe, Marx subscribes to as well.[4]

Marx, like Rousseau, declares as the essence of the state nothing other than the will of the actual people. As he puts it, "democracy is the essence of all state constitutions" (Marx [1843] 1979, 30). All other forms of political life are derivative forms of democracy, which, according to Marx, "stand to the other constitutions as the genus stands to its species" (ibid.). However, unlike a genus that counts as merely a classificatory principle, democracy is a genus that "itself appears as an existent" (ibid.). Democracy is the true universal form of political life that can achieve concrete existence, so that it is only in a democratic political order that we find a form of political community that corresponds to its essence. All other constitutional forms fail to correspond to their essence. Responding to Hegel's claim that sovereignty resides in the state and not the people, Marx retorts,

> As if the actual state were not the people. The state is an abstraction. The people alone is what is concrete. (Ibid., 28)

What makes democracy the essence of all state constitutions? In the most basic sense, a state is nothing other than its people. The objective material content of the state is the life of the people. Everything that happens in the state is ultimately the product of the agency of the people, and it is the people that is, ultimately, the addressee of the totality of the determinations of the social order. Democracy realized is the in-itself and for-itself of the people. "Here, not merely implicitly and in essence but existing in reality, the constitution is constantly brought back to its actual basis, the actual human being, the actual people, and established as the people's own work. The constitution appears as what it is, a free product of man" (ibid., 29).

In a democracy, the whole people exercises the absolute authority to determine the fundamental values, laws, and institutions that form the political constitution. Thus, for Marx, all other forms of political life—in which sovereignty is exercised by any agent or group of agents other than the whole community—will be untrue to their essence, because a particular element of the whole will be given authority over the whole. Marx believes this will guarantee that such an order is grounded in a principle of rule that is inadequate to the content of the system of social relations it organizes. The laws, institutions, and values of the state will necessarily be unresponsive to the actual will and interests of those to whom it is addressed.

Thus, even as "democracy is the truth of monarchy," "monarchy is not the truth of democracy" (ibid., 29). Monarchy is a system of rule in which one element of the whole has exclusive power to determine the law that shapes the life of all members. It is a form of political rule, therefore, that negates its content because it does not and cannot internalize the knowledge, interests, and will of the whole community within itself. Such a political state will necessarily be a system of domination that fails to satisfy the interests of its members. Contrasting monarchy and democracy, Marx proclaims:

> In monarchy the whole, the people, is subsumed under one of its particular modes of being, the political constitution. In democracy the constitution itself appears only as one determination, that is, the self-determination of the people. In monarchy we have the people of the constitution; in democracy the constitution of the people. (Ibid.)

A rationally integrated social system would therefore be one in which the principle of democracy was fully actualized; one where "democracy is content and form," where the "formal principle is at the same time the material principle" (ibid., 30). Democracy's inherent unity of form and content makes it the "solved riddle of constitutions" and the only political form of life that actualizes the "true unity of the general and the particular" (ibid.).

While Marx takes the actual will of the people to be the essence of the state, Hegel's view, that the universal rational will is the true essence of the state, leads him to judge that the people have to have their will represented by those capable of reasoning and willing from the universal standpoint. The primary condition for effectively willing from the universal standpoint is comprehensive and accurate knowledge of the real interests of the community, the objective conditions of life, and the means for realizing the good. As we will see, Hegel denies that the people are able to satisfy the epistemological condition for achieving the good, and this explains his conviction that they must rely on the universal class and the estates assembly to determine their general interests for them, realizing the general interests of the community in a way that harmonizes with the particular interests of individual social members. By conceptualizing the essence of the state as the universal will, which is rational in and for itself, Hegel is able to say that a people achieves collective rational freedom even though they do not directly control the social system. Marx's alternative, apparently Rousseauian conception of the general will necessitates that a people bear direct control of the social system if they are to realize themselves as free.

Hegel's (and Marx's) Account of Rational Collective Agency

However, that is not the end of the story.

Although Marx rejects Hegel's conception of the state's essence, he does subscribe to Hegel's idea of freedom. As it is Hegel's rationalist idea of collective freedom that Marx believes is realized in a true democracy, we can use that fact to unpack what must be Marx's account of the conditions a political order would have to satisfy to count as a rational organism.

Let us distinguish four aspects of Hegel's rationalist theory of collective freedom: (1) an account of what concrete freedom consists in; (2) an account of the basic conditions that have to be satisfied for concrete freedom to be realized, which is his theory of rational collective agency; (3) a metaphysical account of why concrete freedom is both realizable and actually realized in the existing order; and (4) a theory of how the institutions of the modern state allow the satisfaction of the basic conditions for concrete freedom to be realized. If Marx is going to abandon Hegel's metaphysics but adopt his idea of freedom, it would seem that he would still be committed to some core elements of Hegel's theory of rational group agency, which specifies the basic conditions that a people must satisfy to count as a rational self-conscious collective agent.

To help conceptualize these conditions we can consider Hegel's account of what is required for the state to realize concrete freedom and thus to count as a rationally integrated organic entity. Consider the following two passages from the *Philosophy of Right:*

> The state is the actuality of concrete freedom. But *concrete freedom* requires that personal individuality and its particular interests should reach their full development and gain recognition of their right for itself (within the system of the family and civil society), and also that they should, on the one hand, pass over of their own accord into the interest of the universal, and on the other, knowingly and willingly acknowledge this universal interest even as their own substantial spirit, and actively pursue it as their ultimate end. The effect of this is that the universal does not attain validity or fulfillment without the interest, knowledge, and volition of the particular, and that individuals do not live as persons merely for these particular interests without at the same time directing their will to a universal end and acting in conscious awareness of this end. The principle of modern states has enormous strength and depth because it allows the principle of subjectivity to attain fulfillment in the self-sufficient extreme of personal particularity, while at the same time bringing it back to substantial unity and so preserving this unity in the principle of subjectivity itself. (PR §260)

> The fact that the end of the state is both the universal interest as such and the conservation of particular interests within the universal interest as the substance of these constitutes (1) the abstract actuality or substantiality of the state. But this substantiality is (2) the necessity of the state, for it divides itself up into the conceptual differences within the state's functions; and these differences, by virtue of this substantiality, are likewise actual and fixed determinations or powers. (3) But this very substantiality is the spirit which knows and wills itself as having passed through the form of education. The state therefore knows what it wills, and knows it in its universality as something thought. Consequently, it acts in accordance with known ends and recognized principles, and with laws which are laws not only in themselves but also for the consciousness; and it likewise acts in determinate knowledge of existing circumstances and relations in so far as its actions have relevance to these. (PR §270)

Based on these passages, one can reconstruct Hegel's account of the basic conditions the state has to satisfy to be the rational collective agency of the people, which we can also attribute to Marx. The state must determine and implement laws that advance the general and particular interests of the whole community, which requires that the whole system function (1) in service of the rationally determined general and particular interests of the community (the *good will* condition), (2) on the basis of comprehensive knowledge of the objective conditions of life and the most adequate means to realizing the good (the *genuine knowledge* condition), and (3) with sufficient power to realize the rationally determined ends of the community (the *effective power* condition). In addition, (4) the members of the community must knowingly, willingly, and effectively advance the collective good of the whole as the essential end of their rational activity, through social roles in which they are able to satisfy their particular interests. If these four conditions are fulfilled, then the state will be the rational collective agency of the people in which everyone lives the good life together.

What we must now show is why Marx thinks the institutional structures of the modern state fail to enable the satisfaction of these conditions.

III. MARX'S CRITIQUE OF THE REPRESENTATIVE STATE

Despite his very strong criticisms of Hegel's speculative approach to conceptualizing the nature of the state, Marx did believe that Hegel delivered genuine insights into its real empirical character. In fact, Marx used Hegel's empirical account of the specific logic of the constitutive spheres of the modern state to explain why, on Hegel's own terms, it fails to be a rationally integrated system of social cooperation.

On Marx's reading, Hegel provided a relatively reliable empirical account of the basic structure of the modern representative state and even a reliable account of the antagonistic elements inherent to its form, which serve to frustrate the realization of concrete freedom. Marx agreed with Hegel that the modern representative state is a social system formally committed to advancing the particular and general interests of each and all, but believed that Hegel erred in thinking that the institutions of representation rationally mediate the antagonistic elements of society. Marx accused Hegel of needing to identify the *Idea* as the mechanism of reconciliation of interests, because it is not possible to locate any earthly mechanisms capable of such a feat. Nevertheless, Hegel does articulate a non-metaphysical account of the essential ways in which the institutional structure of modern society facilitates the realization of concrete freedom, to which Marx provides a systematic rebuttal.

Particular and Universal in Civil Society

According to Hegel, the political state is formally tasked with determining and pursuing the general interests of the community through a complex system of representative institutions that grants primary decision rights over matters of general concern to elite professional actors, while the people are allowed to have a subordinate and "rationally mediated" say in public affairs but are denied any democratic rights of political participation. Over against this political sphere is the private sphere, consisting of the family (which I will bracket) and civil society. Civil society is a domain in which individuals are able to pursue their particular interests primarily through a competitive-monetary system of contractual exchange relations, wherein every participating agent serves as a specialized representative of the interests of others and achieves her particular interests through the specialized representative agency of others.

Hegel's defense of the relationship between civil society and the political state is grounded in his theory of rational agency and his basic account of the history of the modern world. For Hegel, the self is composed of two inseparable aspects, the universal self and the particular self

(PR §7). A rational self exercises a will that is a hierarchically structured unity of these two moments. This holds for both the individual and the state.

On Hegel's reading of history, the principle of particularity is the distinctive achievement of the modern world and the element that gives modern societies their strength and stability (PR §260). It refers to the right of individuals to determine moral matters for themselves and to pursue their own private satisfaction in self-chosen ways. It is ultimately thanks to the Reformation that the infinite value of subjectivity came to be recognized as such. Civil society, being the domain in which the principle of particularity is allowed to achieve full development, operates as a relatively autonomous system of social cooperation. In abstraction from the full set of social relations that enables it to achieve actuality, particularity is "opposed to the universal of the will" and entails the indulgent and unrestricted desire to satisfy "its needs, contingent arbitrariness and subjective caprice" (PR §150) It attains its satisfaction through property in things and productive activity.

However, between the "satisfaction of subjective particularity" and the "needs and free arbitrary will of theirs, universality asserts itself" (PR §189). In their attempt to satisfy their insatiable appetite for property and to do as they please, individuals find that they are limited in their productive capacities. To overcome their limited capacities to directly satisfy their particularity, individuals must specialize in particular lines of socially productive activity and cooperate with each other through the system of market exchanges that organizes the social division of labor. In this way, "subjective selfishness turns into a contribution towards the satisfaction of the needs of everyone else" (PR §199). The whole system is one of universal interdependence, in which each agent functions as a specialized representative of the interests of all others. The mediating structures of the market channel the excessive behavior of agents into socially productive directions, as agents are forced to constrain their behavior to accommodate others, to take the opinions of others into account, to learn how to produce in an objective way, and to contribute to the production of value for others and the general wealth of society. Hegel describes the capitalist division of labor as appearing in the form of "universal and permanent resources" in which each can share—conditional on their education, skill, basic assets, and contingent circumstances (including the arbitrary choices of others). Thus, inequality is a necessary result of how civil society operates; and it is a precondition of sharing in the universal wealth created by social cooperation. Moreover, because of the infinite right afforded to the arbitrary choice of individuals, the decentralized structure of social decision-making, and the radical interdependence of the large number of agents cooperating through the division of labor, civil society operates beyond the cognition and intentions of the participants and only facilitates their integration behind their backs.

Hegel accepted from Adam Smith the picture of civil society as a complex, spontaneously organized system of social cooperation upon which everyone is radically dependent, through which each serves as a specialized representative of all others, and wherein individuals are potentially able to satisfy their personal needs and live authentically determined private lives—depending on how they are affected by contingent and arbitrary factors that are beyond their control. But Hegel recognized that such a system cannot by itself fulfill the requirements of being a home for freedom, owing to the role that arbitrariness, contingency, and formally right but egoistic action plans play in determining the patterns of social interaction, the absence of a site of collective self-conscious regulation of its affairs within its domain of operations, and the social pathologies it regularly generates precisely because individuals are allowed to act on the basis of narrow considerations, even though their actions have global consequences. Hegel thought that the political state corrects for these irrationalities, enabling society as a whole to realize itself as a self-conscious collective rational agent. Yet Hegel noted that "in our modem states, the citizens have only a limited share in the universal business of the state" (PR §255), a fact that he thoroughly endorsed.

I'd like to highlight three reasons why Hegel thinks the restriction on the participation rights of individuals is rationally necessary. The first is that in civil society, the members of the mercantile estate (as opposed to the agricultural estate) specialize in the production of use values, rendering them incapable of cultivating the knowledge and skills necessary to reason and will regarding matters of universal concern, which Hegel views as too complex to be capable of being managed by amateurs. For Hegel, as we shall see, only a universal class of professionals devoted to managing modern social affairs can answer to the complexity of civil society. The second point is that individuals outside of the universal class are partly corrupted in their ability to reason and will from the universal standpoint because they are conditioned by participating in civil society to be obsessively concerned with their particular concerns. And the third point is that

Hegel did not believe that the masses are capable of spontaneously acting as a rational collective agent except through representative structures that give them an organized form. Consequently, he defended a political system of representation as the only rational complement to the social system of representation that he took the market order to be.

The Public Good Without Public Participation

Hegel decries the idea of popular sovereignty as "based on a garbled notion [*Vorstellung*] of the people," and contends that the people are not epistemically equipped to fulfill the complex tasks of determining what is in their general interests. As he argues in the *Philosophy of Right,*

> if the term "the people" denotes a particular category of members of the state, it refers to that category of citizens who do not know their own will. To know what one wills, and even more, to know what the will which has being in and for itself—i.e. reason—wills, is the fruit of profound cognition and insight, and this is the very thing which "the people" lack. (PR §301; cf. §318)

In response, Marx asks how the state can endeavor to satisfy the general interests of the people if they themselves do not determine what counts as "matters of general concern." Marx takes Hegel to task for once again mystically inverting the real nature of things by transforming "matters of general concern" "into an independent entity" that needs to realize itself through the actual subjects of the state:

> The subjects do not need the "matters of general concern" as their true concerns, but the matters of general concern require the subjects for their formal existence. It is a matter for "matters of general concern" that they exist also as subject. (Marx [1843] 1979, 61)

In Hegel's account, "the matters of general concern are complete, without being actual concerns of the people. The actual business of the people has come into being without action by the people" (ibid.).

Marx regards Hegel's claim that the people do not warrant a say in determining what counts as their general interests as a consequence of his theory of freedom:

> Precisely because he does not establish objective freedom as the realisation, the practical manifestation of subjective freedom, subjective freedom

> appears in Hegel as formal freedom. . . . Because he has given the presumed or actual content of freedom a mystical bearer, the actual subject of freedom acquires a formal significance. (Ibid., 62)

On Hegel's view of freedom, universal reason, which has being in and for itself, constitutes the true will of the people. The people must, therefore, liberate themselves from their arbitrary opinions and recognize the epistemically superior laws and institutions of the state as constituting the essence of their will. The bizarre result of this theory of freedom, on Marx's reading, is that what Hegel counts as matters of general concern do not reflect the expressed concerns of the people, and what the people express as their concerns do not count as the general concerns of their community. With form and content separated in this way, "the content is complete and exists in many forms," such that there are several agencies "representing" what the general interest consists in, including the universal estate, the estates assembly, and the monarch. With a plurality of agencies claiming to represent the general interest of the community, but in the absence of representatives of the people themselves, conflict among the various political authorities and failure to realize the general interest is institutionally necessitated.

Bureaucratic Knowledge versus Bureaucratic Interests

The primary object of Marx's critique of the representative state, as depicted in Hegel's *Philosophy of Right,* is what Marx calls the bureaucracy [*Bürokratie*].

Hegel describes the universal class [*allegemeiner Stand*] as having "the universal interests of society as its business," which includes maintaining and regulating the common affairs of the community and applying the laws to particular cases in order to bring the particular affairs of civil society in line with the common good (PR §287). He places this responsibility in the hands of the "executive power" [*Regierungewalt*], i.e., the bureaucracy, and justifies its right to operate with relative autonomy in managing the general affairs of the community on the grounds that its members collectively possess comprehensive knowledge of social affairs and an institutionally guaranteed commitment to promoting the public interest:

> In the legislative power as a whole, the other two moments have a primary part to play, namely the monarchy as the power of ultimate decision, and the executive power as the advisory moment which has concrete

> knowledge [*Kenntnis*] and oversight of the whole with its numerous aspects and the actual principles which have become established within it, and knowledge of the needs of the power of the state in particular. (PR §300)

Marx, then, is not wrong to see that Hegel attributed to the bureaucracy the right to determine matters of common concern in abstraction from the people and in antithesis to civil society:

> Hegel brings in the "state proper," the "executive," to "see to" the "general state interest and legality, etc.," within civil society through "representatives," and according to him it is really these "representatives of government," the "executive civil servants," who constitute the true "representation of the state"—not "of," but "against" "civil society." The antithesis of state and civil society is thus fixed: the state does not reside in, but outside civil society. It touches it only through its "representatives" who are entrusted with "seeing to the state" within these spheres. Through these "representatives" the antithesis is not transcended, but has become a "legal," "fixed," antithesis. By means of deputies the "state"—an entity alien and ulterior to the essence of civil society—asserts itself over against civil society. The "police," the "judiciary" and the "administration" are not deputies of civil society itself, in and through whom it administers its own general interest, but representatives of the state for the administration of the state over against civil society. (Marx [1843] 1979, 49–50)

Whereas Hegel claims that the civil servants are able to regulate civil society in a way that brings its operations into harmony with the universal interests of the community because of its cognitive capacity, Marx sees the bureaucracy as a force of heteronomous domination over the sphere of civil society because of the fundamental asymmetry of their interests. Civil society is oriented to the particular, whereas the bureaucracy is oriented to what it takes to be the universal interests of the community. In the autonomy of the bureaucracy to determine the universal interests of the community, Marx sees an entity that has usurped the power of the community, which properly belongs to the people: "The bureaucracy has the state, the spiritual essence of society, in its possession, as its private property." It maintains, obfuscates, and legitimates its usurpation of the state through its apparently disinterested proceduralism, self-sanctioned expertise, and hierarchical structure:

> The general spirit of the bureaucracy is the secret, the mystery, preserved within itself by the hierarchy and against the outside world by being a

> closed corporation. Avowed political spirit, as also political-mindedness, therefore appear to the bureaucracy as treason against its mystery. Hence, authority is the basis of its knowledge, and the deification of authority is its conviction. (Ibid., 47)

Each bureaucratic department receives its mandate regarding some aspect of state affairs to concern itself with, but of necessity it interprets these concerns in terms of its own internal logic, which, Marx seems to suggest, are rooted in the interests of those who staff it:

> The bureaucracy takes itself to be the ultimate purpose of the state. Because the bureaucracy turns its "formal" objectives into its content, it comes into conflict everywhere with "real" objectives. . . . State objectives are transformed into objectives of the department, and department objectives into objectives of the state. (Ibid., 46)

Marx peers through the objectifying formalism of the bureaucratic order to expose what he takes to be its "crass materialism," the "materialism of passive obedience, of faith in authority, of the mechanism of fixed and formalistic behavior, and of fixed principles, views and traditions" (ibid., 47). Members of the bureaucracy submit to the governing logic of their departments, taking for granted what is formally defined as the state's interests and knowledge of how to achieve it. By becoming subordinated to the logic of the system, bureaucrats lose themselves in the process: "actual life is material for the bureaucrat himself, i.e., so far as it becomes an object of bureaucratic manipulation; for his spirit is prescribed for him, his aim lies beyond him, and his existence is the existence of the department." And it appears that even while no one knows what is really going on, everyone grounds their own judgments in the faith that the others on whom they depend are epistemically reliable: "The bureaucracy is a circle from which no one can escape. Its hierarchy is a hierarchy of knowledge. The top entrusts the understanding of detail to the lower levels, whilst the lower levels credit the top with understanding of the general, and so all are mutually deceived" (ibid., 46-47).

There are, then, two main problems with the bureaucratically managed state: it usurps the sovereignty of the people, ruling in service of ends it claims to be those of the whole community but that ultimately only reflect the interests of the bureaucracy itself; and, therefore, it operates as an agent of external domination over civil society. Thus, the bureaucratically managed state cannot count as the immanent end of the social system of cooperation, the ground of freedom rather than an agency of domination:

> This is the enigma of mysticism. The same fantastic abstraction, which rediscovers state consciousness in the inadequate form of the bureaucracy, a hierarchy of knowledge, and which uncritically accepts this inadequate existent as the real existent and as fully valid, this same mystical abstraction just as candidly avows that the real, empirical state spirit, public consciousness, is a mere potpourri of "thoughts and opinions of the many." As it imputes to the bureaucracy an alien essence, so it leaves for the true essence the inadequate form of appearance. Hegel idealizes the bureaucracy, and empiricizes public consciousness. (Ibid., 60-61)

The Estates Assembly

However, Hegel believes that the estates assembly is able to serve as a domain of mediation, wherein a synthesis between the state and civil society is effected, masses of individuals become a self-consciously unified people, and the state achieves consciousness of the particular interests of the individuals and groups who compose civil society. It is, therefore, an essential element in the process by which the principle of universality and the principle of particularity are synthetically realized through the self-conscious agency of the various members of the state. Thus, Hegel might claim, Marx's challenge only holds water if you abstract away from the critically important institution of the representative assembly.

Let us, therefore, consider how Hegel envisions this synthesis to be achieved and then consider Marx's critical account of the estates assembly as a site for the meeting of fundamentally opposed principles. Hegel contends that the synthesis effected by the estates assembly is achieved by members of civil society choosing representatives through their primary work associations; these representatives then rationally deliberate about what the content of the laws should be. Hegel emphasizes that while the representatives of the partial associations of civil society are chosen to reflect the will of their constituents, they are tasked to go beyond the narrow perspective of their members and reason and will at the level of the universal through their legislative deliberations. Representatives of civil society are aided in the process of ascending to the standpoint of the universal by the universal class, who contribute their comprehensive knowledge of the real interests and conditions of life of the state to the deliberative process of law-making. While the universal class advises the representatives of civil society, educating the representatives of civil society to look beyond their narrow perspectives to see society as a whole, the representatives of civil society, in turn, hold the civil servants to account for their activities. Finally, citizens at large are able to bear spiritual witness to the rationality that goes into the making of the laws, which reflects what is necessary for their particular and universal interests to be realized in a systematic way, because of the publicity of the deliberations and the bond forged between themselves and their representatives. They can, therefore, recognize as the essential principles of their substantial will the laws and institutions of the state that define the system of rights and duties.

Marx rejects Hegel's view of the estates assembly and contends that rather than being a site of synthesis between the state and civil society, it is merely a forum in which the contradictory principles of the state and civil society face off and reveal the fundamental conflict between the two domains. Marx notes that there is nothing built into the process of determining the membership of the estates assembly or the organization of its activities that guarantees that representatives will transcend the particular perspectives of their constituents and learn to will and reason from the universal standpoint. In fact, the civil estate's

> political effectiveness and significance is the political effectiveness and significance of the civil estate as civil estate. Hence, the civil estate can only enter the political sphere in a way which corresponds to the differentiation of estates in civil society. The differentiation of estates within civil society becomes a political distinction. (Marx [1843] 1979, 71)

Thus, we should expect to find representatives of civil society entering the estates assembly thinking and willing from the perspectives they have formed within that domain, which is thoroughly distinct from the forms of thinking and willing customary of the universal estate and the monarch. Marx cannot see how these distinct forms of cognitive agency, grounded in heterogenous material interests, can be reconciled; and accuses Hegel of failing to give a concrete account of how this reconciliation is to be effected:

> On the one side are placed, always as identical, state and government; on the other, the nation, resolved into particular spheres and individuals. The

> estates stand between the two as a mediating organ. The estates are the centre where "sense and a way of thinking appropriate to the state and government" are supposed to coincide and be united with "sense and a way of thinking appropriate to particular groups and individuals." The identity of these two opposed senses and ways of thinking, in whose identity the state should properly be rooted, is given a symbolic representation in the estates. The transaction between state and civil society appears as a particular sphere. The estates are the synthesis between state and civil society. But how the estates are to set about uniting in themselves two contradictory ways of thinking is not indicated. The estates are the posited contradiction of the state and civil society within the state. At the same time, they are the demand for the resolution of this contradiction. (Ibid., 91)

Hegel's answer is, of course, that the respective representatives of the people within the estates assembly are supposed to "mediate" between each other. Marx rejects this as only conceivable within the domain of Hegel's speculative logic while being untrue to the real nature of conflict in the modern state, where "real extremes cannot be mediated precisely because they are real extremes. Nor do they require mediation, for they are opposed in essence" (ibid., 88).

The modern state, on Marx's view, is nothing other than a system of essential contradictions grounded in the "the antinomy of the political state and civil society," and this fundamental contradiction is merely "forced to the surface" within the legislature, as it is "the totality of the political state." The participation of civil society in the state, through the representative agency of members of the estates assembly, neither entails a process by which the state arises self-consciously from civil society, nor one by which the institutionally structured conflicts of the various powers that claim to represent the general interest are overcome. Instead, representatives of civil society come with narrow agendas defined by their relationship to civil society, and the estates assembly functions as a site in which opponents battle it out rather than resolve their differences.

IV. KNOWLEDGE OF THE WHOLE

In *The Philosophy of Right*, Hegel presented a systematic interpretation of the modern state as the full actuality of human freedom. This was part of his overall attempt to provide an interpretation of the modern world that revealed the negativity of existence to be merely apparent and ultimately in service of the realization of human freedom. Hegel believed that this interpretation provided us with a perspective on modern civilization that enables us to be subjectively reconciled to the world.

But Hegel did not consider his legitimation narrative to be a noble lie. It represented the reality beneath the appearances, the key feature of which is the principle of representation. The representation of interests, for Hegel, legitimates the modern division of labor by providing social subjects with the institutional framework through which the good of each and all can be systematically realized. But at the center of the system of representation is the universal estate of bureaucrats, which is tasked with governing society from the universal standpoint of the good of the whole, especially by regulating the division of labor so that the excesses of civil society do not threaten to undermine the common good.

What enables bureaucrats to fulfill this supervisory role is their comprehensive knowledge of the whole. Because Hegel finds the masses incapable of achieving this knowledge, he rejects the legitimacy of popular sovereignty. Yet the people are free because, through the representative agency of the universal class, the whole community systematically achieves its particular and general interests. Along with the epistemic capacity of the bureaucracy, Hegel identifies two other essential conditions the universal class must satisfy for its political authority to be legitimate: it must have a good (universally directed) will and the power to carry it out effectively. The absolute power of the centralized state and the control of the bureaucracy over its executive functions ensure that the latter condition is fulfilled. As for the former, the bureaucrats' good will is to be guaranteed by their ethical education, the oversight of the monarch and the corporations, the legislative power vested in the estates assembly, and the fact that bureaucrats are paid a salary sufficient to ensure they do not need to monetize their offices to earn a living.

On the central question of what ensures that the bureaucrats are able to gain genuine knowledge of the whole, however, Hegel offers but a vague account. He seems to suggest that they acquire this knowledge from their university training, their membership in the *Mittelstand*, the accumulated body of social understanding that is articulated within the rule structure of the bureaucratic system, and the experience gained through active participation in the management of social affairs. But Hegel never shows the adequacy of these sociological mechanisms. This is an especially pronounced problem considering that Hegel's opposition to popular sovereignty seems to be grounded in the epistemic inadequacies of the people.

Marx's attempt to criticize Hegel's repudiation of popular sovereignty might have pointed that out. Marx's critique of the bureaucracy, as presented by Hegel, focuses on how it must fail to fulfill the task of being the universal estate because of the inherent partiality of its interests. But it would have been entirely consistent with Marx's critique of Hegel's method to point out that Hegel's deduction of the empirical aspects of the modern state from the doctrine of the concept represents it as a rational organism in which the knowledge, volition, and power of each part is necessarily determined by its function within the whole. Therefore, the bureaucracy is guaranteed to possess the knowledge necessary to serve as the universal estate, even without an empirical demonstration that this is actually the case in the real world. Instead, Marx mocks Hegel for merely describing the bureaucrats in terms of their own self-understanding as adequately knowledgeable, but he fails to directly address the question of adequacy. Ultimately, on Marx's view, what makes the bureaucrats a partial rather than universal estate is that they will in accordance with their narrow interests as members of their bureaus, not that they lack access to adequate knowledge of the social whole.

This reduction of the knowledge problem to a motivational problem is a pattern in Marx's critical theorizing that carries through to his mature writings. We can begin to see it taking shape in his critique of Hegel, prior to its assumption of a central role in his theory of ideas in *The German Ideology*. The reduction of bureaucrats' and, later, others' ideas to their narrow interests might also be seen as a missed opportunity to launch a critique of epistocracy, which has made a recent comeback. Even more than Hegel, contemporary epistocrats simply posit the adequacy of "expert" knowledge, leaving defenders of popular sovereignty to object, as Marx did, to the interests served by experts' ideas rather than to the accuracy of their claims to expertise.

Hegel had simply asserted the inadequacy of the people's knowledge to the apparently complex tasks of modern government. He then simply asserted the adequacy of bureaucratic knowledge to this task, an assertion that Marx seized upon. But Marx failed to ground his derision of Hegel's assertion in anything but his own assertion that bureaucratic interests would trump bureaucratic knowledge.

This absence of epistemological argumentation, however, may be understandable if we attribute to Marx the tacit assumption that knowledge of the whole is not problematic, and thus does not require the specialized education and experience that Hegel thought would ensure its possession by bureaucrats and them alone. Given this tacit assumption, Hegel's critique of popular knowledge would have appeared to Marx as obviously groundless. Furthermore, given this assumption, the people would appear to be unproblematically capable of doing what Hegel falsely claimed that only bureaucrats were capable of doing: grasping the interests of the people as a whole and the means by which these could be recognized, such that they could govern society as reason itself demanded that it be governed: in the universal interest.

NOTES

1. On Hegel's distinction between ordinary reasoning and dialectical reasoning, see Rosen 1984, ch. 3. And for a discussion of the idea of ideology as "necessary false consciousness" see Rosen 1996.
2. For the notion of "pure subjective alienation" see Hardimon 1994.
3. See Tuck 2018 on how Rousseau's idea of the general will was interpreted and misinterpreted in nineteenth-century Germany.
4. Important discussions of Marx's relationship to Rousseau include Colletti 1973; Leopold 2007, 262-71; Levine 1993; della Volpe 1978; and Wokler 1983.

REFERENCES

Colletti, Lucio. 1973. *From Rousseau to Lenin: Studies in Ideology and Society*. New York: Monthly Review Press.

Hardimon, Michael O. 1994. *Hegel's Social Philosophy: The Project of Reconciliation*. Cambridge: Cambridge University Press.

Hegel, G.W.F. [1817] 2010. *Encyclopedia of the Philosophical Sciences in Basic Outline, Part I: Science of Logic*, ed. Klaus Brinkmann, trans. Daniel O. Dahlstrom. Cambridge: Cambridge University Press.

Hegel. G.W.F. [1821] 1991. *Elements of the Philosophy of Right*, ed. Allen W. Wood, trans. H. B. Nisbet. Cambridge: Cambridge University Press.

Hegel [1825] 1995. *Lectures on the History of Philosophy*, vol. 3: *Medieval and Modern Philosophy*, rev. ed., E. S. Haldane, trans. Frances H. Simson. Lincoln: University of Nebraska Press.

Leopold, David. 2007. *The Young Marx*. Cambridge: Cambridge University Press.

Levine, Andrew. 1993. *The General Will: Rousseau, Marx, Communism*. Cambridge: Cambridge University Press.

Marx, Karl. [1843] 1979. "A Contribution to the Critique of Hegel's Philosophy of Law." In *Marx and Engels Collected Works*, vol. 3: Marx & Engels: 1843-1844. New York: International Publishers.

Marx, Karl. [1844] 1979. "A Contribution to the Critique of Hegel's Philosophy of Law: Introduction." In *Marx and Engels Collected Works*, vol. 3: Marx & Engels: 1843-1844. New York: International Publishers.

Rosen, Michael. 1984. *Hegel's Dialectic and Its Criticism*. Cambridge: Cambridge University Press.

Rosen, Michael. 1996. *On Voluntary Servitude: False Consciousness and the Theory of Ideology*. Cambridge: Polity.

Tuck, Richard. 2018. "From Rousseau to Kant." In *Markets, Morals, Politics: Jealousy of Trade and the History of Political Thought*, ed., Béla Kapossy, Isaac Nakhimovsky, Sophus A. Reinert and Richard Whatmore. Cambridge, Mass.: Harvard University Press.

della Volpe, Galvano. 1978. *Rousseau and Marx, and Other Writings*. London: Lawrence and Wishart.

Wokler, Robert. 1983. "Rousseau and Marx." In *The Nature of Political Theory*, ed. David Miller and Larry Siedentop. Oxford: Oxford University Press.

Index

Note: Page numbers followed by "n" denote endnotes.

For Product Safety Concerns and Information please contact our EU
representative GPSR@taylorandfrancis.com
Taylor & Francis Verlag GmbH, Kaufingerstraße 24, 80331 München, Germany

www.ingramcontent.com/pod-product-compliance
Ingram Content Group UK Ltd.
Pitfield, Milton Keynes, MK11 3LW, UK
UKHW022156190926
475702UK00003B/56
* 9 7 8 1 0 3 2 3 5 5 3 1 3 *